Communicate Like a PRO

Communicate
Like a PRO

Tools That Forever Change
the Way You Listen,
Love & Lead

Dr Dennis O'Grady & Riley O'Grady
Edited by Sue MacDonald

ORANGE *frazer* PRESS
Wilmington, Ohio

ISBN 978-1949248-326
Copyright©2021 Dr. Dennis O'Grady & Riley O'Grady
All Rights Reserved

drogrady.com
effectivecommunicationworkshopsdayton.com
marriagecounselingdayton.com

New Insights Communication
7085 Corporate Way
Dayton, OH 45459-4223
Phone: 937.428.0724
Fax: 937.428.0824

Published for the copyright holder by
Orange Frazer Press
37½ West Main St.
P.O. Box 214
Wilmington, OH 45177

For price and shipping information, call 937.382.3196
Or visit www.orangefrazer.com

Book and cover design by Kelly Schutte and Orange Frazer Press

Library of Congress Control Number: 2020915646

Communicate Like A Pro is specifically designed for educational purposes and as such does not
purport to be a substitute for counseling, personal coaching, or psychotherapy.

10% of *Communicate Like A Pro* profits go to life-skills and youth leadership training programs
custom designed for inner city Cincinnati youth.

Printed in the USA on acid-free paper
First Printing

DEDICATION

🗨 I, Dr. Dennis O'Grady, dedicate this book to...

my high school speech teacher, Mr. H.L. Connelly, who encouraged me when I walked around in a shell. In fact, he gave me an acting part as a psychologist in our high school play when I didn't even know how to spell the word! He was the first professional in my life who believed that I could be more than my limited self-concept said I could be.

🗨 I, Riley O'Grady, dedicate this book to...

my high school mentor in the Civil Air Patrol, Mr. James Goodman, who empowered me during a time when I felt powerless. He selected me to lead multiple summer programs and conduct peer leadership training. Those opportunities sparked my love of teaching soft skills and developing youth programming. He was the first person to believe there was a leader in me, and he taught me that the best leaders are expert communicators.

TALK2ME© IS A POWERFUL TOOL TO SOLVE RELATIONSHIP PROBLEMS...

This book is about relationship problem solving. If you have a relationship, and there are problems, this book has the answers and tools that work.

- If you don't appreciate how others talk to you...
- If you become snippy and feel like you can't say anything right...
- If you feel deeper issues in your relationship aren't being addressed...
- If you can't raise certain issues for fear of upsetting your partner or boss...
- If you're having the same disputes over and over and over again...
- If you're not in a good place as a couple and need to fix what's broken and heal...
- If you're communicating past each other...
- If you get combative during a conflict and lose your cool...
- If you get too angry too fast and wish you could take back what you didn't mean to say...
- If you don't wish to keep living in an unhappy state of stress...
- If you feel moody because you can't get along...
- If you don't listen respectfully when someone isn't doing what you want them to do...
- If your language use isn't appropriate...
- If you get angry back with someone who's angry with you...
- If you're sweeping things under the carpet instead of putting them in the trash bin...
- If you can't talk to a professional about your personal home life...

- If you can't figure out someone who constantly gets under your skin…
- If you want to know how to read people better and have more empathy…
- If you desire to take your listening and leadership skills up to the next level…
- If you're struggling with any important relationship…

If you're having a problem with anyone, this book is for you. If you're having a repeated problem communicating with someone, this book is definitely for you. You will learn powerful new ways to think about problems and talk about these challenges.

MAY WE ALWAYS COMMUNICATE

May These Blessings of Better
Communication
Abound Everywhere Today
and Always:

When times are rushed...
May we communicate gracefully.

When times are disappointing...
May we communicate hopefully.

When times are angry...
May we communicate peacefully.

When times are prosperous...
May we communicate gratefully.

When times are fearful...
May we communicate honestly.

When times are bruising...
May we communicate bravely.

When times are tense...
May we communicate tenderly.

When times are boring...
May we communicate passionately.

When times are lean...
May we communicate generously.

When times are tiring...
May we communicate inspiringly.

When times are hopeless...
May we communicate courageously.

And when times are abundant...
May we communicate thankfully.

WHAT PEOPLE ARE SAYING ABOUT THE *TALK2ME©* SYSTEM OF EFFECTIVE COMMUNICATION

"Dr. O'Grady has helped me learn more about myself and how I give and receive communication. He has given me some strategies to better communicate with my husband and resolve and prevent conflicts. He is very easy to talk to and offers objective but compassionate insights as to how to improve the relationships in your life."

—BE, Marriage Counseling client

"As an Instigator, I will definitely be more patient with my children. I will also be more understanding of my wife's soft skin and feelings. It has helped me become a much better, understanding father and husband. This course has really opened my mind up. I'm thankful for you."

—Rob Wilson, Outbound Operations Supervisor, Cincinnati Service Center, Dayton Freight Lines, Inc.

"*TALK2ME©* Technology has helped me to label I-E people quickly and get a framework of how best to talk to them and how they're going to talk to me. I'm better able to see their strengths and not take things too personal. I'm not quite at the Ninja level but I'm getting there."

—TR, Engineer, Wright Patterson Air Force Base

"Dayton Freight's culture has always been rooted in open and honest communication. Dr. O'Grady has developed and taught a series of leadership training courses for all levels of management at Dayton Freight

Lines, a family-owned Midwest trucking company headquartered in Dayton. For 15 years and counting, Dr. O'Grady's positive culture of *TALK2ME©* Effective Communication Laws and Million Dollar Talk Tools have helped us secure our family company for the next generation. We have found that better communication improves profitability and productivity while enjoying the work we do and strengthening our families at home. We know of no other investment greater than that of our resource of people!"

"Like every explorer before him, *TALK2ME©*'s Dr. Dennis O'Grady has courageously identified two communicator types, Instigator and Empathizer. These types do not pigeonhole women into expected communication behavior, and they simultaneously empower men to give voice to their emotional side without fear of being perceived as "soft." In the universe of the Instigator and the Empathizer, people learn to see the value in themselves and learn ways to correct their behavior as seen through the lens of the other's communication style. Instigators and Empathizers are then able to work together, respectful of gender and communication differences."

"I was introduced to the *TALK2ME©* Communication System as a result of my professional and personal relationship of many years with Dr. Dennis O'Grady. Dr. O'Grady has the proven ability to interact, relate, and influence perspectives with regard to physicians, and the challenges of communication in gaining patient satisfaction. There is no doubt the arena of communication can require treading in delicate waters. However, Dr. O'Grady's development of and thorough knowledge about Instigator vs. Empathizer communicator styles and the resulting impact on moods and perceptions of behavior greatly improves doctor-patient satisfaction scores in measurable and sustainable ways."

"Off the top of your heads, how many books can you name that are written by a father and his daughter? Me? Not a single one. Until now. And who better to write a self-help book than two people who've lived, breathed, and experienced firsthand the tangible results."

—Sue MacDonald, Writer/Editor

"Over two decades ago, I met Dennis and began working with the *TALK2ME©* system. I cannot overstate the positive impact it has had on both my personal and professional experiences. As a natural Empathizer, I often found myself "helping" people by telling them how I perceived the world with the assumption that my views (and associated long-winded, "helpfully detailed" explanations) were patently obvious. I was continually shocked when my Instigator friends, family members, and coworkers didn't understand what I was trying to communicate. I was even more surprised to find out that many viewed my long-winded explanations as excuses or weakness, when I truly believed I was helping them see my point of view.

Working with Dennis and *TALK2ME©*, I've gained the tools I need to get my point across to all types of communicators. I've learned to take the time to think through how others may perceive my message, and to tailor it so it is effective in both home and professional situations. At work, I use *TALK2ME©* by thinking through my message, then typically send two-part emails: Bottom Line and Back Story clearly marked. This allows my Instigator coworkers to quickly find the actions that feed their decisive approach (Bottom Line), and my Empathizer coworkers know exactly what is expected of them as well as insight into the full-color picture (Back Story) they often need to feel comfortable with a decision. At home, *TALK2ME©* tools help ensure my Instigator (with a very capital I) husband and I can get to the heart of discussions without losing sight of our shared commitment to our marriage. Knowing how to quickly assess communicator styles has helped me do a better job of connecting with my children and grandchildren, since I no longer assume that everyone sees the world through my eyes, and I take the time to process communication with that in mind. I end up less hurt and more heard, which for an Empathizer is the key to peace."

—Teresa Macalolooy, CEO, Macalogic

"Dennis and his team have been an integral part of the Simms Family's personal and business successes for 30 years. His systems and advice are always well thought out and timely. I am happy to see him continue his family tradition in the communication field with his daughter. Best of luck!"

—Charlie Simms, President, Charles Simms Development

"At Vitangeli Dental we know the importance of keeping a culture of communication present and practiced in our dental office. It is not only important for our team to be able to communicate with each other in a positive way but for our team to communicate with our patients as well. The active listening skills, communicating feelings effectively, and using positive feedback tools presented through the *TALK2ME©* program helped us accomplish this and we continue to use these tools on a daily basis."

—Dr. Louis & Dominic Vitangeli, Creating Smiles, Creating Health

"Tilak Learning Group LLC has incorporated Dr O'Grady's *TALK2ME©* Instigator-Empathizer talk technology into communication courses custom designed and developed for companies around the world. Participants are able to immediately use what they learn on the job and at home. It works across geographies! Course participants tell me the Empathizer-Instigator information has had a huge impact on them. They have deeper insight into their communication style and can now identify the communication styles of others, thus making interpersonal communication easier and more productive. It is a favorite course of mine to deliver and a favorite course amongst the companies to whom I have delivered the course."

—Michelle Jackson CPTD COTP, Owner, Tilak Learning Group, LLC

TABLE OF CONTENTS

INTRODUCTION

BRIDGING COMMUNICATION DIVIDES

"He's such a _____!" "She's such a _____!"

Each of us has colorful words for the difficult people in our lives. But what exactly makes those people so challenging?

What if we told you that the difficult person is your opposite communicator type? Empathizer and Instigator communicators have significantly different verbal and non-verbal communication preferences.

Put simply, it's like you're speaking English and they're speaking in Mandarin. You might as well be talking to a brick wall.

Consider this book your Rosetta Stone for understanding what to say to challenging people.

When you understand the language of your opposite type, you will be able to disarm difficult people and feel more at ease and confident during tense conversations.

Not Your Magic Bullet

No doubt you want a magic bullet that fixes your work and home relational issues. In fact, you often turn to the all-knowing source, you guessed it, Google!

Some of the most commonly Googled, *"How to get people to ___"* fill-in-the-blank statements are:

"How to get people to like you."

"How to get people to do what you want."

"How to get people to respect you."

You want answers and so does the rest of the world.

Before we dive into the answers you crave, we must be honest with you. This isn't a guide that will help you psych out your opponent and bend them to your will.

This book is about helping you create calm and confidence when navigating *everyday* tough conversations and tense situations.

You might be surprised at how much easier it is to get your significant other to do the chores. Or get your subordinates to show up to meetings. Or maybe even get your intimidating boss to give you a promotion.

Let's be honest, any of those small wins would be fantastic. All of them? Well, that would be paradise.

While we don't believe there is a one-time quick fix to make everyone love, respect, and kiss the ground you walk on, there is this one little thing that's backed up by 20 years of clinical and corporate findings.

It's called the *TALK2ME©* Communication System.

💬 What Is the TALK2ME© Communication System?

TALK2ME© was developed in the clinical trenches with couples and counseling clients. As a father-daughter team, we have lived *TALK2ME©* in our own lives.

- Dr. Dennis O'Grady, a 40-year veteran clinical psychologist, discovered common traits that became the two distinct communicator types of Empathizer and Instigator.
- Riley O'Grady grew up with the *TALK2ME©* system and is an interpersonal communication professional, educator, and instructional systems designer.

Dad and daughter O'Grady now work together as a father-daughter training team. This provides us with practical and deep insights into how to help you improve your communication life both at work and at home.

The *TALK2ME©* system has impacted individuals, companies, and marriages. Since 2000, it's been field-tested and applied among more than 50,000 people in couple counseling, hospitals, universities, government, family-owned businesses, and much more.

You probably know the age-old saying, "Treat people how you want to be treated." This turned out to be false. The mantra should actually be, "Treat people how *they* want to be treated."

It's normal to expect others to desire to be communicated with the way you like to, but this is a grave mistake. It's also the root cause of many relationship divides.

TALK2ME© is not a personality assessment. It is a communication system.

It's not driven by gender, race, income, religion, or political beliefs. *TALK2ME©* is a global communication system that respects diversity and accounts for differences that give us a chance to create something new, not divide us. *TALK2ME©* strips away the age-old bias of gender-speak where a woman says and feels things this way, a man the complete opposite.

The knowledge of one's own communication type and the understanding of the other person's communication type eliminate false conflicts driven by unconscious prejudices.

It's a way to solve the frustration and loss that come from business working relationships and personal life relationships when people find faults rather than possibilities in each other.

We've written this book to take you on a journey to grow your understanding of the two different communicator types and help you apply these teachings to change your life.

💬 What's My Type?

Let's get right to it. Communication is difficult. But by consciously using *TALK2ME©* tools, you will become a PRO communicator with a little practice.

But first, you need to know who you are, and to whom you're talking. Are you an Instigator or an Empathizer Communicator? Take the NICI-A (New Insights Communication Inventory-Adult) survey to initially gauge your *TALK2ME©* Communicator Type.

NICI-A

Honestly answer the 15 survey questions below from a mindset of your at-home-natural-self vs. your at-work-professional-self. Answer "yes" if it is true for you most of the time. Answer "no" if it is false for you most of the time.

1. Do you try hard not to hurt anyone's feelings?	Yes	No
2. Are your feelings easily hurt?	Yes	No
3. Do you think of yourself as being too sensitive?	Yes	No
4. Are you surprised when your strong words or actions make someone else feel bad?	Yes	No
5. Do you "give in" to avoid conflict?	Yes	No
6. Do you find yourself helping other people before you help yourself?	Yes	No
7. Did your family or siblings see you as a strong-willed, head-strong individual?	Yes	No
8. Are you unafraid to give your opinion?	Yes	No
9. Do you have the strong drive to be right?	Yes	No
10. Are you comfortable giving blunt feedback or personal critiques?	Yes	No
11. Does your mood dominate your life partner for better or worse?	Yes	No
12. Do you back down when defensive tempers flare-up?	Yes	No
13. Would your partner say you're an attentive listener?	Yes	No
14. In a dispute, would your partner say you interrupt and talk over them?	Yes	No
15. Do you prefer to make decisions slowly and think through all your options?	Yes	No

Communicate Like a PRO

⮾ Quick Scoring Yourself

- Empathizers typically answer "YES" to items #1, #2, #3, #5, #6, #12, #13, and #15.
- Instigators typically answer "YES" to items #4, #7, #8, #9, #10, #11, and #14.

Tally up the number for both. If you score more Empathizer traits, you are likely an Empathizer. If you score more Instigator traits, you are likely an Instigator. We will be filling in the details of these two types as we go along. Simply look for trends at this point. Consider this an initial preview of Empathizer and Instigator mindsets.

⮾ Empathizer Vs. Instigator Mindsets

The eyes you see through determine what you see.

You now know that there are two different types of communicators, Instigators (I-Types) and Empathizers (E-Types). Over the years of doing workshops and clinical work with the *TALK2ME©* System, we have carefully collected the unique verbal responses that distinguish Empathizers from Instigators. Below are typical responses to the 15 survey questions. This will help you begin to determine if you naturally have a more dominant Empathizer or Instigator mindset.

Question 1: Do you try hard not to hurt anyone's feelings?

- *Empathizer*: Yes. I dislike having my own feelings hurt so I do my best not to hurt anyone else.
- *Instigator*: No. I don't consider it my responsibility to candy-coat what I say.

Question 2: Are your feelings easily hurt?

- *Empathizer*: Yes. I can be more critical of myself than my boss or supervisor can be of me.
- *Instigator*: No. I'm told by people close to me that I am insensitive and can be cold-hearted.

Question 3: Do you think of yourself as being too sensitive?

- *Empathizer*: Yes. I can be very sensitive to my home or work climate, noise, and surroundings.
- *Instigator*: No. I live by the motto: "Sticks and stones break bones, but your words won't hurt me!"

Question 4: Are you surprised when your strong words or actions make someone else feel bad?

- *Empathizer*: No. Words matter. Words are sacred to me. You can't just throw around words that you can't take back.
- *Instigator*: Yes. Too many times I have been known to open my mouth and insert my foot.

Question 5: Do you "give in" to avoid conflict?

- *Empathizer*: Yes. I'm a big believer that you catch more flies with honey than vinegar.
- *Instigator*: No. I trust people I can mix it up with. I know where they are coming from.

Question 6: Do you find yourself helping other people before you help yourself?

- *Empathizer*: Yes. I am a big people pleaser.

- *Instigator*: No. I have to look after and take care of myself first in order to be helpful to others.

Question 7: Did your family or siblings see you as a strong-willed, headstrong individual?

- *Empathizer*: No. I'm pretty easygoing even with my siblings.
- *Instigator*: Yes. I was a strong-willed kid and teenager, known to be impatient and direct.

Question 8: Are you unafraid to give your opinion?

- *Empathizer*: No. I have trouble being confident when I should be.
- *Instigator*: Yes. I am not afraid at all to give my opinion.

Question 9: Do you have the strong drive to be right?

- *Empathizer*: No. I don't have to be right all of the time, especially when it means I'll lose friends.
- *Instigator*: Yes. I can easily make a strong case for why I'm right. Even when I'm wrong.

Question 10: Are you comfortable giving blunt feedback or personal critiques?

- *Empathizer*: No. I don't like to give feedback off the cuff. I prefer to walk away and think about things before I'm ready to talk.
- *Instigator*: Yes. I'm quite comfortable criticizing others or critiquing projects on the spot. I'll critique anything.

Question 11: Does your mood dominate your life partner for better or worse?

- *Empathizer*: No. I'm a mood sponge. I can easily read the mood of others and tell where they are coming from.
- *Instigator*: Yes. I'm a mood pitcher. It's not how you feel but what you do that really matters.

Question 12: Do you back down when defensive tempers flare-up?

- *Empathizer*: Yes. I have trouble being assertive when someone is being an aggressive jackass.
- *Instigator*: No. I tend to get aggressive and go on the offensive when threatened.

Question 13: Would your partner say you're an attentive listener?

- *Empathizer*: Yes. Being an attentive listener, even during conflicts, is important to me.
- *Instigator*: No. It's tough to just stand by and listen when you disagree or have something important to say that will fix things.

Question 14: In a dispute, would your partner say you interrupt and talk over them?

- *Empathizer*: No. My partner says I'm too slow to speak up and don't push back when I should.
- *Instigator*: Yes. My partner says I can intimidate them with my superior debating skills.

Question 15: Do you prefer to make decisions slowly and think through all your options?

- *Empathizer*: Yes. I always like to weigh all the options and take time to think before deciding.
- *Instigator*: No. I feel confident in making decisions on the spot. I don't like it when decisions take too long.

⌦ But What If I'm Both Types?

Aren't sure if you're an Empathizer or an Instigator Communicator? If you are on the fence, here is your tiebreaker:

- *Were you strong-willed as a kid?* If so, then chances are you're an Instigator.
- *Were you laid-back and easygoing as a kid?* If so, then chances are you're an Empathizer.

Sure, your communicator style flexes depending on the situation, but we all have a default mode. That's because we're naturally born one or the other. What were you like as a child?

The NICI-A is a tool designed for your new individual insights, group discussion, and teaching purposes. Only Extreme Instigators and Extreme Empathizers answer all the questions perfectly.

For starters, pick either Empathizer or Instigator as your initial communicator style. You can always switch later, based on what you learn in the next few chapters. In fact, we will be guiding you to blend the strengths of both communicator types for your personal and professional success.

Use the chart on the next page to understand the basic contrasting characteristics of Empathizers and Instigators. In your experience, read both sets of side-by-side items to determine what Empathizer-Instigator traits you relate to most strongly.

For example, are you more sensitive to the feelings of others? This is an Empathizer trait. Or are you less sensitive to the feelings of others? This is an Instigator trait. Go down each set of items one at a time and take your time to think about how each item relates to your life. Use the checkboxes below to mark which traits on the Empathizer and Instigator chart apply to you.

Make sure to mark only one per set. For example, you can select the Empathizer trait "feel deeply" or the Instigator trait "think deeply," but not both. Select the single item that most applies to you from each set of choices.

💬 The E-I Spectrum

Empathizer (E-type) Communicators		Instigator (I-type) Communicators
More sensitive to the feelings of others		Less sensitive to the feelings of others
Empathetic		Genuine, will speak their mind
Feel deeply		Think deeply
Struggle with sadness		Struggle with anger
Relationship focus		Problem-solving focus
Slower to make decisions. Contemplate.		Quicker to make decisions. Trigger Puller.
Have a longer fuse		Have a shorter fuse
Give bad news hesitantly	OR	Give bad news bluntly
Dwell more on the past		Dwell more on the future
Were easygoing as kids		Were strong-willed as kids
Uncomfortable invading personal space		Comfortable invading personal space
Prone to writing long answers		Prone to writing short answers
Listen first		Talk first
Dislike conflict		Don't mind conflict
Would rather be competent		Would rather be confident

Which communicator type is best? We get this question all the time! The best type is the one that is positive and balanced, accurate and responsible, and able to flex the muscles of both types, depending on the situation.

Communicate Like a PRO

You, and everyone else you interact with, is on what we call the Communication Spectrum. On the far left of the spectrum are extreme Empathizers and on the far right are extreme Instigators. Where would you place yourself on the spectrum?

It is understandable to feel a bit split between Empathizer and Instigator. You might already be balanced. You could have adopted the traits of your opposite type because of your life experiences, an extreme E or I parent, or your work environment. Many factors and experiences can influence your unique communication style. Still, use the questions from the previous section to explore the Empathizer camp or Instigator camp. This will help you maximize the teachings from this book.

💬 Private Questions You Always Wanted Answers To

Thousands of curious people have asked us the following questions, and we hope to tackle them in this book:

1) *What's the best way to get through to someone who's upset or frustrated?*
2) *How do I actively listen during a conversation when I am excited to respond or don't agree?*
3) *How do I get through to someone who deflects criticism?*
4) *How do I communicate with someone who always shuts it down?*
5) *What are the best approaches to communicate with a constantly negative person?*
6) *How do I listen better to what I don't want to hear?*
7) *What are the "best practices" for better communication?*

Communication is the heartbeat of corporate and family cultures. Listening acts like the lungs that pump the oxygen of fresh moods to the heart. With enough oxygen, the limbs can be strong and move where your mind wills the body to go.

🗨 The Two-Way Communication Highway

Effective communication is two-way. "It's my way or the highway!" is ineffective because it shuts down communication avenues.

Throughout this book, there are references to what we call "The Two-Way Communication Highway." This metaphor is inspired by one of our ongoing partnerships with Dayton Freight Lines, a Midwest trucking company headquartered in Dayton, Ohio.

Two-way communication occurs when both the sender and receiver are involved in transmitting the information. Truckers use two-way communication when they speak to each other on their two-way radios. Effective communication is two-way, but it's also made up of additional ingredients for you to master:

- *Practices Empathy:* An effective communicator seeks to see things through the eyes of the person with whom they are speaking. They display compassion, empathy, and respect.

- *Acts as a Listening Post:* An effective communicator asks a lot of open-ended questions and shows active interest.

- *Engages in Duologue:* An effective communicator believes in back-and-forth communication that's open to thoughts that are different from their own.

- *Uses Your Gut:* An effective communicator understands that people talk with their heads and their gut or heart. They understand that balancing "head talks" with "heart talks" can be a reassuring force when wild emotions take hold. They speak up when their intuition urges them to.

- *Stays Positively Focused:* An effective communicator maintains focus on the communication objective without getting redirected by frustrations and roadblocks.

- *Aims for Transparency:* An effective communicator repeals the self instead of concealing or hiding the self. Instead of stirring the pot, the positive communicator adds to the pot to make the soup even better.

- *Works to Improve:* An effective communicator puts in the consistent hard work necessary to build healthy relationships. The result is gratitude and enrichment for everyone involved.
- *Adopts a Pattern of Healing:* An effective communicator doesn't pursue drama, manipulation, or hurtful patterns of communication. Instead, they identify their areas of improvement and work to heal from unhelpful communication patterns.

The aim of this book is to help you feel calmer and more confident in your conversations, even during tense situations or troubled times. This starts with identifying your personal areas of communication strengths and areas of improvement. If you are unsure, ask a close friend or someone who won't sugarcoat things. As you read this book, refer back to your areas of improvement and use applicable tools to cultivate new habits of effective communication.

Effective Communication Is the Surest Route to Happiness

As you might already know, there is a link between good communication and increased happiness, success, and longevity. While those results have been enjoyed by many clients and corporations, it's our hope that, at the very least, this book will help you gain new insights into what people say and do so you can better navigate tough conversations.

What will you gain?

- You will learn useful tools to put you in control of your mind, mouth, and mood.
- You will know and practice what to say in rough patches when times are tense, and talks are tough.
- You will get a roadmap to stop conflicts, misunderstandings, and blow-ups from happening or escalating.

- You will become a balanced communicator who mindfully employs both Empathizer and Instigator core strengths.
- You will experience a sense of calm, confidence, and increased competence in your everyday encounters.

This book is divided into seven skill-based chapters. Each chapter focuses on learning and mastering core skills that will rapidly improve your communication abilities. We will use real-life stories to anchor these core principles in your mind for ready access when needed.

The 7 Laws of Effective Communication

As a preview of what's to come, here are the *TALK2ME©* Laws of Effective Communication we will be focusing on throughout this work:

- Law 1: Know who you're talking to: An Instigator or Empathizer.
- Law 2: The solution isn't in your view. It's in the other person's view.
- Law 3: Pretending to listen isn't really listening.
- Law 4: Your mood dictates your reputation.
- Law 5: In a conflict, pause before you react with a Communicator Prejudice.
- Law 6: Critical feedback is critical to your growth.
- Law 7: Everybody wants to be a better communicator, but nobody wants to change.

Let's get started. Time to stop doing what doesn't work and instead do more of what does work. Easier said than done, we know, but what do you have to lose?

Communicate Like a PRO

ONE

KNOW WHO YOU'RE TALKING TO: AN INSTIGATOR OR EMPATHIZER

> *"What if there were two distinctly different communication styles that influence the way we talk and how we prefer to be spoken to?"*
> —Dr. Dennis O'Grady, 2001
>
> *"That's interesting. What would you call them?"*
> —Then 8-year-old daughter, Riley O'Grady

Talk to Me

Instigator-Empathizer was a eureka moment born of frustration. Every great insight, I guess, starts with a lightbulb moment when you feel lost and alone searching in the dark.

In the late 90s, I met in Pittsburgh with my therapist and now mentor, Bill, to discuss a new book I was writing about relationship communication.

"I have to be honest with you, Dennis. This material sounds good but it's missing something. You're getting at something that is new and powerful but this isn't it," Bill said.

"What do you think 'it' is?" I asked Bill.

"I don't know what *it* is but you should search for it," he responded. "Search for what you don't know, and you might find it."

I laughed, but I was also simultaneously disappointed and felt frustrated. "What a lot of *it*!" I mused.

As I was driving west on I-70 nearing Columbus, Ohio, into a captivating bright-orange sunset, I asked myself several questions. First, "What if there were two separate communication styles? What would they be called?" And second, "What does psychotherapy research say are the key variables that help clients change and relationships grow?"

As a psychologist, I had witnessed miraculous changes that went against the odds. In fact, that's what inspired me to write my first 1992 book *Taking The Fear Out Of Changing*. People typically come to therapy because of relationship frustration. They feel down and anxious, stuck in the rut of miscommunication patterns. They are ready to change but don't know how, and they need some outside advice. Change starts with asking for help and learning how to speak to yourself and others.

So, I knew from the research that "empathy" shown in the therapeutic relationship was a key trait that helped clients change. I also knew that a second variable that helped clients change was a therapist who was "genuine"—someone who was genuinely interested in the client and willing to be honest and accurate with feedback about the client's self-defeating behaviors. I also recalled how the personality variables of extroversion (energizing by being socially outgoing), and introversion (energizing by going within and being with self) were universal traits that most people relate to. For example, the Myers-Briggs Type Indicator includes these concepts and is used worldwide.

"Think of opposite pairs, Dennis," I told myself as I sifted through my thoughts. "Think of something you've not been taught as a doctor. Think of something that isn't known. What would you call *it*?" I laughed out loud at the possibility of these exploratory, important questions. Finally, I felt like I was on the right track. I didn't know where I was going, but I was moving forward.

Naming something is half the battle. Naming the unknown makes it come to life. It's like digging for treasure in a field. The healing factors of therapist "Empathy" and "Genuineness" continued to roll around in my mind.

The first communicator type I came up with was "Empathizer." These are people who are generally more sensitive across a wide variety of situations. Then I tried to think of what the opposite "genuine" term or communicator category would be.

For starters, I came up with "Genuineizer" to describe this group of less sensitive people. But I didn't like that term so much because it sounded like a meat tenderizer. However, the moniker kind of fits because Instigators are full of zest and a bit salty. Even today I think Empathizers are sweet and Instigators are salty. Both keep life balanced and spicy.

I felt better about coming up with something to justify a long conversation and a cold drive. I was not a happy person or driver, but the start of a system that would unknowingly change my life, and the lives of thousands of other good people, was born on that highway drive. In fact, I would never have guessed that Dayton Freight Lines, a Midwestern trucking company, would hire me to teach their entire company of 4,500 employees and nearly 500 leader managers Instigator-Empathizer feedback skills and watch their profits and growth go through the roof as a consequence.

In finalizing the names for the two communicator types, I asked my Instigator friend, Jim, if he preferred the name "Instigator" or "Initiator." I had been waffling between these two choices. I took long walks to contemplate the two choices, knowing that the shoe had to fit across couples, countries, and companies. While our kids were playing together and we were shooting the bull, I asked Jim which name he liked best. Without hesitation, he shot back, "I like the term Initiator because it sounds more positive." I laughed because I thought "Initiator" lacked the punch and sizzle that I knew Instigators were born to demonstrate. Instigate actually means to make change happen.

The very next time Jim and I got together, I boldly announced that I had made my final decision. "Jim, thanks so much for your input," I teased. "But I've decided to go with the name Instigator because it has the punch and grit that best describes them. It gives a stronger visceral reaction."

Jim quipped, "Oh, good. I think Instigator was the right one. I just didn't like it because when I was a kid my mom would say "Jimmy, stop instigating." I had to guffaw because my mom had said the very same thing to me when I was growing up.

With that decision, the Instigator and Empathizer communicator types were born.

Over the next four years, I counseled hundreds of clients through the lens of Instigator vs. Empathizer talk technology. The puzzle pieces began to fit together. I was sure I was on to something big. It was exhilarating to be discovering something completely new in the field of psychology. A lifetime dream was coming true. However, to be honest, this took a horrendous amount of creative work, and at times made me feel like my brain would inevitably seep out of my ears. But it was worth it. Over the span of four years, I was able to put together a very effective system that was personally invigorating and life affirming for me, my psychotherapy clients, and business training events.

Opposites attract but can clash. Instigators and Empathizers go together like sun and water. Together they create life, and at times that vibrant and volatile mix will include storms and droughts. But I firmly believe that communication could not occur in its fullest form without these two unconscious energies at work. In highly interactive training workshops, I use the metaphor of two hands clapping. Empathizers are the left hand and Instigators are the right hand. It takes both hands clapping to make a sound. Both the right and left hand are required to come together to make any sound. Can you imagine participating in a sporting event where one hand is always tied behind your back? But that's exactly what happens when you're ignorant of how the two types function subconsciously in your life.

As a psychologist and single father, one thing I've learned over my lifetime is that the hardest thing to change is my own mind. Although it's pretty mind boggling, when you stop to think about it, using *TALK-2ME©* tools will change your life. Your personality might be the same, but your actions will be different.

A new day is awakening in you. The light will come on as you engage the Instigator-Empathizer knowledge base that is buried in your mind ready to emerge. Perhaps it will relieve your frustrations as well!

🗩 Relationship Communication Opportunities

In my fifties, I reviewed my relationship life, and I didn't like the tally.

On important occasions, I had clashed with bosses, friends, life partners, and family members over small and large issues that blew up when they didn't need to. At other times I didn't push back when I should have. I wish I could go back knowing what I now know, but I can't undo the past. And truthfully, I wouldn't if I could because my life experiences have helped shape this book.

My daughter and co-author, Riley, has taught me much about intentional listening and "parrot phrasing" (her jesting words) for paraphrasing what I hear a speaker say. And we both are right here beside you as you do a deep dive into this material.

Speaking of diving, let me share with you a little about my experience as Riley's father. When she was child, Riley hated gymnastics and loved scuba diving. I remember Riley perfectly balanced hovering over me scuba diving 50 feet down in warm ocean waters while I was gazing at a sea turtle munching on a bright-colored coral. Riley started diving when she was nine and is now an instructor. You'll be surprised about the importance of underwater, non-verbal communication later on in this work.

In her childhood, we tramped in Ohio rivers and she would fill my hiking pockets with treasured river rocks. Sometimes at night, she would worry about dinosaurs sticking their heads in her upstairs bedroom window to devour her, resulting in me spending many a night camping out on her floor. As a teen, Riley really gained in self-esteem when she joined Civil Air Patrol, a youth leadership training program. She was like a dry plant soaking up nourishing water. Now she's not a kid anymore. In my view, Riley's a remarkable millennial professional woman.

Riley is an educator at heart who designs and delivers life-skills and career readiness programs for youth and adults. She has experience as a North Carolina high school teacher, Miami University of Ohio psychology research coordinator, and as she calls it, an edupreneur. Her youth programs help young people develop self-efficacy—a belief in their own capacity to succeed—by providing opportunities to learn and practice these skills in safe real-life settings.

Riley has developed career and life-skills educational programs for YMCA, Cincinnati State Technical and Community College, and various other schools and nonprofit organizations in Ohio and Northern Kentucky. These customized programs help youth prepare for adulthood by learning fundamental life skills of communication, cultural competence, conflict resolution, and the ability to cope with change. Riley is also a *TALK2ME©* Trainer and instructional systems designer for New Insights Communication. Riley is able to give feedback like a PRO; this book has benefited much from her wisdom, wit and grit.

I brought Riley into this world on a sunny autumn afternoon, and I hope to be with her when I take my last breath. Riley's quite funny and deep. She wrote a poem in grade school called *Grass* that I included in my 2005 textbook *Talk To Me: Communication Moves to Get Along With Anyone*. It had to do with her creative idea that grass in lawns might have feelings when we walk on it. This book wouldn't be close to what it is today without her tender touch, depthful thinking, and critical feedback. In fact, when Riley was eight, we sat in a golf cart in Mexico discussing what to name the two types of communicators, and her hand print color-coded paintings of the two types still hang in my office to this day.

To put things into a family context, Riley is the middle sister of my three daughters. Her older sister, Erin, is a Boston psychologist. Her younger sister, Kasey, is a Phoenix data analyst. Riley furiously loves both of these remarkable young women. The same goes for me, only double. Besides myself, my three daughters were the first people to be directly exposed to and influenced by this brave new world of effective communication. And although I struggled communicating clearly with them during their teenage years, and occasionally still do today, *TALK2ME©* is a light that shines in the darkness pointing the way ahead. Frankly, I don't know where I would be today without this talk technology.

My life has been transformed knowing what makes Instigators and Empathizers tick or ticked off. I understand myself and others...far, far better. Specifically, I've learned how to communicate more effectively when the chips are down and I'm highly stressed. I've learned not to give feedback when frustrated. I've learned listening is the fix. I've learned my mood is largely under my control. I've learned honesty solves problems. I've learned that complaining isn't changing. I've learned I can change myself but I can't change you. I've learned how to step back in a dispute and do what works instead of repeatedly knocking my head against a brick wall. I even enjoy getting along with people I used to consider obnoxious. Are you up for those results?

The main error all of us make is to assume our neighbor is a duplicate copy of our Empathizer or Instigator Type. One size shoe doesn't fit us all. Expecting you to be me is the *TALK2ME©* definition of the brick wall. Overall, as a result of *TALK2ME©* teachings my frustrations aren't as many nor do they last as long. Mostly, I experience a calm confidence and inner peace. And according to my three adult daughters, I'm a better single parent. Mostly. And in the opinions of counseling clients, I'm definitely a more competent psychotherapist and workshop trainer. Moreover, I'm a happier senior citizen interacting in this zany world. Life's not perfect, but it's pretty darn good. But life hasn't always been as sweet. There have been sour times filled with sorrow.

Early on, I was pretty hard on myself. I had to face my errors caused by ignorance and forgive myself along the way for what I didn't know. However, if you're like me, you're going to feel excited when you learn why communication accidents have happened to you in the past in spite of your best efforts. And you will now know how to prevent accidents in the future. You will see and hear the train coming and get your butt off the tracks. You'll have the best of both Instigator and Empathizer worlds at your fingertips. And you'll experience why having one without the other is like having an ocean without land. Ignorance isn't bliss; it just makes a mess. Forgive yourself upfront. You didn't know what you were doing...until now.

I've got a long way to go. When my memories are triggered by my failures to communicate, I still can be brutally self-critical. Admittedly, I used to think being right was more important than having inner peace. I used to be pretty depressed and anxious. I used to think it was normal to get mad when people didn't do what I thought they should do. I used to think it was my job to fix your problems and be a peacemaker. I used to feel hypersensitive when criticized. I used to do the road rage thing. I used to stick with people who didn't respect me. I used to take pride in telling people what I really thought about them but packaged my feedback in ways that clogged ears. Nowadays, I have fewer "out-of-mouth experiences." I don't spout off defensively in offensive ways before I think about how my words will wound. Predictive empathy is a gift we present to you here. Pretty much, I can predict how what I say and do will impact you. You'll soon be able to do the same, too.

Sometimes, I still feel guilty to the gills for my failures to communicate. But I've learned if what I'm doing isn't working, I've got to do something different. I go back to the basics. "Know who you're talking to: An Instigator or Empathizer." When I follow the PRO Laws and Rules, I'm not ever disappointed and barriers fall away. When life is dark and you feel alone and nothing seems to be working, the light will come on to show the way ahead and what needs to change. In my case, I had to bring relationships to a close that broke my heart. I had to give up my woe-is-me anger habit. I had to work on myself instead of telling others what to do. I had to walk the talk. Sure it takes work, but it sure is worth it.

Change is difficult. Give yourself credit for keeping an open mind. This chapter is dense with new ideas and a challenge to get your arms around. But you will hear critical feedback that is critical to your growth. This is the hardest part. Don't give up. Don't get all glum. Just go with the new information for now.

Riley Growing Up With *TALK2ME©*

I was a shy, sensitive kid. Elementary school, like for all young children, is a time to learn basic social skills. Luckily, my best friend was brilliant, boisterous, and bold. Even though we grew up together and shared the same crib when our moms would hang out, the way we approached communication at a young age was very different. Sarah would jump in and take charge. I was reserved and would happily follow Sarah anywhere. It was the perfect match.

One day on vacation in Mexico my dad and I were waiting on my sisters and mom to join us outside. I was usually the quickest to get ready. I sported my seahorse shirt, cargo shorts, and a ponytail. I was a bit of a tomboy. My dad turned to me and said, "What if there were two distinctly different communication styles that influence the way we talk and how we prefer to be spoken to?" I loved these types of conversations with my dad. Even at a young age (I was eight at the time), I felt he valued my opinion and challenged me to think outside of the box. "That's interesting. What would you call them?" I replied curiously.

Many things seemed to click all at once. My friend Sarah was an Instigator Extrovert. My most difficult teacher also was an Instigator. I was thrilled. My dad told me he was still working on the colors for the two types and invited me to make a painting of them. When we got back to Ohio, I went downstairs and started mixing colors and pulled a new canvas. I loved to paint. I started with the Empathizer color and picked ocean blue probably because I loved the ocean. I painted half the canvas blue. Next I thought of my fiery friend Sarah. What color would she be? Sarah was bright as the sun, a beam of light in my life. Burnt orange covered the other half of the canvas and infused into the blue creating a mixing in the middle. As a final touch I added a handprint in blue and one in orange. Perfect.

In elementary school and middle school *TALK2ME*© became just another part of my reality. It was just how I started thinking. It's how I got out of conflicts. It was how I overcame my social awkwardness. It's what I reverted to when I felt nothing else was working. I would pause and think about who the person was, what the desirable outcome would be, and what I needed to do to get that outcome. It was really very simple. I've practiced typecasting since elementary school, and grew accustomed to looking at someone and thinking E or I. It was a fun game that gave me great confidence, especially when I was dealing with a scary adult or a school bully.

Fast forward, my junior year of high school I came to the sunroom where my dad often wrote in the evenings or early mornings. I was in tears, "Dad what if they don't follow me because I'm short or because I'm a girl? I feel like it would just be easier if I was a tall boy!" I had always been self-conscious of my height and was picked on since a young age for it. I was also growing increasingly aware of how gender and stature played a role in perceptions of authority. My sisters and parents are tall and I, regardless of my wishes and prayers, maxed out at 5'2".

My dad smiled at me and said, "Riley you have always been up for a challenge. It's not about your height or your gender, it's about how you communicate. Focus on your communication and being equally confident and competent and people will follow you." So, I put my I-Type hat on and started to blend my communication style. And you know what? It worked. When I believed that communication was the key and didn't get into my head, I was able to focus on performance and subsequently other people cared less and less about my height or gender.

Keeping *TALK2ME©* top of mind got me out of a lot of pickles in high school. It also got me into a few pickles, too, but we'll talk about that later on. I've found that the solution to being a great leader is being a great communicator. Focusing on being a great communicator more than you focus on your age, height, race, or gender is something you can control.

As you can already tell, my nature is an Empathizer. However, in some roles it's expected that I look and sound like an Instigator. Although I was born an Empathizer, I have adopted the habits of Instigators to be a better balanced partner and person. I used to be afraid of conflicts. Empathizers can become lost in emotional fog and doubt themselves when strong disagreements occur in relationships. I used to think if someone was hurt by something I said or did that I was in the wrong and had to make it right. Now I'm not so easily intimidated by Instigators debating skills, or what we call "conversational coercion" later on in this book. Throughout my childhood, adolescence, and now adulthood I've been able to use *TALK2ME©* to navigate the struggles of growing up. I'm not a perfect communicator today, but

I believe a lifetime of work and daily sharpening will get me pretty darn close.

Well, enough about us for now. Let's make this about you.

Although your communicator type matters a great deal, understanding your opposite type matters even more to your future success. Ultimately, this knowledge acts like a ladder that you can use to climb over tall walls that separate people. Conflicts will calm, and true confidence will arise in you.

💬 Will This Work For Me?

George Bernard Shaw said, "The single biggest problem in communication is the illusion that it has taken place." How to know if this work will be of benefit to you:

- If you think you're a pretty good listener but people close to you would disagree...
- If you're feared because of mad moods, or pulled down by sad moods...
- If you finish someone's sentences, or can't speak up assertively when you need to...
- If you say things that make conflicts worse, not better...
- If you're criticized for putting more time and effort into your work than your relationship...
- If you show hypersensitivity to critical feedback and get all twisted up...
- If you flip into another personality when all your buttons are hit...
- If you fear conflict and avoid tough talks because it never turns out well...
- If you know you need to change but you don't know how...
- If you need to understand your defensiveness and improve your way of communicating with other people...

Basically, if you're a human being, then this book is for you. That is, if you would like to try doing something new.

💬 A Brave New World of Compassionate Communication

A broader perspective of the world of communication and how to operate within it cultivates your understanding and decreases your worries. This is true in reference to outer space, foreign countries, and yes, difficult people. Fear, dislike, and conflict are rooted in one simple thing: A lack of perspective. You can't see the forest for all the dense trees blocking your view.

You might be thinking, "Well I know that difficult person really well. Probably too well. That's why they get on my nerves!" In fact, the person who drives you up a wall and down again can be a spouse, sibling, teenager, in-law, boss, random strangers, maybe all of the above.

Let's be clear that your being aware of their strange or annoying behaviors is very different from understanding *why* they do those things, and more importantly, how you can stay calm and create far better outcomes.

Throughout this work, you will see a number of "PRO Rules" that are meant to highlight important communication tools that coincide with the 7 Laws of Effective Communication. Make sure to pay extra close attention when you see them throughout this work. Believe it: The same rules work well both at work and home.

PRO Rules are "rest breaks" on our journey together to keep you energized and focused. Once you know who you are talking to, an Instigator or an Empathizer, you can flexibly follow new "PRO Rules" that will help you feel less stressed and get along better with everyone you meet.

PRO Rule: Treat others the way *they* want to be treated: As an Instigator or Empathizer.

Recently, an Empathizer wife came into her Instigator husband's study, jumped in his lap, and said: "I'm really upset. Will you just hold me?" The Instigator husband reacted with, "Can't you see that I'm in the middle of a work project here? Talk to your friend." The busy Instigator husband meant no harm but really hurt his wife's feelings without intending to. In his defense, the Instigator husband was on a deadline and believed her best friend was a better consoler, anyway. His Empathizer wife disagreed, saying, "I don't know what else to do. You asked me what I wanted for Mother's Day. I want a divorce."

Instigators are big-hearted but can appear cold and robotic in the emotional world of Empathizers. This husband loved his wife deeply and showed it in his work and building a financial empire, yet his wife never heard words of affirmation or affection. She felt neglected and rejected. His defense was to say, "I told you I loved you when we got married. When that changes, I will let you know." This was meant to be funny but came across as sarcastic and rude to his Empathizer beloved. Mistakes like this trigger Communicator Prejudices which can be costly. During our counseling sessions, he learned how listening is the fix. How he doesn't have to fix problems by making suggestions or avoiding emotional conversations that raise anxiety. With more practice, all went along much more smoothly and an unnecessary divorce was avoided.

You will learn how to speak in the two different languages of Empathizer and Instigator to avoid causing clashes, conflicts, and communication crashes.

Law 1: Know Who You're Talking To: An Instigator or Empathizer

In this chapter, you will develop a strong foundation and basic knowledge of how the minds of Empathizers and Instigators work. We hope this will be a lightbulb moment for you.

First off, the *TALK2ME©* System is color-coded to make your learning easier. In a half-day training workshop for a law firm specializing in injury cases, we used orange dots and blue dots to represent Instigator-burnt orange and Empathizer-ocean blue typecasting. After learning of the two types, each participant chose their dot and wore it on their sleeve for the rest of the workshop. This empowered the team to see how communicator type was different from age, gender, personality, economic class, society role, etc. This legal practice is still talking about it more than a decade later.

See colors to help cue your mind. Another type of imagery we use is the two-way communication highway that carries only two colors of cars: Empathizer blue cars and Instigator burnt orange cars. These two colors of cars are equally represented on the road as they are in real life. Burnt orange Instigators' energy burns as bright as the sun. Ocean blue Empathizers' emotions run as deep as the ocean. From this moment forward there are only two types of talkers you need to worry about: burnt orange Instigators and ocean blue Empathizers.

Knowledge of I-E talk technology leads to more love at home and higher leadership scores at work. You will know how to interact with others and interpret their behaviors free of inaccurate thinking and in-effective grudges. Complaining can be draining. But that's what we do when we don't understand what we're talking about.

Here's an example: a robotics engineering company was a client. There was a lot of complaining that everyone was talking and no one was lis-tening. Nothing was working as one expensive program after another was tried and came up bust. Leadership communication scores were in the dumpster, for five years in a row. When I talked to folks, I saw and heard where the communication breakdown was occurring. In fact, the same old "how do you interrupt an Instigator and get their attention" dynamic was work. It was the same dynamic that we previously spoke about with our Instigator-Empathizer couple at home. Different day; same dynamic.

This is what was happening. Instead of emailing, and because offices were in the same walking vicinity, Empathizer employees in particular made communication at work a quick, personal, and face-to-face en-counter. Empathizers like to talk directly to a person whenever possible out of respect for the relationship and because in their view it's more effective. But here's what happened.

When an Empathizer engineer would walk into the office of an Instigator supervisor with an important question to clarify, the Instigator manager wouldn't even look at the person. The Instigator wouldn't turn around and face the Empathizer and smile, look them in the eye to signal listening, or stop working at the computer. This constitutes pure rudeness in Empathizer land. Then the beleaguered Instigator supervisor would blurt out a fast and blunt response and return to work. The Empathizer would feel brushed off and not heard, unimportant, and rudely ignored. Silent resentment accrued. It showed up in the form of low scores on the leadership climate survey.

Due to *TALK2ME©*, I knew Instigators believe they can multitask when they really can't. I also knew that Instigators become anxious when interrupted at work because they fear losing their place in the task and thereby losing precious time. And I knew deep down that Instigators judge their worth by what they accomplish; they start with a blank slate each day to prove their worth. I knew, too, that Instigators didn't know who Empathizers were, nor did they understand the basic truth that a little time spent with an Empathizer today would save tons of resentment, and low scores, on the Instigators leadership survey tomorrow. That's because E-Types just need to feel valued and validated. Just a little bit goes a long way. But who knew? No one had taught Instigators the ropes.

In small groups, I taught a "Stop...Look...Listen...Respond" tool that took a minute to use but would save hours of unintended consequences. Employees also rehearsed a pre-planned response, "I'm wrapped up in this project right now but I will come and find you in 30 minutes. Will that work?" Granted, you have to keep your word and follow through. But as a result, managers' scores went through the roof as measured by an independent Cincinnati research company. In fact, the Human Resources VP who oversaw the project declared, "If we were in the medical field, *TALK2ME©* would be the cure for cancer." And he meant it. All this took was small group half-day interactive training for the 200 supervisor managers to accomplish this outcome.

These tools work equally well at work and home. Think of tough spots you've been in when you've done your best but ended up only feeling frustrated and unappreciated. Instead of defending yourself, or why what you're doing isn't working, free your mind up right now to learn something new to do.

> **PRO Rule:** It's not how you meant the message that matters, but how it was received.

Did you get that? As a PRO, you will learn the tried-and-true methods that make sure your true message and invaluable feedback is heard. You will customize what you say by communicator type to improve your impact and your mood. Your reputation will soar. As a result, you will be heard far more often and feel hurt far less often. And in a conflict, you won't defend your position as "right" when it hurts or offends your partner. You will choose your battles carefully. You will pause before you pounce.

Don't buy the skeptical hype that you can't become a better communicator. But don't just take our word for it. We won't rave or brag about *TALK2ME©* because it's not for everyone. Make up your own mind. Simply use the Laws and apply the System. The results will speak for themselves. The first step is the biggest step of all: Know your type and the type of those you work for and live with. That way, you will learn to speak in their "foreign" language and respect the customs of their country.

We recommend that you keep it simple for now. Before you go on, think of two important people in your life. You, and someone you would like to get along more peacefully with. It could be a life partner, boss, sibling, parent, or friend. Just use the two of you to relate to the material in this typecasting chapter. With a little elbow grease, you will master family and team typecasting in no time at all.

This is the most important step: Know how the two communicator types walk, talk and think. And apply those tools so you and yours feel emotionally safe and happier traveling on the Two-Way Communication Highway. Deeper emotional bonding will result.

We'll help you chart your progress with our summary Chapter Takeaways and Sharpen Your *TALK2ME©* tools exercises at the conclusion of each chapter. These are designed to give you a "thumbnail sketch" of key ideas to keep alive and practice every day. You will learn step-by-step how to apply the *7 Laws of Effective Communication* in your world that work wonders.

In our view, it's not a fair game if you don't know the rules of the game.

🗨 The Clear Difference

The number one way you can identify if someone is an Empathizer or Instigator is to have an awareness of the different traits and communication preferences E-Types and I-Types possess. Let's review the table below to highlight key trait differences between Empathizers and Instigators that reinforce what you learned in the introduction.

Empathizers	Instigators
It's Not a Male or Female Thing	
Mood Catcher	Mood Pitcher
More Sensitive	Less Sensitive
Magnify(+) Negatives Minimize(-) Positives	Magnify(+) Positives Minimize(-) Negatives
Listen First	Talk First
Slow Feedback	Fast Feedback
Trusts Feelings	Trusts Reasons
Sad Triggers	Mad Triggers
Duologue	Debate
Soft Heart	Hard Head
Reveal Feelings	Conceal Feelings

These are universal trait preferences that Instigators and Empathizers default to in order to understand the world and navigate tricky life passages. They are not necessarily true for every situation you encounter. Use them as a guide but keep using your common sense. Good communication is common sense but not commonly done.

Let's dive into the differences between E-Types and I-Types, how to identify if someone is one or the other, and tactics to use when dealing with your opposite type. First, let's explain the differences highlighted in the chart above that are key giveaways:

Mood

- If you are an Empathizer, you are a mood catcher. You take on the moods of others.
- If you are an Instigator, you are a mood pitcher. You transfer your moods to others.

Sensitivity

- If you are an Empathizer, you are more sensitive to constructive criticism.
- If you are an Instigator, you are less sensitive to constructive criticism.

Negativity

- If you are an Empathizer, you magnify negatives in yourself when times are tough.
- If you are an Instigator, you magnify positives in yourself when times are tough.

Positivity

- If you are an Empathizer, you minimize positives about yourself.
- If you are an Instigator, you minimize negatives about yourself.

Listening Attitude

- If you are an Empathizer, you seek to listen first before spouting off.
- If you are an Instigator, you strive to talk first to influence the discussion.

Feedback Style

- If you are an Empathizer, you prefer slow feedback to correct problems.
- If you are an Instigator, you prefer fast feedback to correct problems.

Decision Making

- If you are an Empathizer, you trust feelings to bridge disputes, divisions and make decisions.
- If you are an Instigator, you trust reasons to bridge disputes, divisions and make decisions.

Emotional Triggers

- If you are an Empathizer, when triggered by fear you will feel sad.
- If you are an Instigator, when triggered by fear you will feel mad.

Conflict Style

- If you are an Empathizer, duologues make you feel safe and valued.
- If you are an Instigator, debates make you feel safe and valued.

Connecting

- If you are an Empathizer, you have a soft heart but that can make you appear weak.
- If you are an Instigator, you have a hard head but that can make you appear rude.

Self-Disclosure

- If you are an Empathizer, you reveal feelings to calm anxieties and feel more secure.
- If you are an Instigator, you conceal feelings to calm anxieties and feel more secure.

Remember, both types are equal. One is not better or worse. Each type is a blend of traits and communication preferences. The key is to seek to be a blended communicator.

You are a unique person with a unique background. As such, you have a unique blend of Instigator-Empathizer communication traits that exist along a spectrum.

You can be extremely positive or extremely negative or just plain in the middle neutral. Extreme types intensify and magnify the traits we've listed. Which type is best? A *positive* Instigator or a *positive* Empathizer. Negative Instigators and negative Empathizers are equally bad news bears.

Using a blend of both types' strengths within yourself is best. Did you know what? Secrets be told, each type finds fault with their own type and believes their opposite type is the better one. Strange, isn't it? So, let's compromise and actively use the tools of both types. For where would our world be without the bright sunshine of Instigators? Or where would our world be without the blue ocean waters of Empathizers? Together, each does their part to form solid land for our world playground. Indeed, what a cold world this would be without our beloved opposite other.

It's also important for you to continuously keep in mind that being an Empathizer or Instigator is not gender-driven. It's the first prejudice among many we must take on and conquer. Our extensive "real life" clinical research shows about a 50/50 Instigator-Empathizer split between men and women. This means that if you're a woman, half of your female friends will typically be Instigators and half will be Empathizers. Likewise, if you're a man, half of your male friends will be Empathizers and half will be Instigators. Knowing "who's who" will empower you.

And do be aware that you may select friends and give promotions to people like you who are your I-E mirror type. Birds of a feather, it seems, do like to fly together. In our experience, balanced teams with about an equal mix of both types seem to function best.

Throughout the remainder of this chapter, we are going to use these distinct traits to anchor the discussion on Empathizer vs. Instigator and how to typecast. Let's start by exploring a clinical example of a "mixed" E-I couple.

🗩 Marriage Counseling: Opposite Sides of the Same Couch

Joe and Amy appeared to have a picture-perfect marriage. They had a Golden Retriever, suburban house, stable careers, and adorable children. That, of course, didn't explain why they found themselves in Dr. O'Grady's office, awkwardly seated as distantly as possible from one another on the same couch.

"She is absolutely impossible and never listens," Joe confessed with eyes down looking away from his wife. "We just fight all the time now—I mean it's starting to affect my work and the kids, so I thought..."

"So, you thought you would call a shrink?!" Amy interrupted looking disgusted.

They say opposites attract. While true for Joe and Amy, these differences were now leading them down the road of many couples who argue like them—divorce.

This makes sense when you know who's talking. Amy was a fiery Instigator while Joe was a laid-back Empathizer. Both partners did not understand why their opposite reacted the way they did and what could bridge the divide. It seemed like pure lunacy. This, of course, caused increasing tension disrupting satisfaction for both partners within the marriage.

How did this couple get here and what can be done to salvage the situation?

In the next few sections, we will help you dive into the differences between E-Types and I-Types and how to get through to your opposite when in tough situations, such as the one Joe and Amy faced.

💬 Breaking the Empathizer Code

Let's start by looking at Joe. How are male or female Empathizer Communicators wired?

Joe will be self-critical. He will magnify negative feedback, even negative comments made by Amy that are inaccurate. His feelings will get hurt easily. Joe will dwell on past mistakes and might get criticized by Amy for not being able to move on.

Joe will also be very sensitive to the moods of others. He has the natural ability to read people. This also means he absorbs the moods of others like a sponge.

Joe will feel in the wrong when something goes wrong in the relationship. As someone who is focused on relationship harmony, he assumes he ought to know what to do to make others happy.

Joe will be slow to speak up or give constructive criticism to Amy. Since nothing is said, Amy is likely to assume she has done no wrong and incorrectly think Joe is happy.

When encouraged to be honest and blunt with Amy, he will say, "But I don't want to hurt Amy's feelings and make her feel bad." Or he will say, "Look. I've told her before, but she just blows me off. I'm not going to waste my breath. She won't hear what she doesn't want to hear."

Wired as an Empathizer, Joe believes in the code of decency. He will dislike "extreme" or negative Instigator men and women who are cold, blunt, selfish, or mean.

As a weakness, Joe will stew on his resentments toward Amy. Things she said or did that disrespected Joe, such as overspending or threatening to leave him, will be received by Joe as slights and rejections until the "last straw" makes him blow. When he finally blows up, because his Inner Instigator came out, this will shock Amy. Then he will feel bad that he lost it and Amy will make him feel even worse for dumping his frustrations on her.

Joe will typically default to feeling sad. Joe is a mood catcher while Amy is a mood pitcher. He will feel down when things aren't going the way he expects them to. Whether fair or unfair, Joe will feel bad and responsible for his partner's blunt complaints of unhappiness.

Empathizers also have notable strengths. Joe will love ferociously, forgive quickly, be loyal, gentle, patient, and kind to those he cares for. He will be told he is a great listener and a good friend. Joe stands for equality, compassion, and teamwork.

Looks can be deceiving. He will act easygoing, laid back and have a positive outlook even when Amy has stepped hard on his toes. And Joe will wish he had more confidence and less self-doubt. He will negatively believe, "I'm not good enough. I could do so much better." He will also struggle to feel OK when people dislike or disagree with him. Joe as an Empathizer will strive too hard to be approved of.

Joe will have grown up being the sensitive member of the family who hurts when others hurt. And because words are gospel to Empathizers, Joe will think before he speaks, and thereby avoid saying hurtful things to others. Joe also won't forget sharp-tongued words Amy throws at him in anger.

About 50% of the people you know and now interact with are Empathizer men and women. Again, it's not a male or female thing. It's just how E-Types are naturally wired.

Let's practice what we're preaching. We've used opposite-compiled "personality" trait lists for you to review and revisit. Instigators typically scan the lists lightly because they prefer a *Reader's Digest* version. Empathizers prefer to dig in to get the fuller *War and Peace* book version. Notice which style of knowledge acquisition you prefer. Can you change it? As a reader, do what suits you or try reading the lists from alternate Instigator-Empathizer learning preferences.

How Empathizers are Wired

If you're an Empathizer, you were born and are hard-wired to approach life from these vantage points:

- Tuned-in sensitive
- Picks up the mood of others
- Accepts fault too easily
- Excessive self-criticizer
- Excellent listener
- Defaults to sad when stressed
- Stunted self-confidence
- Loyal to a fault and faithful friend
- Represses justifiable anger
- Acts too nice when discounted or dismissed

Knowing someone is an Empathizer will help you amplify their strengths and avoid their pet-peeves.

Checklist for Interacting With Empathizers

Empathizers will sense you're speaking in their language, will feel emotionally safe, trusted and respected when you:

- Smile and be warm
- Listen carefully
- Don't gruffly interrupt

- Don't argue or talk over
- Repeat what was just said
- Ask questions to clarify views
- Compliment tons
- Criticize little
- Pre-plan feedback to have the best impact
- Ask: "How could I do better by you?"

Resort to these communication basics with Empathizers when the train is threatening to go off the tracks.

⤬ Breaking the Instigator Code

Let's take a look at Amy now. How are male and female Instigator Communicators wired?

To Amy, being respected is more important than being liked. In her relationship with Joe, she will take pride in telling it like it is, being blunt, acting genuine and being authentic. "What you see is what you get," cautions Amy. This is often the motto of Instigators. Political correctness, kissing up, and telling you what you want to hear is loathed by Instigators. They prefer to say it how it is. No sugarcoating.

Joe will complain that Amy talks at people instead of to people. But Amy is a natural-born leader who is prone to being large and in charge. She knows what she wants and needs, and goes after it.

As a habit, Amy magnifies positives and minimizes negatives. This makes Joe think she's not listening, being selfish, or sporting an inflated ego.

Amy can be too blunt or say things she later regrets. She is a quick decision-maker and a bold risk-taker. She can come across abrasive or strong-willed when she wants to get her way. She won't take "no" for an answer.

Amy thinks of alternate routes to solve problems. She values doing things efficiently and not wasting time. She will stare you down, roll her eyes expressively, and get right to the point. She is comfortable interrupting and would prefer to jump in, so she doesn't forget her point.

As an Instigator, she will speak up, shake hands hard, and be passionate about her beliefs. Amy will pride herself on being right most of the time.

She dislikes showing her "soft side" for fear of being taken advantage of. Amy is a mood setter. Like a thermostat, she sets the mood temperature in her home. Amy can even talk herself out of a bad mood, saying: "If I can't do anything about what went wrong, we just have to move on and forget about it." This can make Joe feel like she's sweeping important issues under the rug.

Joe doesn't realize that Amy can handle focusing on only one criticism at a time. He needs to learn to keep feedback criticisms short and simple and singular. Although super-confident on the outside, inner insecurity is Amy's vulnerability.

Although Amy has a big heart, she's often viewed by Joe as less demonstrative, on the cold side, robotic, or hard-headed. As an I-Type, Amy is impatient and easily gets mad. She will tell Joe exactly what she's thinking and not hold her punches. Amy can dish out genuine negative feedback without feeling, a behavior that disturbs Joe.

Amy is a world-class debater who easily wins arguments with Joe, even when she's in the wrong. Being less sensitive has its advantages. Joe might tease her that she would make a good attorney. Winning is important to Amy and she doesn't like weakness or whining. Secret insecurities of "never quite measuring up" plague her.

Amy's an Alpha mother and spouse who struggles with feeling loved and secure. When in conflict, Joe will jab, "It's always your way or the highway!" Amy can't quite believe that anyone would love her unconditionally. Amy measures her worth by how much she accomplishes.

Instigator females are maligned as being bossy. But Instigator views are often just what it takes to change things or to get ahead in the workplace. Instigators are born that way. It's just how I-Types are naturally wired.

How Instigators are Wired

If you're an Instigator, you will approach life from these vantage points:

- Builds self-worth by solving problems
- Hides hurt
- Acts confident when nervous
- Sets mood tone in the home
- Hypersensitive to partner and kids
- Won't seek help because is overly self-reliant
- Shrugs off constructive criticisms
- Appears thick-skinned but has a tender heart
- Defaults to mad when sad, hurt or scared
- Low self-esteem as a communicator
- Will break rules to get way
- Fearful of being controlled
- Doesn't need others' approval

Do these traits describe you or someone you know?

💬 Checklist for Interacting with Instigators

Instigators will sense you're speaking in their language, and will trust and respect you when you…

- Aren't afraid to disagree
- Get to the point
- Look them in the eye
- Speak in a confident voice
- Tell your truth
- Push back when challenged
- Tease and joke
- Paraphrase views
- Give one criticism at a time
- Say what you need
- Respect short attention spans

- Trust problem-solving skills
- Account for insecurity vulnerability

Speak in the feedback style that Instigators prefer, and Instigators will respect and listen to you more.

💬 Different Strokes for Different Folks

Instigators and Empathizers also have distinct preferences when it comes to feedback, decision making, listening, mood, and many other activities or tasks. For example, Empathizers are approval seekers who feel motivated by sincere compliments. In contrast, Instigators can act like a bull in a china shop and tend to distrust sincere compliments.

Here are how some of these peculiar I-Type vs. E-Type aspects will come across when you remove the blindfold:

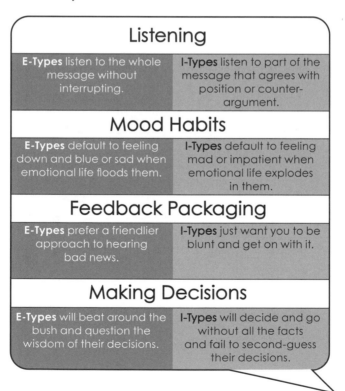

Listening

| E-Types listen to the whole message without interrupting. | I-Types listen to part of the message that agrees with position or counter-argument. |

Mood Habits

| E-Types default to feeling down and blue or sad when emotional life floods them. | I-Types default to feeling mad or impatient when emotional life explodes in them. |

Feedback Packaging

| E-Types prefer a friendlier approach to hearing bad news. | I-Types just want you to be blunt and get on with it. |

Making Decisions

| E-Types will beat around the bush and question the wisdom of their decisions. | I-Types will decide and go without all the facts and fail to second-guess their decisions. |

Instigators push hard to create forward movement as if their very life depends on it. In contrast, Empathizers don't sweat the small stuff and just want Instigators to be happy and approve of them. This can make Instigators come across as bull-headed while making Empathizers look like pushovers who are easy-to-manipulate.

Your Strengths and Blind Spots

Based on your Empathizer or Instigator type, there is a corresponding set of strengths and blind spots for you to be aware of. We want to help you build awareness of what each type is good at and what each type is bad at. See if you can identify the strength, weakness, or "blind spots" and areas of improvement that you would like to add to your life.

Strength-based approaches generally ask, "What's right?" while deficit-based approaches ask, "What's wrong?" *TALK2ME©* does not fall on either side of these extremes. It's not in the sugar-coated, feel-good, strength-based camp nor is it in the hyper-critical, nitpicky, deficit-based camp. We are not going to sing Kumbaya and we are also not going to beat you down like a school bully would. It's not about who's right or wrong but about what works best for you and yours.

TALK2ME© helps you identify your strengths and areas that need improvement. It lights the way ahead. It also helps you become aware of the unique traits of Empathizer and Instigator Communicators to feel more confident and in charge.

What are Your Strengths? What are Your Blind Spots? And What Can You Do Better?

Following is a short list of contrasting strengths and areas of improvement. Throughout this work, we refer to areas of improvement as "blind spots" since they are often areas the individual is unaware of or "blind" to. Use the list below to identify the traits you possess and review it with a friend, colleague, or partner.

If you're an Empathizer, your strengths are:

- Intuitive
- Big-hearted/Compassionate
- Hard-Working
- Reliable
- Patient
- Good Listener
- Laid Back
- Thoughtful
- Approachable
- Inclusive

If you're an Empathizer, your blind spots might be:

- Overly self-critical
- Tends to ignore accomplishments and greatness
- Can be taken advantage of
- Overly sensitive to what people think about them
- Minimizes the positives and magnifies negatives
- Stays quiet when it's time to speak up
- Gives too much, resulting in feeling drained
- Overly cautious decision-making
- Being too "nice" causing a loss of authority, control, or getting pushed around
- Driven by feelings when the situation requires analytical or logical analysis
- Defaults to sadness and negative self-talk during tough times

As an Empathizer, which strengths and blind spots do you feel apply to you? What have you heard that would improve your communication game?

If you're an Instigator, your strengths are:

- Honest
- Motivated
- Accountable
- Decisive
- Tough/Strong
- Not fearful/Confident
- Eager to take control
- Level-headed
- Logical
- Optimistic

If you're an Instigator, your blind spots might be:

- Can be hard-headed, combative, or debate when it's inappropriate for the situation
- Does not listen closely and gets distracted by a busy mind during conversations
- Conceals feelings causing an appearance of being cold
- Constantly seeks external accomplishments that never seem to satisfy
- Attempts to solve issues beyond personal control
- Can be overly demanding of themselves and others
- Optimistic to the point of being unaware of issues or areas of improvement
- Can be overly critical and judgmental of others
- Struggles to give up control and can be dominating or a "control freak"
- Defaults to anger and resentment during tough times

As an Instigator, which strengths and blind spots do you feel apply to you? What have you been told would improve your communication game?

Consciously choosing to adopt and use the strength sets of both types works best for everyone.

⌕ Adopt the Strengths of Your Opposite Type to be a More Effective and Flexible Communicator

Because balanced communication is best, here are traits that Empathizers and Instigators can adopt from their opposite communicator type list.

Adopting these positive traits of the opposite type often "cures" the blind spot or negative trait previously possessed. Empathizers often possess positive traits that are the antithesis of a negative Instigator trait, and vice versa. For example, E-Types are good listeners while I-Types struggle to listen. Or, E-Types let things get to them too easily while I-Types are thick-skinned.

If you're an Instigator, choose one of these Empathizer strengths to adopt:

- A willingness to listen
- Showing a consistent compassionate interest in the inner lives of co-workers, subordinates, and partners
- Tuning in to emotions
- Openness to receiving input on areas of improvement
- Being confident enough to ask for help or admit mistakes
- Becoming more approachable
- Seeing things from the other person's point of view
- Withholding judgment
- Doing a better job expressing positive feelings
- Being less aggressive
- Showing patience
- Staying calm and relaxed

- Being more caring, nurturing, and supportive (not as apt to crush someone)
- Giving more compliments instead of criticisms
- Being intuitive (checking/trust your gut as well as logical data)

If you're an Empathizer, choose one of these Instigator strengths to adopt:

- Being straightforward and blunt
- Being more confident
- Being assertive
- Being outspoken
- Becoming more thick-skinned
- Not allowing the opinions of others get to you
- Speaking up when something needs to be said
- Being more directive and demanding
- Becoming more analytical and break problems down into parts
- Getting to a decision and sticking to it
- Being ambitious, timely, and focused on achievement
- Being confident and "faking it" even when feeling inadequate
- Not listening or tolerating negativity or negative people
- Asking for what you want and deserve
- Leading with a strong sense of authority

Which strengths of your opposite type will you choose to adopt to use in your life today? These unique strengths, blind spots, and areas of improvement influence the perceptions Empathizers and Instigators have of one another.

The Instigator-Empathizer Dance

Not everything is rainbows and butterflies between Empathizers and Instigators. As you noticed from the example mentioned earlier with the couple, Amy and Joe, the differences between E-Types and I-Types can cause division...job loss...or divorce. Here are just a few of the ways I-views and E-views can co-create standoffs that spiral out of control:

- As the Instigator judges an Empathizer as too wordy and beating around the bush...
  The Empathizer judges the Instigator as too close-minded and not listening.
- As the Instigator rudely talks over and debates...
  The Empathizer shuts up and shuts down.
- As the Instigator doesn't tune in and paraphrase what's being said...
  The Empathizer gives up trying to get their point across.
- As the Instigator gets louder to make a passionate point...
  The Empathizer feels intimidated and pressured to go along.
- As the Instigator thinks everything is OK...
  The Empathizer increasingly feels very NOT-OK.

Listen to Hear

Not listening is the root cause of many conflicts. That's because active listening requires you to listen to what's being said, not just what's in your head. If you're an Instigator, you will fail to listen and cause conflict by...

- Not tuning in
- Prejudging the Empathizer as too wordy
- Assuming you know what the Empathizer is going to say
- Rudely interrupting or talking over the other person
- Getting all "huffy"
- Loudly repeating your point like a broken record
- Being a solutions pusher but dismissive of people

If you're an Empathizer, you will fail to be heard and cause conflict by...

- Giving up trying to get your point across
- Prejudging the Instigator as too close-minded
- Assuming the Instigator will disapprove of you or your view
- Getting all intimidated
- Not requiring what you said to be paraphrased by the other person
- Quietly going along but fiercely disagreeing
- Not pushing your solutions so you won't upset people

These conflicts are why the skill of typecasting is one of the most important communication skills you can acquire. Typecasting will help you identify who you are speaking to so you get better results.

🗩 Introduction to Typecasting

Typecasting is the act of assessing if someone is an Empathizer or an Instigator. This is an acquired skill you will pick up progressively. You can typecast someone by doing the following:

- Using formal assessment tools such as the NICI-A
- Asking questions about their communication preferences
- Assessing which traits they possess
- Paying attention to nonverbal cues and behaviors
- Identifying keywords or statements
- Attending to someone's "mood temperature"

Failure to communicate causes misery. Typecasting the person you are talking to helps you to sidestep or reduce issues before they arise.

An Empathizer sister said of her religious Instigator sibling: "She's such a bossy know-it-all. She always thinks she's right and can do no wrong. I don't like going to church with her because she acts so fake. My sister says I'm just being selfish and ungodly if I refuse to go. I wish I would have told her off, but I feel in the wrong for not wanting to go to church. But it's just too much to argue with her."

We're going to show you better ways to talk to yourself and others when you feel wronged. Let's give you a sneak preview of tools we're going to teach you how to use:

- First, by typecasting, difficult conversations will go much more smoothly. You will think before you react emotionally.
- Second, instead of stewing about a transgression, you will pre-plan your next move. You will respond effectively instead of reacting defensively. You will pause, take a step back, and think clearly about what you will say.
- Third, you will be grateful for the difficult person in your life. Yes, that's right...grateful! Difficult people are the sand in your oyster shell that creates pearls of wisdom. This sounds corny, but it's true. You will sharpen your communication skills under fire.

Training Your Mind to Spot an Instigator or Empathizer

The best technique to typecast someone as an Instigator or Empathizer is to use a combination of methods. As a start, let's take a look at the following sixteen real-life quotes below. Ask yourself, "Is this an Instigator or Empathizer? What does that mean?"

1. "I spend 11 minutes on what my son's basketball team is doing wrong and one minute being positive about the 15 points that he scored. It's easier for me to find the flaws in everybody else." Answer: Instigator. As a group, Instigators quickly see the negative pieces of what others could do better and quickly speak out about it.
2. "I was pretty sweet and nice in my first marriage. I made excuses for my husband's drinking. I was taken advantage of as a result." Answer: Empathizer. Because Empathizers want peace, love, and harmony in relationships, they can be walked on by others.

3. "My wife goes from zero to screaming about my not helping her with the laundry and the house not getting clean by itself." Answer: Instigator. As a group, Instigators divert to defiant anger when people don't agree with them.

4. "Just so I don't have to hear them yelling anymore, I will give in and do what they want." Answer: Empathizer. Empathizers fear anger and will withdraw or become anxious when confronted harshly.

5. "I'm the most impatient person on the face of the planet. I have to get to all the events, be first in line, and can't stand slow drivers in the passing lane on the highway." Answer: Instigator. Instigators struggle with impaticncc, have a constant sense of urgency, and are extremely task-focused.

6. "It's a constant back-and-forth about whether or not to write a book or get a new job." Answer: Empathizer. Empathizers have trouble making decisions and like to take things slow.

7. "It frustrates me when people sugarcoat or beat around the bush and don't tell me upfront what the problem is." Answer: Instigator. Instigators have confidence in their problem-solving abilities and like to get to the point.

8. "Harsh words can cut like a knife. If you hit a man below the belt, he will feel emasculated." Answer: Empathizer. Empathizers respond better to soft words and shows of support as sources of motivation.

9. "I think it's rude to be late. I am on time for most things or ten minutes early." Answer: Instigator. Instigators feel anxious when not accomplishing goals in time-efficient ways.

10. "I feel stress and anxiety when people act cold or aloof, as if they don't like me." Answer: Empathizer. Empathizers need the approval of others to feel OK about who they are.

11. "In my dating profile, I tell people don't ask for more pictures, don't ask for money, and don't ask me a question about politics if you don't want to hear the answer." Answer: Instigator. Instigators who feel insecure come across too blunt and strong.

12. "I add lots and lots of emojis to my texts so as not to unintentionally offend the person reading them." Answer: Empathizer.

Empathizers are slow to give assertive critical feedback that might cause conflicts.

13. "I get teased by my wife that I'm the wife in the marriage because I'm tuned in to how others feel." Answer: Empathizer. Empathizers are naturally warm, compassionate, nurturing, relationship-centered, and caring.

14. "I'll tell it like it is. I don't care if you like me or dislike what I'm saying. I'm not here to win a popularity contest." Answer: Instigator. Instigators take pride in being genuine and giving critical feedback others are too afraid to provide.

15. "I've learned a new language. It's not mechanical. Everything used to be mission-centered—my focus was only on the mission." Answer: A trained Instigator. Instigators who adopt the strengths of Empathizers are more effective, calmer and happier. So, too, are their partners and children.

16. "I've learned a new language. I don't take things so personally. Everything used to be feeling-centered—my focus was on the relationship." Answer: A trained Empathizer. Empathizers who adopt the strengths of Instigators are more effective, confident and happier. So, too, are their partners and children.

These examples show the differences in the mindsets, preferences, and perceptions of Empathizers and Instigators. It shows how a choice in "key statements" and "keywords" are dead giveaways for someone's communicator type.

Celebrity Typecasting

Let's have a bit of fun "typecasting" some famous cultural icons you might know, whether you're a Millennial or a Baby Boomer or somewhere in-between. Would you agree or disagree with our typecasting? If so, how come?

Empathizers	Instigators
Winnie the Pooh, Eeyore (*Winnie the Pooh*)	Tigger, Owl (*Winnie the Pooh*)
Jon Snow (*Game of Thrones*)	Tyrion Lannister (*Game of Thrones*)
Meg Griffin (*Family Guy*)	Stewie Griffin (*Family Guy*)
Donald Duck (Disney)	Mickey Mouse (Disney)
Lady Gaga (Singer)	Kanye West (Singer)
Paul McCartney (Beatles)	John Lennon (Beatles)
Luke Skywalker (*Star Wars*)	Han Solo (*Star Wars*)
Forrest Gump (*Forrest Gump*)	Lt. Dan (*Forrest Gump*)
Odie the Dog (*Garfield*)	Garfield the Cat (*Garfield*)
Charlie Brown (*Peanuts*)	Lucy (*Peanuts*)
Franklin D. Roosevelt (President)	John F. Kennedy (President)
Goose (*Top Gun*)	Maverick (*Top Gun*)
Elton John (Singer)	Mick Jagger (Singer)
Frodo Baggins (*Lord of the Rings*)	Gandalf (*Lord of the Rings*)
Rocky Balboa (Fictional Boxer)	Muhammed Ali (Famous Boxer)

From now on, when you watch movies or TV shows guess what communicator type each character is playing. How would you typecast your favorite musical artists, actors, or public figures?

⬭ Riley's One-Minute Typecasting Strategy

Think fast! Are you speaking with an Empathizer or Instigator Communicator?

Sometimes you don't have time to give someone with whom you have no relationship history a lengthy assessment. A PRO can typecast anyone within less than a minute without the aid of assessment questions. Quick typecasting can help you feel at ease during a family or couple discussion, an important interview, business negotiations, or any situation where communication skills are critical to success. It can mean the difference between making a good first impression, getting hired for a dream job, or nailing an important presentation. Most importantly, quick typecasting helps you feel at ease during what would otherwise be a tense or uncomfortable situation. I (Riley) have always found quick typecasting to be one of my secret weapons when going into situations I feel stressed about, so I'd like to share with you how I do it.

Over my lifetime, I've loved playing the game of, "Are they an E or I?" I consider myself exceptionally good at this acquired skill. Growing up, I typecasted my teachers, friends, and strangers. When life gets tough, I feel that knowing who I'm talking to is a critical skill to my survival, ability to compete and success.

As a training facilitator, I pay special attention to the communicator type when participants enter the room. For example, I was working at a community college working with a group of career coaches and academic advisors. As people filed into the room, I attended to the "mood" temperature of the people in the room. Are they warm or cold?

An Empathizer was the first person to walk into the training room. She came in with a smile and warmly introduced herself. She made a quick effort to get to know me personally, which led to a discussion about my Shetland Sheepdog, Kai, and a conversation about our mutual love for dogs.

During this conversation, another person walked into the training room. She moved purposefully and had a neutral expression on her face. I welcomed her and she asked me a question about the training. A firm handshake and intense eye contact sealed the typecasting.

Empathizer Giveaways:

- Warm and friendly demeanor
- Smiling
- Desire to make you feel comfortable
- Make an effort to get to know you personally
- Ask you about your day

Instigator Giveaways:

- Neutral or intense facial expression
- Purposeful or powerful walk
- Focused on the task at hand
- Speaking loudly
- Making jokes or using sarcasm

Because Empathizers want you to feel welcomed, they greet you warmly. Empathizers, male or female, want you to feel comfortable, accepted, and at ease. E-Types give you the benefit of the doubt. Empathizers believe in treating people kindly, almost as they would a friend, even if they don't know you yet. In truth, Es often do this because they want to be liked. Empathizers want verbal and nonverbal validation that you accept them. Ultimately, Empathizers believe everyone deserves respect until something is done to lose it.

In contrast, Instigators often go into meeting someone with a sense of neutrality or uncertainty. Instigators don't care if you like them. Instigators don't know at first if they like you. I-Types will spend time analyzing you to determine what they think about you. Instigators will see how you handle yourself and if you can withstand hot water. Often an overly friendly demeanor is distrusted by I-Types since it's seen as not being sincere or genuine. It's believed to be fake, a lie, and something to be distrusted. "How can you like me that much when you don't even know me?" I-Types skeptically think. You have to win I-respect. It's not a given.

E-respect is given equally to everyone but can be challenging to recoup if trust, kindness, or sincerity is mistreated. On the other hand, I-respect is something that you earn that always reflects their genuine opinion of you. I-respect is lost when someone isn't comfortable in their own skin or doesn't seem genuine.

💬 Speaking in the Language Style of Both Types

Once you learn how to identify E-Types and I-Types, the next step is to learn how to speak to both types in any sort of stressful situation. You must learn how to navigate tough conversations for the benefit of everyone.

Let's be honest, changing your communication habits will take a little work but give yourself some credit here. You've done far harder things. As one Instigator leader said, "This is all about doing the hard stuff right instead of the easier stuff wrong."

You can start creating better communication outcomes:

- Make a habit of typecasting everyone you meet
- Speak to your opposite type in their language style
- Accept that Empathizers and Instigators have opposite preferences
- Adopt the strengths of your opposite type
- Work on improving your communication blind spots

You are likely familiar with the definition of a dead end: Doing the same thing over and over again expecting a different result. Yes, this might be the most overused cliche, but it stands true in communication. If you aren't getting the outcomes you desire, you are better served by switching your routine instead of repeating it. When what you're doing isn't working, do something different.

In the next six chapters, we explore the differences between Empathizers and Instigators and how to tailor your communication to attain far better outcomes. We'll do this by focusing on the primary communication "pain points" people most commonly encounter, such as differences in perspective, listening, and mood.

⍰ A Word to Our Readers

As you work through this material, you will likely take time to reflect a lot, and that's a very good sign. You will begin to cross over between types and walk on either side of Talk Street. Not every trait you encounter will be a perfect fit. That's to be expected. You will be the final judge of which type you are. And don't freak out if you find that you're one type at work and the opposite type at home. Right now, look for the similarities, not for the exemptions to the rules. And don't let the names of Instigator and Empathizer throw you off.

After hundreds of training workshops and thousands of coached clients, no one liked their name initially. After all, Instigators have empathy, and Empathizers can be insensitive. Just go easy on yourself for now. If you're engaging and using this material, and we really hope you will, you will be challenged. But when others don't behave as you would like them to, you will soon know exactly what to say and do to get the best results for everyone.

You need repetition or practice to up your game. For this to work, you need to work at it. It's not natural. It's like nothing you've done in the past. For my (Dennis) part, as a doctor of psychology, I had to toss out much of what I thought was the right thing to do in favor of what actually worked better. Soon you will pre-plan and practice exactly what to say and do when the heat is on and mistakes are costly.

Good things take work. And that being said, Riley and I are here for you.

💬 Key Takeaways: Do You Know Who You're Talking To?

- Apply Law 1: Know who you are talking to: An Empathizer or Instigator.
- *TALK2ME©* is an easily applied strength-based system but it takes work.
- Treat others the way *they* want to be treated: As an Instigator or Empathizer.
- It's not how you meant the message that matters, but how it was received.
- You were born to be the communicator type you are. It's your natural style.
- You carry both Empathizer and Instigator strengths inside of you, ready to activate.
- Being an Empathizer or Instigator type isn't better or worse; just different.
- 50% of the battle is to know your audience: Instigators or Empathizers. This is the first step in effective communication. It's a step that can't be skipped.
- The ultimate goal is for you to blend your Empathizer and Instigator dominant and dormant Communicator Styles.
- Instigators excel when listening before speaking. Empathizers excel by speaking before listening.
- Instigators are dinged for not being more approachable. Empathizers are dinged for not being more assertive.
- Although Instigators set the mood temperature in a room like a thermostat, a chilly atmosphere will make the warmest Empathizer go cold.
- Being able to understand and speak equally well in both language styles of Instigators and Empathizers will make you feel more confident, calm and in control.

Interface with the material in ways that make these concepts come alive in your life. That's sometimes done by disagreeing with the material to find out how it's real. Sometimes it means identifying the painful patterns in your life that can be changed with a little elbow grease.

💬 Law 1: Sharpen Your *TALK2ME©* Skills

Use these activities to start embedding your knowledge of *TALK2ME©* into your everyday life:

Activity 1—Say "Empathizer" and Say "Instigator" Out Loud: Because Empathizer and Instigator can be a mouthful, say those words out loud. Then use our nicknames of E-Type for Empathizer-type and I-Type for Instigator-type communicator or E and I for short. Your superconscious mind has a library of data in storage to help you. Use your new vocabulary to become a mindful communicator.

Activity 2—Tap Into the Mindset of Your Opposite Type: Pop the question in your mind when you greet a clerk in a checkout line or talk to someone new on the phone or when reading online posts. "Are they acting like an Instigator?" Or, "Are they coming across like an Empathizer?" "And, how can I know for sure?" Be curious about your fellow travelers on the two-way Communication Highway.

Activity 3—Watch a Movie to Separate Gender From Communicator Type: Watch a favorite movie. For example, take one of the greatest sports films of all time, the 1976 movie *Rocky*. Typecast the leading characters as Empathizers or Instigators. Then insert the label of Instigator or Empathizer before their name when you speak, such as Empathizer Rocky, Instigator Apollo Creed. Or, Empathizer Adrianne, and her brother Instigator Paulie. Instigator trainer Mickey will fill out the bill. Changing your thinking will change your life.

Activity 4—Growing Up Years and Conflict Style: As children, siblings see Empathizers as more sensitive and Instigators as less sensitive. Think about your growing up years and being in a conflict. Did you react like an Empathizer who is sensitive to loud voices, being interrupted and threats? Or did criticism bounce off you like water from a duck's back because you were known as an Instigator who set the family mood? Matching parent-teen communication styles for disciplinary purposes works best due to this hidden factor.

Activity 5—Typecasting Those You Lead, Live With, and Love: Practice seeing those you love through your new lens of Empathizer and Instigator. Take a go at typecasting the people you know best. Does your life partner fit the description of an Empathizer or Instigator? Easy now. People can be one type at work and another type at home. Do your best to remove the prejudiced lens you look through. What about your parents? How about your children? How is each of your children different on the dimensions of Empathizer vs. Instigator? How about your boss or supervisor at work? Your best friend? Even though I-E is a huge change of view to get your arms around, you will grow accustomed to using *TALK2ME©* Tools in no time at all.

Activity 6—Accounting for Relationship Rules and Expectations: Think about the rules that govern your relationships. What rules do you follow during a conflict? Do you follow the rule of being nice and caring when times are difficult and conflicts arise, as Empathizers do? Or do you follow the rule of being blunt and honest when talks turn tense, as Instigators do? Each type uses opposite problem-solving approaches and tactics. The opposite ways Instigators and Empathizers attack problems unintentionally cause walls and create divides.

Activity 7—Who Steps on Your Last Nerve: Think of someone in your life who steps on your last nerve, someone you have a difficult time respecting, liking or getting along with. Diagnose their communicator type as an Instigator or Empathizer. Are they your opposite type? Armed with your new typecasting knowledge, how might you respond differently to them in the future so they won't prick you like a porcupine or get under your skin? Resentment is triggered by the subconscious prejudices you carry toward your opposite type.

Activity 8—Respecting Boundaries and Testing Limits: Look at how people test the limits with you. For example, if you tell an Empathizer not to cross a line, they will cautiously step back. If you tell an Instigator not to cross a line, they will step on or over the line, and say: "This line?"

(Stepping on it.) "Is this the line I'm not supposed to cross?" (And walk over it.) You will feel far less frustrated because you will see that most issues aren't personal. They're the result of not recognizing the others' communicator types.

TWO

THE SOLUTION ISN'T IN YOUR VIEW
IT'S IN THE OTHER PERSON'S VIEW

"Could a greater miracle take place than for us to look through each other's eyes?"

—Henry David Thoreau, Essayist & Poet

Higher-Level
Creative Solution

C

Exchanging Views

B
Belu
Empathizer View

A
Alpha
Instigator View

The More Ways We Have to Communicate, The Less We Do

Do you get frustrated trying to get through to someone who isn't listening? Ever been hit with an angry text? Have you felt afraid to speak up to a boss or life partner for fear of retribution?

Join the club. Every day, you make a million important communication decisions that impact your mood, success, and happiness. Your need for effective communication has become even more vital due to the ever-growing list of ways to communicate.

The more ways you have to communicate—text, email, Facebook, mobile phone, videoconference, Snapchat, etc.—the more opportunities you have to miscommunicate.

Too much of a good thing, it seems, can be a bad thing. Trouble brews when you listen to respond instead of using intentional listening skills to understand. Frustration fuel fears and keeps you from hearing what's actually being said.

The solution? Regardless of the format of the communication, see the conversation through *their* viewpoint as an Empathizer or an Instigator to reduce miscommunication and frustration.

The need for clear communication is even more imperative when scuba diving. As a PADI Scuba Instructor, I (Riley) have a number of diving stories. Some funny. Some otherworldly. And others that are not for those with galeophobia—a shark phobia. The following diving story captures the importance of viewpoint. It shows how the same event can be viewed in two entirely different ways. It was an unforgettable diving experience that took place at the Newport Aquarium in Kentucky where I worked as a Dive Safety Officer.

Shark Attack

Have you ever been attacked by a shark? I have. At least that's what it looked like to onlookers who saw a sleek 7-foot shark trying its hardest to latch on to my fins and legs.

The looks of horror that I received from the other side of the Plexiglass wall in the Newport Aquarium shark tank reflected what you might expect from quality extras on the movie set of the 1975 Spielberg movie hit *Jaws*. "Dun dun... dun dun.... dun dun dun dunnnn nnnnnnnn!"

I looked back through the thick Plexiglass tank wall at the crowd beginning to form. Teens started recording videos and pointing at me. Parents shielded their children's eyes. More and more people gathered and stared, their mouths gaping wide and eyes glued to the unfolding scene.

Before you get too concerned for my surviving this unfolding "shark attack," it's important to let you know that this zebra shark was less like Jaws and more like a sea puppy. We called zebra sharks the clowns of the tank. They are more Goldendoodle than cold-blooded killer.

But here's the point: Misperception creates miscommunication. What you think you see is often a distorted view of reality. And the biggest distortion of all arises from Instigator and Empathizer fear-driven fallacies that can fog perception.

The Springtime Zippies

Did the shark threaten my safety as the shocked onlookers assumed? Nope. It was springtime and the sharks experienced what my boss, Jen, affectionately named the "springtime zippies." It was mating season and the tank was filled with male sharks.

The "zippies" manifested in several peculiar ways. The sharks would charge at one another and beat up on each other in displays of dominance. Territorial brawls broke out. Gang-like territorial scenarios were frequent occurrences.

Given the intense conditions, new divers were forbidden from entering this tank during the zippies season. Still, the glass in the tank needed cleaning, and a "gut pickup" of lobster shells was overdue. So, being one of the more experienced divers that day, I entered the tank with my diving buddy. My adrenaline was pumping. I was excited about this challenge. You could say I'm a bit of a thrill seeker, so entering a tank full of misbehaving testosterone-jacked sharks was, well, exhilarating!

Fast forward 20 minutes later. The clown-like zebra shark was going after my leg and fins repeatedly. I used my yard-long dive pole to gently maneuver him and keep him at arm's length. He had clearly confused my legs with a mate. It was like a dog going after their owner's leg to hump! I couldn't control my laughter to the point my mask began to flood a bit.

As trained diving professionals, we expect this odd behavior during this season, are prepared mentally for it, and deal with it straightforwardly and assertively. The shark was not going to hurt me. In fact, the aquarium has zero incidents of divers getting hurt by sharks.

Alas, this didn't stop guests from being horrified at something that looked so unusual. They clearly thought the shark was attacking me and trying to have a taste of my leg.

Once the shark came to his senses and swam off, the crowd appeared to cheer triumphantly. From inside the tank, I delivered a nonverbal, diver "OK" signal to convey that there was nothing to worry about. I didn't want them to think the shark was violent. He just wanted some love!

Why Viewpoint Matters

When you are unaware of the communication style of another, perceptual distortions can make things appear scary and threatening. Just as in the aquarium example, the diver's reality and that of the uninformed crowd were drastically different.

This is analogous to understanding your opposite communicator type. If untrained, it can feel like you are navigating a sea of bloodthirsty sharks.

Perception matters, and the meaning you give an event dictates the next actions you do or don't take. If you operate without a clear understanding, unthreatening things can appear threatening or the reverse, and you can react incorrectly.

So, what's the solution to misperceptions that cause unintended problems and consequences? Knowing the solution is in the other person's view, not your view!

The aim of this chapter is to help you understand the verbal and nonverbal mechanisms used by your opposite type so you can view things through their perceptual lenses. Dive into (see what I did there?) how your opposite communicator type views the world. By working to understand Empathizer and Instigator habit patterns and partners, you can relax because you really know what's going on. You will make the most effective moves for each unique situation.

If humans can communicate with sharks, then Empathizers and Instigators can communicate with each other. It's time to do a perceptual 180-degree shift. Instead of being the bystander looking in through the Plexiglas, put on your dive tank and learn to swim with the sharks.

✒️ Law 2: The Solution Isn't in Your View. It's in the Other Person's View

Empathy for a view that's different from your own is a hallmark of the PRO communicator. Empathy is the willingness and ability to walk in the shoes of another. Things don't always have to go with the way you think they should. You open your mind to alternative explanations. You allow yourself to question your own ideas and expand your view.

By analyzing human behavior through the I-E lens of Instigator vs. Empathizer mindsets, you will be more approachable. The results of "changing your mind" and literally expanding your mind will surprise you. Changing one's mind is the hardest thing to do.

Until now, no one has explained to you how Empathizers and Instigators have opposite views regarding what constitutes proper relationship conduct. It's like each has their own secret code of appropriate behaviors and cultural norms. This is just like differing viewpoints of what is considered "good" and "bad" behavior in the United States compared to other parts of the world.

For example, not tipping in the United States is frowned upon, while leaving a tip in Japan or South Korea is considered insulting. Throwing a baby shower is a fun custom in the United States, but other countries find it strange or rude. Giving a thumbs-up in the Middle East, Latin America, Russia, and Greece have the same meaning as holding up a middle finger in the U.S. It's good to know what you're doing and saying when tensions mount and souls are tired from trying.

Just like visiting a foreign country, if you don't follow your opposite communicator type's communication norms, you might find yourself in a tough, tense, or awkward encounter, not knowing where you went wrong.

So, what are the benefits of practicing thinking in opposing Instigator-Empathizer (I-E) mindsets? For starters, it keeps things simple and focused on the positive. You feel less frustrated and more productive. You enjoy interacting with people more. You stew less about how others do or don't treat you. And that's because you know how to listen to hear when emotions roar as loud as a tornado instead of spouting off saying things you'll regret later.

Sure, being a PRO communicator takes practice. It's a lot like learning to swim or practicing free throws in basketball. First, you want to practice in easy situations when no one is watching or judging you. Then you take on more difficult challenges during practice games. Eventually, you're able to make swish shots in the final minutes of a big game when the crowd is roaring and a great deal is at stake.

A change of view will do you good. Try a day looking exclusively through either the Instigator or Empathizer lens. What's the communicator type of the person you are talking to and how do they respond to what you say?

The Dangers of Misperception

Perception is everything. Emotions dictate outcomes. The emotion of resentment ruins relationships and personal health.

The first golden rule is to know the insider trade secrets of your own Instigator-Empathizer communicator type. The second golden rule is to know the insider trade secrets of your opposite type. Misperception causes you to make incorrect decisions and react too defensively or inappropriately to others.

> **PRO Rule:** Know how your opposite communicator type views you from their world.

There are dangers in your misreading of an event. Inside the Newport Aquarium shark tank, ironically, the large sea turtle, Denver, was the cause of most mischief, not the sharks. Denver was the boss of the tank, and the divers and sharks all knew it. He was famous for mischievously stealing dive fins, throwing temper tantrums, or picking on the sharks.

In one instance, he attempted to steal Scuba Santa's hat by pulling at the ball of the hat that was tied around Santa's neck, an act that nearly strangled him. The kids laughed at this playful interaction; from the surface, I monitored the situation horrified. It was one of my first days on the job and I was not going to be the Dive Safety Officer who was responsible for Denver strangling Santa in front of a crowd of children. That'd be some bad PR. Luckily, the safety divers stepped in and Denver swam away on his way.

This demonstrates how you often look right past the biggest danger and instead focus your fear on something that plays to your prejudices. Often, what you fear isn't such a big deal, and what you fail to look at often is the purveyor of pain. The sharks were pretty tame compared to the rambunctious sea turtle. It's all in how you view things. Have you ever felt threatened by someone who isn't a threat, and the other way around? Of course, you have. We all have made mistakes in perception that are costly.

When you use *TALK2ME©* tools, you more accurately understand both sides of the Instigator vs. Empathizer storyline. This includes verbal and nonverbal defensive habits used by both types.

The key to changing painful patterns? Immersing yourself in how your opposite Empathizer or Instigator partner views the world and not panicking when things get challenging.

🗨 Tall Walls of Resentment

President Ronald Reagan echoed freedom and summoned change during the famous Berlin Wall speech on June 12, 1987. He intoned, "General Secretary Gorbachev, if you seek peace, if you seek prosperity for the Soviet Union and Eastern Europe, if you seek liberalization: Come here to this gate. Mr. Gorbachev, open this gate." The crowd cheered loudly during a long pause and then Reagan commanded, "Mr. Gorbachev, tear down this wall!"

The Berlin Wall was an 11-foot concrete barrier to divide West Berlin and East Germany from 1961-1989. At least 140 people were killed or died at the Berlin Wall. Unknown numbers of people suffered or died from distress and despair separated from loved ones. It didn't matter if you had family on the other side. If you tried to cross, you risked getting shot. It was a separation of people.

Humankind has a love-hate relationship with walls. Can you think of some famous walls? The Great Wall of China where many worker bodies are buried. The border wall President Trump campaigned on to control immigration from Mexico into the USA. And if you're a *Game of Thrones* fan (Riley!), you know of the colossal 700-foot ice fortification, "The Wall," to keep the "civilized" people in Westeros apart from the uncivilized "Wildlings" and the walking-dead-like White Walkers.

> Samwell Tarly: "*The White Walkers sleep beneath the ice for thousands of years. And when they wake up...*"
> Pypar: "*And when they wake up... what?*"
> Samwell Tarly: "*I hope the Wall is high enough.*"

Tall walls are meant to keep others out, but they often come crashing down (as in the *Game of Thrones*), at times violently, in fire and blood. Perhaps, walls aren't always the best solution to all conflicts?

There is another kind of wall, though. The biggest walls that divide us in relationships are invisible. These invisible walls are built brick by invisible brick out of small resentments. The worst kinds of walls are those you cannot see.

Resentments build when you expect me to be like you, or the reverse. When you don't do as I expect you to, wearing my classic Instigator-Empathizer pair of glasses, I get upset. But is that really necessary?

You get too attached to your views. If you get over your own ego, you see that your attachment freezes your problem-solving abilities and doesn't help anyone. Here's the truth:

> **PRO Rule:** We're all difficult in the eyes of our opposite type but not in our own view.

Let's play a game. Go through each scenario below and guess which communicator type may hold that particular view of the situation. Your job as a PRO is to see the diamond from all angles. Two conflicting views of the same event can collide to create "resentment walls" between Empathizers and Instigators. What kind of wall do you run into with your partner?

Nagging Scenario

View 1: You're frustrated that you have to repeatedly remind your partner to do _____. Take out the trash, change the toilet paper and not put it in backward, take off their shoes at the back door, or put the dishes in the dishwasher correctly, etc. You feel disrespected about something petty.

View 2: It's a small thing. It's not a big deal. You're making a big deal about nothing. I'll do it on my own schedule. You're a big nag bag. You treat me like a child. I already have a mother.

Interrupting Scenario

View 1: You're in the middle of making an important point and your partner interrupts. You feel frustrated because you haven't finished your point. It makes you lose your place in the conversation. You feel disrespected because you perceive your partner wasn't listening to what you had to say, that your partner was instead listening only to debate with you.

View 2: If I don't say something now, I'm going to forget what I have to say. This has become a drawn-out story. They don't respect my time. I'm getting irritated, they're going on and on and not getting to the point.

Being Late Scenario

View 1: You're running behind schedule. You hit the snooze button on your alarm. There was more traffic than expected on your way to work. You hurry into the meeting 15 minutes late and apologize.

View 2: The rest of us got here on time. Why can't you? You're always late. It sends the wrong message. You don't respect our time. Instead of apologizing, just get here on time next time.

Money Equality Scenario

View 1: You're the main caregiver for your family. You manage the household and get the kids to all of their events. You don't feel appreciated for how much time you put into raising healthy kids and keeping the household running. You're never "off work" because it's a 24-hour job.

View 2: You're the main breadwinner and provider for your family. You resent your partner's over-spending and not working part-time to help cover expenses. You also resent that your partner expects you to have the energy for them after a long day, do household chores and help with the kids when you need to recharge your battery.

Negative Mood Scenario

View 1: Your partner is in a nasty mood when they come through the door late from work. They don't say "hi" and walk right past you wearing an angry face. You were excited to see your partner but now feel ignored. You begin picking up your partner's bad mood.

View 2: You need to unwind because rush hour traffic was brutal. It was a non-stop day at work filled with crises. You feel sad but you hide it to be strong for your partner. Because home is a safe place to let your hair down, you expect your partner to understand your preoccupied mood.

Were you able to categorize viewpoints into an Empathizer view versus an Instigator view? Did you avoid the traps of role, gender, or mood attitude? Or did you take sides instead of seeing the merit in each view? As we like to say, "That's a valid view." Would you like the answers to this puzzle?

If you categorized all "View 1" scenarios as Empathizers and all "View 2" scenarios as Instigators, you're correct. See, you can shrink people too!

The root cause of most of your conflicts are different but subconscious expectations held by Instigators and Empathizers. Small resentments fester and grow larger. Pebbles of resentment grow into larger rocks and boulders that can be thrown around. But as everyone knows, boulders can roll back down the hill, crushing you and yours.

Resentments build tall walls that you can't see over, making it impossible to connect with your partner. The higher levels of resentment you carry inside of you, the less joy you will feel about life and living with your partner.

🗨 Classic Epathizer vs. Instigator Viewpoints

How can you put your new knowledge of the differences into perception into good use?

Here's a tool to apply to viewpoints of E-Types and I-Types. Use this when you get stuck in a conflict:

(1) Identify their type
(2) Think about what they are thinking through their perception
(3) Decide the course of action that will result in the most positive outcome

Here are twelve initial perception categories. This makes the subconscious more real, more conscious to you. When going through these, apply your new tool by thinking about how these differences in view have unearthed conflict in your life.

Anger Viewpoints

The I-Type View: Anger isn't a choice. It's how I automatically react to something that bugs me.
The E-Type View: Anger is a choice. I'm more likely to get angry at myself than others.

Achievement Viewpoints

The I-Type View: Being super-productive and accomplishing things are more important than feeling peaceful or happy.
The E-Type View: Being peaceful or happy is more important than being super-productive or accomplished.

Arguing Viewpoints

The I-Type View: Arguing as a couple doesn't scare me at all.

The E-Type View: Arguing as a couple scares me and makes me feel vulnerable.

Listening Viewpoints

The I-Type View: My partner would describe me as a part-time listener instead of a full-time listener.

The E-Type View: I always listen closely to my partner, even when it hurts me.

Change Viewpoints

The I-Type View: Change is an adventure. It doesn't bother me at all.

The E-Type View: Change can make me fearful of the "what ifs."

Likeability Viewpoints

The I-Type View: I don't care what people think of me. It doesn't matter if they like me.

The E-Type View: I often worry about what people think of me. It bothers me if I think I'm disliked.

Insecurity Viewpoints

The I-Type View: If I feel insecure, I choose to fake it until I make it.

The E-Type View: Admitting outwardly to feeling insecure is a show of strength.

Intimacy Viewpoints

The I-Type View: It's scary getting close to someone.

The E-Type View: It's soothing getting close to someone.

Competition Viewpoints

The I-Type View: I can be combative and competitive. Rarely am I a pushover.

The E-Type View: I'm unaggressive and noncompetitive. Some say I'm "too nice" or a pushover.

Assertiveness Viewpoints

The I-Type View: I push back when I feel put down. I speak up for myself.

The E-Type View: I can be pushed around. I don't speak up for myself enough.

Feedback Viewpoints

The I-Type View: I give out negative feedback quickly and bluntly but I'm a little slower to share positives.

The E-Type View: I give out a lot of positive feedback but I'm a little slower to share negatives.

Honesty Viewpoints

The I-Type View: I just tell it like it is and let the chips fall where they will.

The E-Type View: I share my honest feelings hesitantly to ensure I don't hurt the person I'm speaking with.

See the differences? These differences are precisely why what you are doing with your opposite type isn't working.

This awareness will help you function better in a conflict situation. You will be free to be you if you're aware of Instigator and Empathizer mindsets that distort what you say or do.

💬 Change Your View to Change Your Life (DENNIS)

When visiting the Grand Canyon on a family summer vacation, I stood with my arm around Riley, looking across the breathtaking vista. At the time, she was a fifth grader.

My mind was set on cheering up pre-teen Riley because she was a recently certified scuba diver and had been outvoted for an ocean vacation to enjoy her diving skills. She had some mixed feelings about "family stuff" at that time.

Even though the scenery was so awe-inspiring that I was at a loss for words, my mind continued to jump all around. I started playing with my perspective and view. I would turn around and look at the plain asphalt parking lot view behind me adorned with scraggly pine trees. Dullsville!

Then I would pivot and look at the multi-colored layered view of one of the greatest wonders of our natural world. I mused: "Whoa! What a difference looking in a 180-degree opposite view makes. Change your view of what's real and life really takes off!" Meanwhile, Riley was looking glum and glummer.

I decided to give it a go and cheer Riley up. I cheerfully said, "Riley, isn't that an amazing sight. The Grand Canyon is huge and so layered with beautiful colors!" Missing the ocean, Riley sarcastically said: "It would look a lot better, Dad, if it were filled with water so I could go scuba diving." We both laughed at her quick wit and quip. But point well-spoken from the soul of a sassy but respectful pre-teen.

My first reactive negative thought was that Riley wasn't being appreciative of the money spent on this vacation, and that hiking in Sedona, Arizona, and seeing other sights wasn't such a bad trip.

PRO Rule: Change your view to change your outcomes.

But Riley was just being honest. She was being an intuitive Empathizer. Her feelings weren't wrong. And she was grateful not spiteful.

But Riley wasn't happy with all that was going on and wasn't about to hide it when asked how she was doing. In truth, this period of time was tough for our family. Even young Empathizers are ethical. She didn't need a lecture. She needed me to be approachable and willing to listen.

I needed to change myself and my attitude. I could ruin this vacation with a few harsh words. I needed to adjust my attitude on the spot, or I was going to get resentful and say something stupid. I needed to drop my judgment fast, and become more empathetic and understanding, to serve her better as her dad.

I changed my view of Riley being "unappreciative" and "not getting past feeling sensitive." Instead, I viewed her as an E-teen who needs a supportive E-father response right now. I needed to be sensitive to her thoughts and moods. I felt better as a result, things got better between us, and Riley seemed to get her mood back on track instead of looking at what she had lost.

I looked through her eyes instead of the lens of my own bossy or threatened Dad ego.

Change your view and you will change your life. Keep on looking at the same old tired view, and you won't see what is just outside of your peripheral view.

- When you're triggered by a negative Empathizer, use a positive Empathizer mindset to respond.
- When you're triggered by a negative Instigator, use a positive Instigator mindset to respond.

Most communication challenges with difficult people are caused by ignorance of Empathizer-Instigator feedback preferences that invisibly impact moods and attitudes.

💬 Classic Instigator vs. Empathizer Defensive Resentment Walls

There are two sides to every story. You know your side. Getting defensive and putting up walls in your relationships can have the unfortunate consequence of building resentment on both sides. Practice being curious about how the situation might be viewed from the other side. What perspective might you be missing because you're all worked up?

View frustrations through the lens of the person you are talking to and see what they see. What are your communication defense walls as an Instigator or Empathizer team player? Reflect on a handful of times at work or at home when you were in an argument or the things you said did not create the outcome you desired.

Do you build many of these defensive walls in order to protect your self-worth?

Instigator Defensive Walls	Empathizer Defensive Walls
Being too blunt	Being too nice
Becoming overbearing	Beating around the bush
Nit-picking others	Picking on self
Pushing too hard	Not pushing back
Being a compulsive fixer	Being a compulsive pleaser
Steamrolling	Recoiling to a safe space
Hiding insecurities	Fear of appearing inadequate
Becoming mad when hurt	Becoming sad when hurt
Moodiness	Moodiness

These defensive habits are maladaptive behaviors that often do the opposite of what needs to be done. They self-sabotage the results you desire. An Instigator might turn to micromanage employees and become overbearing, resulting in decreased productivity instead of improving productivity. An Empathizer might get pushed around so they default to being even nicer and not pushing back, resulting in a decrease in respect instead of an increase in respect.

In fact, this is exactly what happened to me (Riley) as a first-year teacher at a leadership academy in North Carolina. As a first-year Empathizer high school teacher, I really wanted my students to like and respect me. My students had a way of pushing the limits, and I was hesitant to correct them publicly or send them to the office. I enjoyed making lessons fun and ran a looser classroom environment. I didn't know why a handful of my students just wouldn't listen to me when I would correct them. I spoke with my mentor, a senior level teacher at the school, and shared my concerns early into the school year.

Thank goodness for that expertise in classroom management. As a classic old-school Instigator teacher, I was told I needed a "sacrificial lamb." The next student who didn't listen to my instructions needed to be punished and sent directly to the office. This would demonstrate to the class that I meant business. I was told I was being "too nice" and that I needed to push back. And I was advised that my rebellious Instigator students would never respect or listen to me until I did so. Throughout that year, as an Empathizer, I had to constantly remind myself that it was *good* to correct bad behavior. It was *not* being mean. As an Empathizer, I always have to be aware of my tendency of being too nice, especially to those who take advantage of my niceness.

The solution to a problem is to move beyond your habitual defenses to understand what's really going on in the private inner world of your opposite communicator type. I would have never reached my strong-willed Instigator students if I didn't start speaking to them in their language. They felt most comfortable with a teacher who had clear rules and reinforced them accordingly.

⤺ Lowering Your Defensive Walls

What are your defensive walls? There is great wisdom in your communication slip-ups. When emotions hold influence over you, it's common to default to your extreme E-Type or I-Type communicator defense habits to feel secure. The ironic thing is when you go to the extreme side of the communicator spectrum, you are prone to doing more of what won't work well. For example, an E-Type during a conflict with an I-Type will do more "niceness" when in reality, the I-Type might prefer "bluntness," which is the E's exact opposite. If you are seeking respect from your opposite communicator type, practice doing the inverse of what you would reflexively choose to do in order to reach through to your I-Type.

Choose to slide along the E-I spectrum like the keyboard on a piano. Depending on the song, play high notes, low notes, or a combination of both in the tempo and tune. Your antagonist just might lighten up their mood and start to dance.

> **PRO Rule:** Resentment respects no one.

If you're an Instigator, chances are you will come down too hard when you perceive that someone isn't respecting you. In contrast, if you're an Empathizer, you need to set limits to show how strong you are when you are feeling taken advantage of.

Here's a brief exercise. Which classic trait do you exaggerate to feel safe and in control during a conflict? As an Empathizer or Instigator, go down the paired list below and check one box in each pair that best represents you:

☐ I withdraw
☐ I push forward
☐ I got quieter
☐ I get louder
☐ I back off
☐ I argue harder
☐ I flip moods
☐ I act like it doesn't bother me
☐ I get pleasing
☐ I get bossy
☐ I listen too much
☐ I won't listen

☐ I underuse anger
☐ I overuse anger
☐ I act like a mouse hiding in the house
☐ I act like a bull in a china closet
☐ I come across too sensitive
☐ I come across too stone cold
☐ I pout
☐ I shout

Scoring: Did you notice the trend? The classic Empathizer view came first and the classic Instigator view came second in the series. These paired opposite views escalate conflicts but can be controlled by you when you notice these conflicting energies.

You need to be constantly aware of walls you might run into when feelings are fever pitched. Walls keep in all sizes and shapes. Plexiglas, a force field, a tall brick wall, or a thick fence of trees to mark the boundary of a farmer's field all serve the same purpose: They keep you from hearing and connecting with the person you would like to get closer to.

Next, we will show you a 15-step self-calming empathy exercise to help calm your nerves and switch views.

⤳ The Mental Empathy Exercise

When you are frustrated and enter into an "I'm right and they're wrong" conflict in which everyone loses, imagine Riley's earlier story of the Plexiglass wall in the aquarium shark.

1) Take a deep breath and exhale fully and completely.
2) Tell your mind to "Be calm..."
3) See the wall in your mind. What does it look like?
4) Decide the Empathizer-Instigator side of the wall you're occupying.
5) Let go of the compulsive need to argue about or defend your view.

6) Imagine the viewpoint of your "antagonist" on the other side of the glass.

7) Ask yourself: "How would they see what's happening here?"

8) Switch to the view of your opposite communicator type.

9) Ask yourself: "If I were them, what would I expect me to do or not do?"

10) Consider your options: "How could I behave differently here that nets a decent result?"

11) Relax your view. When you're part of the problem, you can be the solution.

12) Is what you're seeing really a threatening shark attack or a sea puppy?

13) Decide what new action you will take from your calmer mood state.

14) Wait until you calm down prior to speaking with the other person.

15) Think before you talk, and listen instead of defending.

Easier said than done. The key is to consciously take time to calm down first. You can't create positive outcomes when in a negative headspace. Then you must identify the other's communicator type and see things through their perspective. Think empathetically about their point of view rather than defensively. Finally, you get clear on what result you want and the things that would need to be done to create that outcome.

See through the defensive walls of Instigators vs. Empathizers to respond with empathy, not judgment. *Respond* to provocations rather than simply reacting defensively to them.

⟲ Empathy: Can You Walk a Mile in My Shoes?

Empathy, feeling connected to another person's struggle, breaks through communication impasses and resolves even long-standing conflicts. Not easy to do as we hold so tight, like a death grip, to our favorite views of what's right and who's wrong. But viewing life through the lens of your opposite communicator type will free you to feel empathy and come up with new solutions to old stalemates.

As a senior psychotherapist, I (Dr. O'Grady) am trained on how to listen deeply without bias and show genuine empathy to the pickles we humans put ourselves in. Empathy is aroused when you are aware of the type of talker you are interacting with and appreciate their inner life view. Growth happens when you can look clearly through a view contrary to your own without getting anxious.

I always learn new views from my clients, as long as I don't feel compelled to preach to or admonish them. It took me a long time to learn that just because I'm showing empathy by listening doesn't mean I'm approving or condoning the action under discussion. This has helped immensely with delicate issues of dishonesty, politics, religion, and marital affairs, just to name a few.

PRO Rule: Don't view the person as the problem. It's the pattern, stupid.

The common catchphrase for empathy is "Can you walk a mile in my moccasins or shoes?" Elvis Presley's 1970s song, *Walk a Mile in My Shoes*, captures the need for being empathetic toward all our fellow human travelers, especially our opposite (not opposing) communicator type:

> *"If I could be you, if you could be me*
> *For just one hour, if we could find a way*
> *To get inside each other's mind*
> *If you could see you through my eyes*
> *Instead your own ego I believe you'd be*
> *I believe you'd be surprised to see*
> *That you've been blind*
>
> *Walk a mile in my shoes*
> *just walk a mile in my shoes*

Before you abuse, criticize and accuse
Then walk a mile in my shoes"

To walk in the moccasins of another person without judgment is truly at the apex of challenging communication skills. Our goal is to be fully able to walk in both Instigator and Empathizer shoes. Is that your goal, too?

💬 Before You Abuse, Criticize and Accuse... Walk a Mile in My Shoes

This idea of walking in someone else's shoes has given birth to a light-hearted workshop activity. You can receive good results, too, by mentally walking through it with us. The activity goes like this:

The Shoe Exercise Instructions: I will give these instructions to you twice. After I finish repeating the instructions for a second time to be sure you're clear on what to do, then I will say "Go!" Follow my exact instructions. Ready? OK. Here we go...

When I say "GO" you are to take off one of your shoes and pass it to another participant in the room. I repeat, take off one of your shoes and pass it to another participant in the room when I say go. GO!

Here's what typically happens. Chuckles and sideways glances commence as participants awkwardly take off a shoe, pass it to a partner, and set it on the desk or floor before them. Next, I ask everyone, "How would you feel about putting on the shoe you've just been handed?" Occasionally, it's also fun to tell them we are now going to go walk a mile around the outdoor track. Guffaws and looks of disbelief result.

In the exercise, most shoe colors don't match. There is the issue of slip-on shoes and shoelaces. Men's shoes tend to be larger than women's shoes. Footwear ranges from steel-toed boots to high heels. You get the feel (and smell) of things here, right?

What does this shoe metaphor have to do with Empathizer and Instigator communicators?

Well, if you've ever had the experience of someone rubbing you the wrong way, similar to walking with a sharp pebble in your shoe, your communication will be hobbled before long. Here are a few ways we recap this training activity after the workshop group has had an opportunity to relax a bit:

1. Tripping Up Wearing the Wrong Shoe

No one was told whether to take off their right or left shoe in the training instructions so there's some random chaos. You might have two right shoes or two left shoes. What to do? It's hard to know how to behave if you don't know whether you're talking to a "leftie" Empathizer or a "righty" Instigator.

2. One-Size Fits All

No one-size shoe fits every person. Using a one-size-fits-all method will cause rubs, frustrations, and trip-ups. Doesn't this explain many of the fusses we get into with our opposite type without knowing why?

3. Different Shoes to Fit Different Occasions

Shoes are diverse and come in different colors and styles. Your tennis shoes are a great fit for the gym but might be an odd choice when going to a wedding. Communicators come in all colors, personality sizes, income levels, professional backgrounds, genders, generations, etc. What each one of them has in common is that they are either an Instigator or an Empathizer. Tailor your communication to suit the situation and the person you are speaking with.

4. Select Shoes That Work Best For You, Your Purpose, and Your Safety

Shoes should be a personal choice that is selected for the purpose, occasion, safety, look, and feel. Being flexible and aware of choices is what fixing communication stumbles is all about. If the shoe fits and fits your purpose, why not wear it?

No two shoes look alike and typically won't match, given chance events. Why not adjust your style to "fit" the person to whom you are talking?

5. Walk to New Areas Instead of Staying Stuck

Your comfort zone can be a coffin. One question asked during training is, "Who did you give your shoe to? Why?" Oftentimes, people in class give their shoe to the person closest to them. Empathizers aligned with Empathizers and Instigators aligned with Instigators. Only on rare occasions will a shoe go flying to the other side of the room. Get out of the comfort zone of your natural communication style and start mixing in traits of your opposite communicator type.

6. Now We're Talking

Empathizers and Instigators wear different shoes. Assigning blame is a distraction from healing pain. This explains why people you are so carefully trying to communicate with aren't receiving your message.

The fun empathy exercise will make you think twice whenever you're hitting a difficult patch. Simply by posing the question "What is their type and why do I think so?" will trigger more compassionate empathy. This removes the hobbling sharp pebbles of prejudices from your shoes.

Know this: The biggest communication mistake you can make is to ass-u-me you know what someone is thinking or feeling. Split the word ass/u/me apart and see how assuming will make an "ass" of "you" and "me." Get out of that narrow view that will constrict your empathy and your options. Each respective type feels respected when you have empathy for their world view. Now that you know there are two types of Empathizer and Instigator "shoes" to select from, we are confident you will trip up far less often.

⚬ Empathizer View of Rude Instigator Anger

Anger is the root cause of dysfunctional Empathizer and Instigator relationships. Empathizers fear Instigator anger and Instigators know it. Unhealthy anger is used to get your way at the expense of a peaceful relationship.

Empathizers view angry words from the mouth of Instigators as rude, uncivil, and uncalled for. They indicate lack of emotional maturity and control in the Empathizer world. Anger is the most common relationship wall that divides and separates you from others when you want to get along.

Instigators default to fake anger as a bad habit that intimidates Empathizers. When anger or strong words are used, Empathizer partners will view anger as rude and will shut down, withhold ideas, stop being affectionate, and decrease their efforts to be helpful. Instigators then perceive they have "won" and nothing is wrong, when in fact everything is wrong. Tall walls are being built.

An example of Instigator anger was a female partner who was fixing the sink. Her partner came on the scene asking if she could take a break or needed anything. The female Instigator snipped, "Look. Can't you see I'm in the middle of something here? You're being selfish wanting my attention right now. Just leave me alone so I can finish this task, and then we can talk." What appeared to be a simple case of frustration turned into her partner again feeling unimportant. And by now you know how grudges grow.

Empathizers believe, "Why talk if I'm always wrong?" Or, "It's not worth saying anything when my ideas always get shot down." An Instigator's fiery passion for a particular topic, love for debate, or their need for control in a conversation can shut down Empathizer partners, subordinates, or co-workers. In extreme cases, Instigators can spout angry words without realizing the devastating effects it has on respect, likeability, and trust.

Here are a few examples of what defensive Empathizers have said about angry Instigator partners:

- It's not smart to speak up around here. I feel like a subordinate.
- My partner is bossy and doesn't understand my viewpoint.
- I can easily be over-talked or out-argued, so I just stop standing up for myself.
- Because everything about me is viewed negatively, I've put up walls of mistrust.

- I feel like I'm constantly doing things to please my partner to pacify their anger, but nothing is ever good enough.
- My partner hits the ceiling and shouts me down whenever I say "No" to whatever they want to do.
- Because my partner is unapproachable, overbearing, and unavailable I don't believe they will ever change.

Resentment is the #1 cause of relationship standoffs and breakups. Hidden conflicts drain Empathizer moods and scare Instigators when they can't fix them.

Granted, Instigator partners won't take a step back when they see something that needs improvement. They'll just tell it like it is and take the heat. They will charge the hill taking gunfire for the greater good to fix the problem. This tactic can backfire and hurt the Empathizer and the relationship mood.

The solution to perceptual differences of anger is to inoculate negative moods and communicate to the other person in a way that resembles their natural communicator type. Easier said than done, we know. If anger, sadness, or other strong emotions are taking hold of a conversation, it's better to cool off and come back to things later. When the conversation starts up again, it's important to be aware of your dysfunctional defensive communication habits and avoid them before they sabotage the conversation.

💬 Showing Empathy toward Views Opposite of Your Own

EmPATHy is the path to truly understanding your partner, family, friends, boss, subordinates, and anyone else. It's the ointment that helps to heal a wound caused by words and actions. Empathy puts you on the frequency of your opposite type to accurately receive their broadcasts.

People who struggle with giving empathy are also very judgmental of themselves. You need to be OK with your quirks. You also all need to identify ways to grow more advanced in your communication skills. Accept the unique differences that set everyone apart. If cynical snarky comments wound your relationships and make your partner bleed, how can you understand them better from the opposite view?

Here are a few classic examples in Instigator-Empathizer unions that highlight clashing Empathizer-Instigator views and what the mid-ground "Balanced I-E View" is:

You're Too Sensitive

Instigator View: "It's nothing personal. What I said wasn't meant as an attack. Why can't you just get over it?"

Empathizer View: "Harsh words can cut like a knife. If you didn't mean it, then why did you say it?"

The Balanced I-E View: I accept Empathizers are more sensitive. I also accept that Instigators are less sensitive.

Just Make a Decision Already

Instigator View: "Why can't you make up your mind? It's not that difficult."

Empathizer View: "It's better to take time and do it right rather than make expensive mistakes that need to be corrected later on."

The Balanced I-E View: I accept Empathizers make better decisions when they are given space and time to reflect upon and weigh their options. I accept that Instigators feel it's better to make a quick gut decision and correct mistakes later.

Stop Beating around the Bush

Instigator View: "Just get to the point. Don't waste my time by beating around the bush."

Empathizer View: "It's better to pick your words carefully so you don't offend someone and hurt the relationship."

The Balanced I-E View: I accept Empathizers need to explain their point carefully and in greater detail. I accept that Instigators want to hear the conclusion or headline first to have an idea about what to do.

That's Not How I See It

Instigator View: "The best outcomes come from putting the idea on the table then debating the right course of action."

Empathizer View: "The best outcomes come from taking turns to respectfully listen to a partner's views."

The Balanced I-E View: I accept Empathizers need to be asked more questions to draw them out, not shut them out. I accept Instigators need to mix it up to be confident that their conclusions are the correct ones.

You're Obsessed With Winning

Instigator View: "Winning is everything. You motivate others by criticizing their performance. Everything is a competition."

Empathizer View: "I hate competition. Why can't we all just get along? I care more about harmony than winning."

The Balanced I-E View: I accept Empathizers make the mistake of being too nice and always trying to be a mediator and peacemaker. I accept that Instigators make the mistake of being too blunt and competitive.

Why Can't You Just Get Over It?

Instigator View: "Because we discussed it and I apologized, just put it in the past and forget about it."

Empathizer View: "If we discuss it and don't change the root of the problem, it will crop up again in the future."

The Balanced I-E View: I accept Empathizers need to work through present emotions to let go of the past. I accept Instigators prefer to forget about the past and focus on the future being better.

There's No Time to Waste

Instigator View: "A sense of urgency matters. It's better to create momentum, even if it's in the wrong direction. You can always pivot and go in the right direction. The only failure is the failure to take action...any action...NOW."

Empathizer View: "It's better to take time and do it right rather than hurrying and rushing too fast without thinking through what the consequences will be."

The Balanced I-E View: I accept that when Empathizers feel rushed, they choke. I accept that Instigators feel anxious when things aren't moving forward fast enough.

Stop Interrupting Me

Instigator View: "If I don't interrupt you, I'll forget the important thing I have to say."

Empathizer View: "Interrupting is just plain rude."

The Balanced I-E View: I accept Empathizers may keep their best ideas secret if I keep interrupting them. I accept Instigators have a short attention span and want to make progress happen fast.

To get respect, show respect. By showing respect to your opposite type, you are showing respect for your own strengths and Achilles' heels. Words have the power to wound or heal. Wounding words come from a place of hurt and they spread bad moods around. Healing words come from a place of hope and they spread good moods around.

Empathy comes from walking in the shoes of your opposite type. Hearing, feeling, and seeing the view of our opposite balances your energy and neutralizes prejudices that blow off your talking legs just when you're hitting your stride.

🗨 Do You Need Sensitivity Training?

Sensitivity training, originating from Kurt Lewin's 1946 workshop series, was huge in the 20th century and is still used today. The training goal was to make people aware of and sensitive to others.

We believe that Empathizers need "Insensitivity Training" while Instigators need "Sensitivity Training." We aren't referring to the sort of training Lewin created, but instead training that balances Empathizers and Instigators and deepens empathy. Among other traits, Empathizers need to learn to be less sensitive while Instigators need to learn to be more sensitive.

Below are lists of desirable soft-skills Empathizers and Instigators would acquire if trained to be a less sensitive Empathizer and a more sensitive Instigator:

🗨 Insensitivity Training for Empathizers

1. Make a decision quickly.
2. Don't second guess your decision.
3. Pump up your mind with self-congratulations.
4. Be less sensitive to others' opinions about what you should do.
5. Drive through any adversity and don't worry about "But what IF…"
6. If your decision doesn't work out–cheerfully make another decision.

There is a time to be sensitive and a time to let what people think roll off your back. If you're an Empathizer, do you fear turning into a heartless jerk if you follow the above suggestions?

🗨 Sensitivity Training for Instigators

1. Delay making a decision.
2. Reflect on alternative choices.

3. Critique the downsides of the various choices.
4. Seek out others' advice about what decision would be best for you to make.
5. Check into your vulnerable feelings.
6. Allow someone else to make the decision for you.

There is a time to be sensitive and feel what you do without self-shaming. If you're an Instigator, do you fear becoming a spineless doormat if you follow the above suggestions?

When you start adopting the characteristics of your opposite I-E type, it is fairly common that you will often overdo it and shoot past where you eventually need to be. The key is to not go to extremes but to do more of what your opposite would do: balance your communication style and avoid going to extremes.

Empathy is like a muscle that grows larger with use. By acting like your opposite type on key dimensions, you will have more empathy for their view of what works in their world.

Insensitive Empathizer vs. Sensitive Instigator Training Challenge

Here's a practical way to try out switching your view. Go out to dinner with your partner. Use your opposite view in looking at the menu and ordering food.

For example, the Insensitive Empathizer will only take a few seconds to look at the menu and then confidently decide. In reverse, the Sensitive Instigator will stare at the menu, read every option, and compare them before deciding.

How did this new view impact you emotionally? Process your experiences with your partner.

In summary, know what bugs your opposite type. Respect their limitations and pre-wired perspectives.

💬 Show Empathy: "Let Me See If I've Got This Right..."

"Clarify and confirm" check-ins do two things. First, they slow your mind to hear multiple levels of a message. They also help you make fewer false assumptions by helping you understand their viewpoint while the conversation is rolling along.

You say:

- "Let me be sure I'm getting this right. Are you saying…"
- "I appreciate your directness. To sum up what you're saying…"
- "I want to make sure that I'm understanding you. The main point you're making is…"
- "This is important to me. What you're saying is…"
- "I'm sure you're right. How can I be of most help right now…"

During diverse times and in the midst of divergent conversations, you want to get on the same social wavelength. An empathetic, not sarcastic, tone keeps open lines of communication. Keeping a neutral and caring tone of voice opens new viewpoints.

Use this tool when you feel a conversation could go sideways if you don't ask for clarification. Pick one statement and try it out in a close relationship. Find out for yourself how it can smooth out relationship problems at work or at home.

💬 Conflict Remedies

There are some easy and proven techniques you can use when you find yourself in conflict. Of course, these are easier said than done, but they are nonetheless helpful if applied. Here are five mindful remedies to keep top of mind when you find yourself in the midst of a conflict that causes relationship breakdowns:

1. **Listen.** You will listen intently and not interrupt or talk over your partner.
2. **Engage.** You will give your partner a balanced mixture of positive and negative feedback.
3. **Think.** You will take time to reflect upon your partner's point of view that's frustrating you.
4. **Empathize.** You will tear down Plexiglass walls by repeating back what your partner is saying.
5. **Change.** You will take the surest route to happiness which is to grow and change.

The solution to conflicts is not in your view, but in the other person's view.

Blend the Strengths of Both Types for Success

In summary, resolve to be a blended communicator who sees things through both an Empathizer and Instigator perspective.

Two key changes will magnify your hidden strengths and minimize perceived weaknesses:

- **Empathizers Need To Speak Up and Tell It Like It Is.** Assertive Empathizers will stop fearing their greatness and feel good enough.
- **Instigators Need To Listen Up and Hear It Like It Is.** Approachable Instigators will stop fearing their vulnerability and feel worthwhile.

Thousands of clients testify to eureka moments when shifting their perspective and adopting the strengths of their opposite type.

Communication is wanting to be heard and the willingness to listen. You can fuse the best of both worlds, one that harmonizes the Instigator and Empathizer contrasting views. Use this list to balance your communication and overcome blind spots:

The Balanced Instigator	The Balanced Empathizer
SLOW Stop talking so fast.	**FAST** Stop talking so slow.
COMMA Add more details.	**PERIOD** Be brief. Use a period.
SAY HELLO Smile. Be approachable.	**NO HELLOS** Chin up. Be direct.
RIDE Listen don't lead.	**DRIVE** Confidently stand ground.
GENTLE Be mindful of hurts.	**ASSERTIVE** Be tough in tender ways.
SOFT Be a velvet glove.	**HARD** Be a steel fist.
HEAR Listen to feedback.	**SPEAK** Give correct feedback.
EMPATHIZE Be caring and kind.	**INSTIGATE** Be large and in charge.

Notice that these traits run opposite of one another. Doesn't that explain why it's so easy to get our tongues twisted?

Try actually walking in the shoes of and talking like your opposite type. Make a habit of acting like your opposite type in different situations. You can do this when checking out at the grocery. Talking to a coworker. Leading a team meeting. Talking to your kids.

Just keep at it. If you're an Instigator, you will find yourself smiling, feeling calmer, and empathizing more. People will no longer perceive you to be an insensitive jerk.

If you're an Empathizer, you will find yourself speaking up, feeling more confident, and taking charge. People will no longer perceive you to be a nicey-nice pushover.

Success starts with just a few small changes. What small changes will you make in your communication habits to get better results with the people you love and work for?

💬 Key Takeaways: Change Your View to Change Your Life

- Apply Law 2: The solution isn't in your view. It's in the other person's view.
- Perception means more than facts.

- Know how your opposite communicator type views you from their world.
- When you are unaware of the communication style of another, perceptual distortions can make things appear scary and threatening.
- The solution to a problem is to move beyond defensive Plexiglass walls to understand what's really going on in the private inner world of your opposite communicator type.
- Everyone is difficult in the eyes of your opposite type but not in our own view.
- Knowing someone is an Empathizer or Instigator will help you amplify their strengths and avoid their pet peeves.
- Change your view to change your outcomes.
- Resentment respects no one.
- Disappointing expectations cause resentment. Resentment is the #1 cause of relationship standoffs and breakups.
- Hidden conflicts drain Empathizer moods and scare Instigators when they can't fix it.
- Instead of preaching about how your views are correct, walk in another's shoes by listening to them.
- Don't view the person as the problem. It's the pattern, stupid.
- Assigning blame is a distraction from healing pain.
- Learning to act, walk, and talk as your opposite type will boost your mood and better your outcomes.
- Communication littered with Empathizer and Instigator (E-I) perceptual prejudices can be like walking blindfolded through a minefield.
- Instigators need to make room for Empathizers to offer their viewpoints.
- Empathizers need to stop viewing themselves as "lesser than."

💬 Law 2: Sharpen Your *TALK2ME©* Skills

For a change of view, challenge your preferences that can hide prejudices by doing the opposite of what you ordinarily would do.

Activity 1- Conflict Viewpoint: Next time you are in a disagreement or conflict with someone, identify their communicator type and review lists in this chapter. Can you see the conflict through their point of view? Say their view out loud. How can you show empathy by matching their view? What would you do or say differently? Seek a creative solution by viewing the issue through the other person's Empathizer-Instigator lens.

Activity 2- Decisions...Decisions: If you're an Empathizer who's asked where you would like to go to dinner, make an immediate decision, voice it confidently, and don't change your mind or second-guess yourself. If you're an Instigator, allow your partner to order dinner for you without your input. How do you feel walking in the shoes of your opposite now?

Activity 3- Love Texts: If you're an Instigator, write a long text full of sincere compliments or affirmations to your Empathizer partner during a time of day they won't expect to receive it. If you're an Empathizer, write a short text to your Instigator partner giving recognition for actions they've done to make your life better.

Activity 4- Parking Spots: When you arrive at work, park in a different location far away from where you usually do. If you don't drive, get to work 30 minutes early. Stroll around the office or work area and go out of your way to talk to people you ordinarily don't talk to because you arrive later. Change your routine so that your view won't get stuck in a rut.

Activity 5- Emails: Before you begin to email someone, identify their communicator type and email them in their preferred style. Short emails for Instigators, longer emails for Empathizers. Before getting down to business, remember their type and choose the right format. If they're an Empathizer, start the email with a connecting statement, such as, "I hope you're doing well." If they're an Instigator, get straight to the point and use numbered or bulleted lists to make it clear what you want.

Activity 6- Musical Reviews: Listen for 30 minutes to a type of music you can't stand. Try country western, rap, heavy metal, jazz, soul, folk, classical—any music genre you are convinced you won't like. Listen to the lyrics and try to get into the mix without judging or condemning. Why is it so difficult to keep an open mind to what you believe you dislike when you don't have any direct experience with it?

Are you ready for a change of view? Being open-minded to a view different than you're comfortable with doesn't mean that you're endorsing that view. You're stretching your mind and keeping your brain young. There are plenty of other ideas. Watch movies that you think you'll dislike, try out a place to eat in an area you ordinarily don't go, or walk around a college campus and ask permission to sit in on a class. Volunteer in a soup line, root for a sports team you think is inferior, watch a different news channel, or take a minute to talk to somebody at work you ordinarily pass by. Mix it up. If you're like many people, you're scared out of your mind on this big rock in the sky, just trying to get by one day at a time. Don't take life too seriously, as if your view is the only view worth knowing about. An old cigarette commercial had the (wrong) tagline, "I'd rather fight than switch!" In the *TALK2ME©* world, switching your view is good. Switch your view when it suits you. You aren't married to your perspective.

Yes, you'll be stretching the mental speeding limits and family rules you grew up with here. Doing the new is uncomfortable. We're asking you to be a bit more comfortable being uncomfortable. But if you're saying, "I can't do this because I don't approve of it and never will… and this talk of changing my views is setting me off …and asking me to change makes me feel like the fault is all me!"…then we have more work to do.

THREE

PRETENDING TO LISTEN ISN'T REALLY LISTENING

"Most people do not listen with the intent to understand; they listen with the intent to reply."

—Stephen Covey

Are You in the Mood to Listen?

"Mood spelled backward spells what? DOOM."

I (Riley) wrote the word MOOD in all caps dramatically on the board in a high school class of seniors at Simon Kenton High School in Northern Kentucky. The teens in the class appeared unphased, overcome with post-lunch comatose, and worst of all, senioritis. Some even had their heads down or headphones in.

After five visits to this high school class, it was clear that no more lessons on soft skills could be taught without addressing the elephant in the room. No, not the burned-out teacher. Not the fact that they were permitted to use cell phones. Not the fact that they were considered by the school to be the "problem" students.

It was their listening or lack thereof. No learning can take place without listening. And no listening can take place with a negative mindset.

"Listening is an attitude," I explained, "What people haven't taught you before is that poor listening stems from our moods, attitudes, and desire to focus our attention."

"But what if I just don't want to listen?" One of the students asked.

"What outcome do you want? When you listen, you get better outcomes, and people will listen more to you," I explained. "Listening is the key to getting respected and liked. It's the key to getting what you want from others."

"But what if I don't like them?" Another student chimed in.

Finally, they were getting curious. Heads that were down started to pop up around the classroom like whack-a-moles. Earbuds came out. Phones were set down. I had about 10 seconds to snag their attention or lose their focus indefinitely.

"You all have people you don't like or don't respect. This is because you often don't feel liked or respected by them," I pointed out. "The only way you can change this is by initiating respect through listening. This is because…"

"I would never do that! I'm not going to fake how I feel," one student interrupted passionately. "If you are mean to me. I am not going to be nice to you. You have to earn respect."

"An eye for an eye. And what happens then?" I asked, looking from student to student. "The whole world is left blind, goes the saying. Not listening does more than hurt your opponent. It will come back and hurt you." I looked around again.

"When you don't listen or show respect to someone it's a reflection on you. It takes a strong sense of self-respect to be the bigger person and be the first one to show respect," I continued. "Respect doesn't mean being fake or not standing up for yourself. Why let someone else dictate your mood? Isn't it better to *not* let them get to you? Isn't it better for you to take the higher road?"

Silence, but still not convinced. Now in debate mode, we continued with one student's comment, "But you didn't understand! They don't deserve to be listened to if they won't show me the same respect."

"You can show respect and not like someone. You don't have to like people to show respect and listen," I went on. "You will have to deal with many people you don't like. In the military, they talk about saluting. Even if you don't like someone higher ranked than you, you still salute their rank. Not because you like them, but because you respect their rank. This is the same as listening to people you dislike. You do it because it's in your best interest and because not listening is a reflection on you. Their behaviors are a reflection of them. If they are mean, that's on them. If you are mean back, that's a reflection on you. You don't have to be fake nice; you just have to be neutral and show them common decency through doing things like listening."

To this day it's unclear how many of the students were convinced of what was said that day. At the very least, it started a conversation about listening, which led to a discussion about the causes of poor listening, only one of which is mood.

🗨 Listening Creates Change

Listening creates change. That's why people don't listen well. No one likes change, usually because of a fear of the unknown or fear of failure. Instigators particularly feel like "listening failures" and subsequently lack confidence in their ability to listen.

Listening builds bridges of trust and respect when nothing else is working. Not listening builds tall walls of resentment that are hard to climb over. It is why couples seek divorce. It's a root of workplace dysfunction.

PRO Rule: Listening is the fix.

When listening stops, it's a sign that things need to improve; otherwise, the metaphorical timebomb begins ticking down. Like a James Bond movie, your mission "possible" is to fix the root of the listening problem before the relationship blows up in your face.

The resolution to your listening issue is different, depending on your communicator type and the type of person you are speaking with.

- *Irritated Instigators complain:* "But if you don't speak up and tell me what needs to change, then how can I do anything about it?"

- *Frustrated Empathizers reply:* "I tried to tell you, but you kept interrupting me and didn't act interested in what I had to say."

This chapter's teachings are all about listening strategies that are specially tailored for Instigators and Empathizers. If you are a poor listener, it's important to realize listening is a skill that, like working a muscle, can be exercised to strengthen and improve it. While Instigators more frequently struggle with listening, Empathizers suffer from an opposite listening hang-up. Empathizers listen to things that would be best ignored, such as, unhelpful negative comments. They also don't speak up enough.

How does this translate into everyday practice? Empathizers excel if they are assertive and make sure their message is heard. And Instigators excel if they are receptive to answers and views other than their own.

🗨 Talk First vs. Listen First

Not listening or partial listening is a bad habit. What needs to happen so you can get on the same "trust and respect" relationship page to solve problems?

- As an Instigator, you will earn Empathizer respect when you listen well and don't interrupt or contradict.
- As an Empathizer, you will earn Instigator trust when you show confidence by getting right to the point and don't beat around the bush.

Power is conferred by your position or title, but authority is earned by using your relationship communication skills.

Net effect: Listening both solves pesky existing problems and prevents future problems.

Most people aren't accustomed to being listened to and heard. By occasionally paraphrasing what's being said, the speaker will feel valued and validated, cared for, and cherished. To do this, you need to change your listener attitude. Listening after all is an attitude and a skill.

💬 Law #3: Pretending to Listen Isn't Really Listening

Half-listening occurs when you're trying to solve another issue in your head while someone is talking to you. Because we can only do one thing well at a time, it's important to choose to listen to hear instead of just pretending to listen.

It's normal to have a busy mind that gets distracted during conversations. Even the best listeners experience this. What matters is how many times you are willing to continue to recenter your mind on the speaker instead of drifting away in your own thoughts. This activity is analogous to meditation. Meditators bring themselves back to their breath each time they inevitably drift off in thought. You bring yourself back to the speaker by getting curious about what's being said again and again, just like the best listeners do. You don't give up, you don't judge, and you don't interrupt.

The truth is, we can tell when people aren't really listening. It's clear in their expression, distraction, or lack of curiosity. They look more like a bobblehead. The wheel appears to be turning but the hamster is dead... or perhaps the hamster is on another planet. Intentional listening is a feat that requires you to recenter your mind even when it feels like a spinning tornado.

> **PRO Rule:** Intentional listening is the greatest gift you can give another human being.

Not listening adds gasoline to the fires of resentment. This is particularly true of couples when the decisions of one individual dominate the other partner at the expense of strong bonds, intimacy, and an equally loving relationship. This is called "conversational coercion" and we will be describing this dynamic and solutions to it later in this chapter. Change means having the courage to try something new. Are you ready to change?

In fact, your couple and family life will benefit most from using our Instigator-Empathizer listening tools. Feeling heard fuels passions. To illustrate this point, we're going to tell you a story about a mixed Instigator-Empathizer couple, married for 20 years and growing apart.

The Ketchup Story

What's your love life got to do with ketchup? Our next true-life couple story has a moral to it that you won't soon forget.

It all started in an effective communication workshop of all men. It was co-led by our *TALK2ME©* male and female leader team. The subject was "What's in it for me to communicate better with my wife?" As usual, describing the benefits is much less impactful than experiencing the results firsthand and making up your own mind. It was late in the afternoon on the second day of training. For class participants, the *TALK2ME©* principles were coming alive to apply at home. It was time to change old views with new insights.

The discussion focused on how to handle complaints. Complaining is socially acceptable anger that inhibits change. One 40-something Instigator trainee, Rob, started off by mimicking how his wife Rita always nagged him about joining her early every Saturday morning for grocery shopping for the family. The guys groaned and laughed in anxious unison because they instantly recognized this type of pattern in their own relationship lives.

Complaining Is Socially Acceptable Anger

They also spoke up honestly about their view of nagging. The Instigator View: "Most guys resent being nagged by a wife dressed in his mother's clothing. I already have one mother. I don't need another one nagging me non-stop. I'll get to it but in my own time!" Of course, these ways to handle the complaining game don't work. And the fire of love grows smaller behind resentment walls that grow taller.

A little history here. In all fairness, Empathizer Rita tried many approaches to get Instigator Rob to go grocery shopping with her. She would ask nicely. She would reason with Rob that shopping as a team would take less time. Rita even shared feeling lonely because of a lack of time spent together as a couple and her belief that shopping would make up for lost time. Eventually, Rita felt worn down by Rob's refusals and resorted to nagging. Still more nagging, and still nothing worked. Rob wouldn't budge and defended his view. They couldn't seem to find a compromise to move past the Plexiglass wall that was keeping them apart. Rita was growing angry because she perceived that Instigator Rob wasn't listening to what she needed and no longer cared.

Meanwhile, big-hearted Instigator, Rob felt justified that sleep was required to rest up for the hard work week ahead. He remained fixated on his view no matter what Rita would say or do. Rob argued strongly that it was only right for him to have one day of the week to sleep in since he was the sole financial provider for their family of four. Rita reacted to this ploy, by saying: "I don't get any day to sleep in because I'm working at home every day, all day every day." A distancing pattern of Empathizer-Instigator standoff, nit-picking and defensive arguing developed. Negatives filled their relationship with tension. Time for a change of view to see what was possible!

⌕ Listening a Minute Longer Is a Guaranteed Fix

Because Instigator Rob thought he was right, he wasn't listening to what actually needed to be fixed. Rob simply didn't know what to do differently. He needed firsthand experience with a new approach. So, I asked Instigator Rob if he was up for a homework assignment that would get far better results for him with his wife.

"Can you guarantee this will work?" Rob poked at me with a sly grin that amused the class.

I shot back: "I absolutely guarantee it will work if you use a positive attitude and follow these mile markers. Here's all you have to do to change your view:

1. Ask your Empathizer wife in a soft voice if you can go shopping with her on Saturday.
2. Be ready. When Rita acts surprised and asks you why the change of mind, just say you've thought about her concerns, and think she's got a good point. You want to spend some overdue time being together. (The guys cut up here because they teased Instigator Rob that Empathizer Rita might have a heart attack or think he had been out drinking or carousing.)
3. Get up early without being nagged on Saturday. No griping or deep sighing as if you're going through labor pains.
4. Be in a cheerful attitude the whole time. NO grumpiness or acting like it's killing you to lose an hour of sleep to be nice to your wife.
5. And NO expectations. Go just to go. Don't go to get something back in return. Don't go and collect resentments while shopping. You are giving your beloved the gift of your time. Leave it at that.
6. Shop for groceries, make small talk, and simply be with your wife. You don't have to solve any problems or do anything special or remarkable. Challenge yourself to change your view that shopping is boring.
7. Simply listen to your wife. In fact, concentrate on Rita's face when she speaks. Show her that you're listening intently to whatever she has to say.
8. No smart-aleck jokes, arguing or debating, or getting all cynical or snarky. Zip those lips. If you don't have anything nice to say, don't say anything at all, and just smile warmly.

"OK, Rob. Got it? Now repeat your marching orders," I said. And Rob repeated them perfectly.

But as an Instigator, Rob also wanted to have the last word. He kicked up a bit of a fuss that he had to act fake and pretend he's in a good mood when he's dog-tired.

I reacted instantly, "But that's what you do at work. You give your all at work. Your partner, the love of your life, the mother of your children who adores you like no other, does the same at home and deserves as much."

Rob laughed about my dramatic intonations but trusted me and was curious about how his change of attitude would impact his wife's view of him as being uncaring, hard-headed, and insensitive.

💬 Let's Go to the Supermarket

Rob did as promised and asked Rita if he could accompany her on the upcoming Saturday grocery shopping trip while their two growing teenagers with wolf-size appetites were at practice. When Rob told Rita of his intent to go, he was a little taken aback when she reacted with a big smile and an even bigger hug. "That would be just great, honey!" she purred. "I can't wait. This will be like a date." Rob smiled back meekly but wasn't so sure about that.

Saturday morning arrived and Rob awoke in a sour mood. He really didn't want to go grocery shopping on this cold morning. He preferred to stay in the warm bed and keep on snoozing. But he remembered his promise, and if for no other reason, he wanted to prove me wrong so he could immediately put this whole shopping nonsense to bed. And he also remembered that a sour-mood attitude would doom the whole experiment, so he pretended to be chipper when he interacted with his wife. He still felt annoyed and secretly grumbled under his breath when she wasn't in sight.

At the store, Rita grabbed a cart and got busy on her shopping routine. Rob remembered his assignment was simply to observe, not judge or fuss, and to listen intently to whatever his wife said. Rob mused how he might be able to catch a nap at home before their two rambunctious teens returned to ransack the refrigerator. Rob noticed how Rita was focused, efficient, and had a routine to maximize her time and stick to the shopping list. She chatted nonchalantly as Rob dutifully pushed the shopping cart after her, making sure not to run the cart into Rita's backside or stub his toes on the squeaky cart wheels.

💬 Change of View

Then came the ketchup aisle. Rita intently gazed at the rows of ketchup choices. Rob had no idea that ketchup came in so many options. What is the difference between fancy ketchup and regular ketchup? Why so many flavors and shapes of bottles? Is there a National Ketchup Day? Was it true what his buddy said that McDonald's replaced Heinz ketchup with their own mixture, resulting in the loss of business? What's the big deal here, anyway? Ketchup is just crushed and squashed ripe red tomatoes. Rob was beginning to lose his cool, feeling irritated and frustrated with his Saturday morning time being wasted by his wife.

Then Rob heard Rita talking out loud to herself. She was arguing with herself about which ketchup would be the best pick. Rita knew the tastes of each family member and was comparing them so she could come up with a choice that pleased everyone. Then she compared ketchup quality to price. Rita tried to stick to a budget to respect the hard-earned money her husband brought home, even though prices kept going up. Then she read the labels of two promising choices out loud. "I think this one will make everyone happy," Rita chirped, aware that she had been lost in thought, and Rob was staring at her.

"What's the matter," Rita said. "Oh, I get it. You're probably thinking we should have checked out of here 30 minutes ago. I'm sorry. I know you're not used to this and it's pretty packed in here on a Saturday." Then Rita noticed Rob's eyes were misty.

Rob was deep in thought. He hadn't even realized how much love and attention Rita put into shopping. He didn't know she took her shopping role so seriously to the health, wealth, and happiness of their family. Rob was stunned. Talk about the "change of view." His view of Rita and shopping shifted 180 degrees. Rob saw what he hadn't seen before because he never gave it much thought. His memory flashed back to all the times he would sarcastically chime in only to complain about how much money Rita was spending on groceries every week. "You would think we're feeding an army. Isn't there a way to spend less?"

Rob felt embarrassed. His feelings tangled and tumbled in his mind. Rita stared at Rob with a mixture of curiosity and compassion. She knew Rob wanted to be the strong one. She knew her guy would ordinarily conceal and not reveal his feelings; she understood that's just how he rolled. But she wasn't ready for what happened next.

"Baby, I'm amazed how much love you put into all this. I had no idea. I feel like an idiot. If you put that much love into ketchup, I know you must put a whole lot more love into each one of us. I'm so grateful for you." And then Rob looked at Rita with soft eyes.

Rita was joyfully stunned. Rob's words held so much power and meaning. She knew he meant what he said, and from his point of view, his words and feelings were all pretty mushy stuff. Rita didn't want to put him on the spot and fire a bunch of questions at him. So she simply smiled, took Rob by the hand, and squeezed it warmly. Then they finished shopping and checked out and headed home.

Rita and Rob playfully interacted in the kitchen as they quickly put away the groceries. The boys weren't due home for another hour. Rita grabbed Rob's hand and pulled his arm heading toward the bedroom. Rita teased, "This shopping spree has really put me in the mood." Rob didn't resist and was grateful because their sex life had been slipping. They had a delightful time together and went about their weekend activities in a happier mood as they welcomed the boys home.

💬 Moral of the Ketchup Story

What does this true-life Ketchup Story have to do with communicating effectively? How does listening change the view of the peoplescape?

Ears stuffed with cotton are guaranteed to create resentment in your partner and drain the intimate connection between the two of you. By listening, you will hear legitimate complaints and suggestions, and you'll implement solutions that you've long overlooked.

You have two ears and one mouth. That means you can listen twice as much as you talk. Earlier we said that benefits accompany the art of Instigator-Empathizer communication definitely accrue over time. Listening open-mindedly to a partner's view is an aphrodisiac. But you've first got to give a fair trial to the tools to find out in real time that they work for you and yours. "Listening a minute longer" and "listening to understand" are attitudes that you use actively. That's why it's called "active listening" and requires focusing your mind instead of drifting off.

Here are the reasons why listening is the avenue for your greater relationship satisfaction:

- Better listening equals better moods and outcomes.
- The main mistake you make is to listen to what's in your head instead of what's being said to you.
- Intentional listening builds a culture of trust and respect.
- Listening intently to views contrary to your own doesn't mean you condone those views.
- Repeating back what you heard lowers the drawbridge between partner islands.
- Instigators could be fairly critiqued for listening only to what they want to hear.
- Empathizers could be fairly critiqued for listening to garbage that they ought to take to the curb.
- People don't listen so they don't have to change their ways.

What you've been wanting in your relationship life will arrive when you listen intently to your life partner, or anyone, and don't react with a predetermined E-I prejudiced viewpoint.

🗩 You Can't Listen If You're Talking

Quieting the mind is essential for effective listening. Listening to what's in your head vs. what's being said is the number one listening mistake everyone makes. It's common sense but not commonly done. You can't listen if you're talking. If you feel pressured to prove a point, stop talking and start listening to slow the train down and change tracks.

It's normal to default to not listening. None of us have been trained to be good listeners. Practicing listening requires you to refocus your mind when it drifts off. It also requires you to manage the temperature of your mood and stay calm when passions are rising. As a rule, upset Instigators will talk more than listen. Upset Empathizers will withdraw and be silent.

The main technique to bridge the communication gap in a conversation is to listen to your internal dialogue. When you're thinking about other things instead of listening to the speaker, you must choose to bring yourself back and center your mind in the conversation. This is why we say that "listening is an attitude." Calming your mind and slowing down the train rumbling through your brain is a requirement for rigorous listening.

All of us go back to an ego-centered me-first attitude that puts cotton in your ears. Everybody is a bad listener. What really matters is to catch yourself in the act of not listening to refocus your attention again on the person who's talking to you.

Instigators often feel they're inferior listeners and that there's no hope in even trying to get better. That's a shame because skills improve dramatically when practiced. Empathizers know they are excellent listeners but don't speak up strongly enough about their creative ideas. This is a shame, too, because it creates an unbalanced team.

But how do you catch yourself in the act of not listening to refocus your attention back on what the speaker is saying?

- Listen to your inner world. Is your mind drifting off?
- Stay curious about the conversation. Why did you drift off? What was being said?

- Was something being said that you didn't want to hear?
- Could the point that you didn't hear be the solution to a thorny relationship problem?
- Remind yourself that listening is a priceless gift you give to another person.

💬 Listening Is a Dance

Two-way communication is like a dance. You must be in the moment and moving to the sound of the music. There are three levels of listening. Use these levels to grade where yours is during the conversation. The higher level, the better the listening and the better the results. Whether you are an Empathizer or Instigator, you can use these levels to evaluate your listening.

LEVEL 1 SELF-DRIVEN LISTENING: You're thinking through your perceptual lens about you. Your concentration is distracted by "What will I say next?" "What do they think of me?" "What will I have for lunch?" You're thinking about yourself and not listening where they're coming from. You are listening to respond, debate or your mind has wandered. Your listening is "ego-centered," meaning you are focused on you and your thoughts. This the default mode we all slip back into.

LEVEL 2 PARTNER-DRIVEN LISTENING: You're focused on the other person and the words they are saying. Internal chatter is free of "What's in it for me?"

LEVEL 3 RELATIONSHIP-DRIVEN LISTENING: You're aware of what isn't being said, the other person's body language, and are flexibly shifting between I-E mindsets. It's a heightened state of awareness and connectivity. Your mind is calm and open to "What will I discover here?"

Sports Example: UCLA basketball legend Coach John Wooden was an I-Type coach who, according to his players, was known to be such a deep listener that his intensity was scary. He also consistently produced winning teams that outperformed other teams with more raw talent.

If you're an Instigator, it's natural that you might feel doomed because "I just am not a good listener" and there's not much you can do about it. That's just plain false.

It's worth keeping in mind this sports example when you feel like you're losing the talk game. Countless other successful I-Type communicators have honed their listening skills; you can, too. You will soon discover that listening is the key to I-Type success. It balances your intense drive for success and helps you grow into the next most successful version of yourself.

We've all experienced these three different levels of connectivity. Be a mindful listener to connect with the players in your life at deep levels.

Avoiding Common Listening Mistakes

What are the powerful principles of a poised communicator? Look through the eyes of your opposite to see the truth you can do something about. As you learned in the last chapter, you're difficult in the eyes of your opposite type but not in your own view.

People are only difficult when emotions are difficult to handle. Difficult people give you the opportunity to expand your life view and coping skills.

- INSTIGATOR MISTAKE: When you raise your voice to get your point across, you lose respect and get labeled as an arrogant person.
- EMPATHIZER MISTAKE: When you speak softly, you are perceived to be weak and your opinions are seen as untrustworthy.
- INSTIGATOR MISTAKE: When you interrupt or talk over people, you're viewed as bossy and selfish.
- EMPATHIZER MISTAKE: When you don't speak up forcefully to share where you're coming from, you create anxiety and lose influence.

What listening mistakes do you make? Better yet, what listening mistakes does your partner tell you that you make?

💬 What Do Instigators and Empathizers Need from Each Other?

Conflict causes hurtful feedback, and hurtful feedback causes conflict. What each type needs from the other to get along better:

- If you're an Instigator, you will be viewed as approachable and available when you listen up. By listening to all the facts, you won't make hasty and faulty decisions.
- If you're an Empathizer, you will be viewed as assertive and directive when you speak up. By speaking up without all the facts, you will advocate for your own careful and wise decisions.

Talking without hearing is empty air. If a tree falls in the forest and no one is around to hear it, does it make a sound? If you took a philosophy class at some point in your educational journey, you likely heard this question as a thought experiment about observation and perception. The same goes for listening. If someone says something, and no one is listening, was anything communicated? Without getting into a philosophical debate, you can surely agree that without listening, you aren't communicating and frustrations will multiply.

PRO Rule: Problems can't get solved until hot emotions cool off.

Listening is a little thing that matters a lot, and when you listen, you can communicate. Be a flexible communicator who uses the strengths of both types to get the job done. If you choose only one communication skill to develop, choose the skill of listening. Without listening, we can't hope to be communication experts and make the impression we desire in our work, in our families, or in the world.

💬 Top Listening Complaints

Let's take a moment to review the top Empathizer complaints of Instigators and then review what Empathizers can do to up their listening game in the eyes of Instigators.

Complaints by Empathizers about Instigator listening:

- Instigators push aside your comments
- Instigators shoot the messenger, and then take credit
- Instigators become hot heads when an opposing view intersects
- Instigators go in for chest pumping to emotionally support a viewpoint
- Instigators bait people to test how they will squirm or react, and then they lean back and smirk

In hundreds of classes, Empathizers are never dinged for being poor listeners. It seems impossible but true. Instigators, on the other hand, are the first to say that their listening skills need improving.

What's the first step to change? Admitting the issue. "Hi, I'm an Instigator, and I'm a poor listener." Rigorous honesty solves problems.

Yes, although this is cliché and echoes the power of Alcohol Anonymous meetings, it's still on target. Just because you are a poor listener doesn't mean you are destined to always be a poor listener. Like meditation, listening is a habit that is learned. It soon will become second nature like breathing.

Next time you have trouble focusing during a conversation or notice your attention drifting, bring yourself back to the person talking. Just like bringing yourself back to your breath during meditation, refocus your mind back on the person talking. Once you practice this, you will become a naturally more engaged listener.

Complaints by Instigators about Empathizer listening:

- Empathizers should stop listening to trash
- Empathizers need to loosen up and learn to verbally spar with Instigators
- Empathizers have to speak up more; otherwise, no one will know what they are thinking
- Empathizers give the silent treatment instead of saying what's wrong
- Empathizers need to shrug off teasing and get past the past
- Empathizers allow people to verbally hurt them, which is why hurts keep happening
- Empathizers need to take responsibility and stand up for themselves to be respected

Instigators have a point: "If you don't have enough respect to speak up for yourself, why should I?" As a rule, Empathizers do need to speak up more. E's do need to learn how to filter out the things that aren't true. E's do need to tell their truth when pressured not to.

Moreover, if you're an Empathizer, chances are you are great at listening but overvalue and magnify critical feedback. This tendency reduces your confidence and self-esteem. Also, Empathizers tend to listen too much and silently disagree without speaking up. This will cause a loss of respect from Instigators because it raises their anxiety and gives them too much free rein to dominate you and others.

Change happens when you set appropriate listening boundaries and push yourself to take accountability for what you can do better. This arises from the helpful feedback you hear.

The next set of listening rules stems from countless training classes where people have courageously shared what works when conflicts heat up. This is the time you will make costly mistakes you can't take back. These "tough love" rules aren't evidence of your failure. They are designed to stop you from opening the metaphorical can of worms.

💬 Tough Love Rules for Instigators to Connect With Empathizers

Instigators dominate situations. It's their nature to lead passionately and work hard and fast to fix problems. Their worth depends on it. Unfortunately, an urgency to fix problems limits listening. In fact, Empathizers often have the solution to problems that Instigators face, if you take time to ask them for their input.

If you're an Instigator, use these rules to get your message heard and gain the respect you desire from Empathizers. This blunt advice is coming from countless Empathizer clients, corporate leaders, and everyday people.

- *Shut up:* Get off your high horse and listen.
- *Don't interrupt:* Listen for a change to what you don't want to hear.
- *Don't roll your eyes:* It's rude and people lose respect for you.
- *Don't talk down to me:* Show compassion. Seek first to understand.
- *Don't talk over me:* Be tolerant by accepting others for who they are.
- *Don't finish my sentences:* Demonstrate patience.
- *Don't preach to me about what you won't do:* Hypocrisy stinks.
- *Don't say how to do it better:* Be humble because you know so little about everything that's going on in the world.
- *Don't dictate how you would have done it:* Stop neurotically trying to fix people to distract yourself from fixing yourself.
- *Stop trying to dominate the situation:* Puffing out your chest to hide insecurities comes across as fake, arrogant, and unconfident.

💬 Tough Love Rules for Empathizers to Connect With Instigators

Empathizers take a back seat in situations. It's their nature to work collaboratively and come to solutions collaboratively. Unfortunately, listening to everything can delay decision making. In fact, Instigators know that making a decision, any decision, is important to problem-solving momentum.

If you're an Empathizer, use these rules to gain confidence when speaking with Instigators. According to Instigators, Empathizers need to be more assertive and get to the point faster.

- *Interrupt:* Speak up and talk over the conversation dominators for a change of pace.
- *Use your lion gaze:* Speak directly, with your eyes locked on the listener.
- *Don't fidget:* Be poised and assertive; otherwise, I-Types will view that as weakness and pounce.
- *Get to the point:* Be fast and brief and write out critical comments in advance.
- *Be a fixer:* Come up with a solution to any complaint and repeat it like a broken record.
- *Louder:* Raise your voice one level to grab and hold the attention of a distracted Instigator.
- *Stick to your point:* Make one point at a time and reiterate your point until it sinks in.
- *Joke around:* Take a joke and make a joke. It's not a personal attack but a way to connect.
- *Speak-up:* If you don't say anything is wrong, the assumption will be that nothing is wrong.
- *Let it go:* Don't get hung up on things; it doesn't help. Move on and get over it.

Instigators Excel When They Adopt Empathetic Listening Attitudes

The solution to most problems is listening to accurate information in a relatively calm mood and non-biased mindset. Instigators push back hard in our workshops and want to know the exact steps they can take to become a better listener.

We know the challenges you face. How do you clear your mind to hear? How do you give your entire attention to the speaker when you're interrupted in the middle of an important task? How do you keep composed and not oppose the speaker when you hear feedback that you don't want to hear? How do you let go of needing to be right and correcting the speaker in a harsh way? These are all real deals in the real world of communication.

PRO Instigator communicators can make a speaker feel like a first-class teammate by using this simple but disciplined active listening checklist:

- Breathe
- Say to one's busy mind, "Be calm and listen up"
- Remove environmental distractions
- Concentrate on the message, not on mannerisms
- Don't have multiple conversations
- Ask curious questions
- Bring your drifting mind back to focus
- Paraphrase often to encourage more talking
- Stick to one major topic at a time
- Withhold judgments
- Lead the person to the conclusion rather than outright telling them or jumping in
- Admit when your attention has drifted
- Ask, "What do you most need me to hear to be helpful?"
- Inquire, "And what else have you been thinking about this?"
- Close the conversation, "I'm glad we had a chance to talk."

It's normal to have your highly active mind get distracted. It's normal to want to jump in and solve things. Stay focused.

Remember, the best solution for someone else is their own solution. Help guide them to their solution. It empowers the person you are speaking with and creates the best results while simultaneously building bridges of trust and respect. Avoid constantly giving advice, especially to those that don't need or want it. Sadly, your pearls of wisdom may get trampled in the mud. Instead, engage the listener by listening to yourself and asking curious questions.

TIPS TO CALM YOUR MIND: If you find your mind extra distracted and active, clear your mind before a conversation with a brain dump. Write down anything you have to do after the conversation or anything that's on your mind. Clear your mind of irrelevant distractions before the upcoming conversation. Next, review in your mind the purpose of the upcoming conversation. What outcome do you want? Finally, take a few moments to close your eyes and do nothing. These techniques can be especially effective before a tough conversation or business meeting. These are instances when your mind is extra hyperactive, thanks to adrenalin. Take five and calm your mind.

Clear your mind to clear the way to higher levels of effective communication.

Empathizers Excel When They Adopt Instigator Listening Attitudes

Empathizers are deep listeners who have a tendency to listen to trash and get pushed around. If you're an Empathizer, listening doesn't require you to feel down and absorb inaccurate feedback that siphons off your energy. Adopting Instigator attitudes about listening can help balance your listening attitude.

PRO Empathizer listeners get their voice heard by using this simple checklist:

- Speak up with an affirmative tone (not mousey)
- Hold eye contact and hold a confident posture
- Have the courage to speak up right away when something needs to be said
- Don't fear the results or "What IF...." yourself before speaking your truth

- Stop listening to things that are hurtful or unhelpful
- Repeat or restate key points as needed
- Confirm the other person heard you by asking a question to clarify understanding

TIP TO SPEAK UP: Give compassionately honest feedback without being held up by your fears. If you feel something needs to be said or challenged, just say it. Next time you have something important that needs to be said, take a moment to write it down or act it out with a friend or loved one. Then, say it to them straight. Instigators appreciate it when you see through the BS and call them on something. You will be shocked at how easily it's taken when you say what you need to say bluntly and accompany it with your E-type empathy.

If you're an Empathizer, you don't have to stop being a great listener to start adopting these Instigator selective listening tactics. By matching styles and using I-techniques to balance your communication, you will gain Instigator respect.

Next, we're going to discuss the elephant in the room that disrupts listening and relationship satisfaction. We'll help you take a closer look at listening disruptions and how to correct them to create Instigator-Empathizer synergy. Like a pyramid, one side of the base is the Instigator view, and the other side of the base is the Empathizer. These energies combined arise to form the point of the pyramid. Instead of "my view" vs. "your view," the third view is "our view," which is the higher-order problem-solving reality.

Conversational Coercion: Getting Your Way at the Expense of Relationship Synergy

Conversational Coercion is a debate tactic that works in the short run to get your way during a heated disagreement. Unfortunately, it's also the leading, hidden cause of a resentment wall that has graffiti written on it in red paint with the angry despairing words: "It's always your way or the highway. And that makes me lose trust and respect for you."

Conversational Coercion is strategically manipulating the outcome of a conversation to gain the upper hand in order to get your way. Instigators are naturally fierce debaters who think well on their feet during a crisis or heated exchange.

For example, shouting "You're not listening!" is manipulative when, in truth, your partner is listening but not agreeing with you. It is a classic example of how *Conversational Coercion* erodes trust and respect in your relationships. This "steamroller technique" of decision-making leaves Empathizers outside in the cold feeling alone.

Watch for *Conversational Coercion* and you will see it wherever you go. In political debates about what is right or wrong to do regarding national health care insurance options, in courtrooms with lawyers arguing the mental sanity and competency of a co-parent, in major finance spending decisions with strapped couples, and in family squabbles about when aging parents will be able to see their grandkids or not.

To better understand this dynamic, let's dissect a specific real-life example of *Conversational Coercion* that occurs in the homes of many couples. You will learn how an Instigator subtly coercing an Empathizer partner is the secret behind understanding of our earlier Ketchup Story about Rob, who rationalized to Rita why it wasn't logical for him to go Saturday grocery shopping with her. You will recall that Rob got his way but it was at the expense of a harmonious marriage filled to the brim with sexual energy.

In the couples realm, I (Dennis) worked with an I-E couple for a series of sessions over several years. The wife, Suze, was an Empathizer educator. The husband, Steve, was an Instigator family doctor. They came up with the term "conversational coercion" to describe how he was able to debate like an attorney to push and get his way. Unfortunately, the "successful" act of "winning the point" and persuading Suze to do something against her will, or getting out of doing something for Suze that Steve didn't want to, was at the expense of the relationship connection and intimacy.

Suze's Empathizer view: "Steve uses intense passion to explain a point of view. He uses so much physical and vocal energy that I am convinced to agree. I am afraid to disagree because I won't hear the end of how he's being inconvenienced. I am afraid to disagree because he will get in a bad mood so I just go along to get along. Then I resent it later on."

The drive to be right undercuts your partner's need to be heard, appreciated, and loved.

Steve's Instigator view: "As an Instigator, I'm an excellent debater and persuader. I fashion arguments and cite facts to support my position. I believe that communication is a chess or poker game. You've got to play to win the point. You know how to force agreement or make the other player come up with a counterargument very quickly, or a siege will follow. It's all about who cares more to win the point. Who will be the last one standing? Who will not surrender the point? Who will have the last word? I will!"

Many creative solutions at work and at home bite the dust due to the *Conversational Coercion* dynamic. Two minds indeed are better than one when it comes to helping each partner express their honest view. Your job is to help a partner up, not out of, their independence.

Bottom line: When decisions are tainted with the prejudice of triggered emotion, you won't arrive at a mutually satisfying, forward-thinking solution or win-win strategy. No one will listen and no one will be listened to.

In short, this coercive relationship pattern wins the battle but loses the war. It chokes your trust connection, restricts creative team problem-solving, and sows seeds of resentment. When you take an Instigator and Empathizer and combine their strengths without judgment or manipulation, you create creative problem-solving that's synergistic and takes the team or couple to a higher level. Good moods ripple out.

🗩 The Recovering Instigator Debater

If you're an Instigator, being able to get your way via being a better debater is addictive. Like a sporting event, winning the point fuels chest thumping and fist bumping. So how do Instigators let go of always needing to get their way when it helps their ego but hurts their happiness?

Humbly admitting you are part of the problem is the solution. Steve joked that he and Suze uncovered these secrets of Informed Instigator during their marriage counseling sessions with me:

- I am a tough debater, but I realize I also limit discussions and options.
- I have no doubt that good defense, The Deflecting Defense, is a good first-strike offense.
- If you don't agree with me, I claim to be misunderstood.
- I become frustrated that I'm not hearing from you what I want to be hearing.
- I steer you into a position that limits your options.
- I shouldn't choose Empathizers' positions for them. But I do.
- I know I can talk circles around my opponents.
- I limit the options so severely that my Empathizer partner has to fight their way out of a corner.
- I can focus the topic on a negative point and draw everybody into the fray.
- Not only do I define the issue, but I also attempt to define what you will think about it.
- I use verbal intimidation and redirecting. I will exert pressure and create the urgency to hurry up and decide because time is wasting.
- I am like a dog on a bone, and my need to dominate is incredibly exhausting to everyone involved.
- Being hard-headed is a real energy-drainer, and it causes extreme relationship friction.
- I strong-arm Empathizers when I say authoritatively, "Here's the issue . . . and here's what you think about it!"
- I will take cheap shots when you don't agree with what I'm selling you.

Said Steve: "If there isn't an emotional bond or connection, *Conversational Coercion* doesn't work as well. But I usually employ this approach anyway when someone isn't buying into my plan because I get the results I want. Although I can get my way, I'm learning it is at the expense of finding a better way. I jail rather than liberate. Our relationship connection becomes a burden rather than a blessing."

Showing disapproval of Empathizers to manipulate the desired result is emotional blackmail.

Conversational Coercion occurs between Instigators, too. False conflicts that erode trust and respect flare up as harsh threats are made. The subtypes of *Conversational Coercion* to be aware of include Decisional Coercion, Identity Coercion, Mood Coercion, Social Opinion Coercion, Financial Coercion, Sexual Coercion, and Health Coercion. Overall, there are many different types of coercion that can occur in controlling relationships when you look for them.

In sum, *Conversational Coercion* is using words, delivery, debate, argument, or emotional blackmail to manipulate the other party into acquiescence. You may get your way today, but you will lose the trust and respect of your partner tomorrow.

💬 Instigators: How to Listen to What You Don't Want to Hear

We won't soft-pedal this truth: Instigators benefit from communications coaching as much as Empathizers do to help change their view of the world. It's true that hindsight is 20/20 vision.

> **PRO Rule:** Listening doesn't mean agreeing.

Do you want to be right or do you want to be loved? If you can't have it both ways, which road will you choose to take on the communication highway? Here are ways to tell and sell yourself on letting go of being right and listening to what you don't want to hear:

- Is it worth being right if it costs me love and honesty?
- Is it worth being right if it costs me respect and trust?
- Is it worth being right if it causes my partner to be a hostage with their mouth taped shut?
- Is it worth being right if it puts me in a bad mood that raises my blood pressure?
- Is it worth being right if I have to yell or cuss to get my way?
- Is it worth being right if my kids are afraid of me and slink away when I come home?
- Is it worth being right if my love life tanks because my partner resents me?
- Is it worth being right if divorce papers come at me out of the blue?
- Is it worth being right if my coworkers feel bad or unappreciated?
- Is it worth being right if my advisors are afraid to tell me the truth that I need to hear?
- Is it worth being right if I'm not able to relax and be happy with who I am and what I've got?
- Is it worth being right if I don't like who I see when I look in the bathroom mirror in the morning?

Which one of these irrational thoughts applies to you when you're mad or blue? Recall, it's not how you meant the message that matters, but how it was received. Measure the effectiveness of your actions by the impact of your words on the receiver. Viewing results rationally and factually is accountability in action.

Recall the PRO Rule from chapter 1; it's not how you meant the message that matters, but how it was received.

The compulsive need to be right is all wrong for your happiness and health. Do you want to be right or do you want to be loved? I know, I know. "But why can't I have it both ways?" spouts off the Instigator like a big bellowing whale. If you can't have it both ways, which road will you choose to take on the communication highway? We recommend you choose love, peace of mind, and the happiness that comes from being a poised and mature communication PRO.

It's never too late to change how you are received up to and including our last dying breath. But why should we wait that long?

⤺ What Do Empathizers Want from Instigators during Heated Disagreements?

You're learning to walk in the shoes and look through the eyes and view of your opposite communicator type. Here's what Instigators need to know about what Empathizers want during intense times of respectful disagreeing:

- Empathizers want Instigators to actively listen to them.
- Empathizers want their opinions to be worth something to Instigators.
- Empathizers want Instigators to hear and disagree without shouting.
- Empathizers want their views to be respected, understood, and appreciated.
- Empathizers want to speak assertively without the fear of put-downs.
- Empathizers want to know their feedback is having an impact.
- Empathizers want to receive genuine credit when warranted.
- Empathizers want their wisdom to be recognized, considered, and utilized.
- Empathizers want engaging duologues, not distracting monologues.
- Empathizers want responsible honesty during times of conflict.

If you're an Instigator, pick one of these areas to assertively practice this week. Give the respect you expect and you will be aptly rewarded.

Respect is both given and earned through the intentional act of listening.

Empathizers desire to speak up and have their feedback heard by Instigators without stubborn pushback that shuts down talks. Both types need to be able to process negative or positive feedback without taking it too personally or too impersonally. Respectful communication is built on a foundation of trust, listening, and paraphrasing skills, and it's fortified with an open exchange of ideas.

Devote your communication life to the high art of listening when escalating feelings are interceding in and ruining difficult talks. Instigators and Empathizers alike want to have genuine and trusting experiences with each other, during which we can be open and honest for the benefit of everyone.

⌬ Mood Distorts Your Listening IQ

As you have learned, Empathizers and Instigators face different but equally difficult struggles to maintain effective listening skills during stressful times. Regardless of your type, a bad mood decreases your listening IQ, compromises your listening skills, and frankly turns you into a listening idiot.

What does mood have to do with your Listening IQ? Everything. One of the most frequent questions at our workshops is, "Sure. It's easy to listen to people talking calmly. But how can I get people to listen to me when they're in a grumpy mood?"

In tough situations, when your mood temperature rises, stick to the basics of good listening-speaking skill sets. By sticking to the basics, you will access a mindset that arises from your active application of Instigator-Empathizer talk technology:

- **Apply Law #1:** Know who you're talking to: An Instigator or an Empathizer. Which type are you talking to? And why does it even matter?
- **Apply Law #2:** Remind yourself that the solution isn't in your view, but in their view. Are you walking in their shoes?
- **Apply Law #3:** Pretending to listen isn't really listening. Are you hearing the truth of what your partner is trying to tell you?

The *TALK2ME©* Laws weave together like strands of a strong rope bridge across a canyon. They all connect and link together and work in harmony to solve problems. Listening is an attitude.

Listening doesn't inflame moods but puts you in a more neutral mindset when the heat is on and emotions are threatening to trample outcomes.

Question: "How can I get more people to listen to me?"

Answer: "By applying the laws and actually listening more to them! By focusing on the conversation, asking good questions, and periodically paraphrasing the message you hear."

Everyone craves to be seen and heard. When people listen to you, you will feel visible and seen instead of treated like a ghost. The most common greeting in the African Zulu tribe is "Sawubona." It literally means "I see you, you are important to me and I value you. All my attention is with you. I see you and I allow myself to discover your needs, to see your fears, to identify your mistakes and accept them. I accept you for what you are and you are part of me." This greeting calms and centers the mind. As a member of the human tribe, you become both a willing leader and a follower who makes devout friends.

With all the talk around the importance of listening, most people still fall short. That's alright, as long as you have an attitude to flex this critical soft-power muscle.

Basic Listening Strategies: How to Fix the Listening Problem

Balancing the two styles comes from your understanding of both specialized I-E listening styles and picking the one that best suits your situation. Experiment. Regardless of your type, keep this list to remind you of essential listening techniques that will guide you during tense conversations:

- Clear your mind. (Anxiety is normal. Breathe!)
- Give your entire attention.
- Listen to hear.
- Seek first to understand.
- Listen a minute longer.
- Don't interrupt.
- Listen to the message's mood tone.
- Keep an open mind.
- Smile through the phone or text.
- Always remember that listening creates change.

Listening alone solves many problems. When you listen, people feel a sense of belonging and shared caring. By listening, you get to know the person better, and they perceive you to care more.

Rewarding Listening Checklist to Encourage Change

Listening changes the listener. That's why you resist listening. You fear change, fear the unknown, and fear failure. Here's what you can say to keep a conversation flowing along like a river instead of a flood:

- *Ask Curious Questions:* "What is your take on this _____?"
- *Paraphrase:* "So what you're saying is _____."
- *Clarify:* "Let me make sure I'm understanding you. You're saying _____. Is that correct?"
- *Confirm:* "We agree that these are the next steps to take. Did I hear you right?"
- *Ask to Interrupt:* "Would it be OK if I interrupt you here so I don't forget my point?"
- *Apologize-for-Interrupting:* "I'm sorry that I cut you off. I didn't intend to. Please go on."

- *Reward:* "That was a really good point you made. Let me think about that some more."
- *Rebuke:* "You don't have to raise your voice to get your point across with me."
- *Thank:* "Thank you for making time to listen to me. I value your contributions and what you have to say."
- *Silently Affirm:* "I'm giving myself a pat on the back for listening to what's hard to hear. My listening and emotional IQ are on the rise."

Listening takes courage. You learn when you listen, and you don't learn when you don't listen. Let's dive deeper into core listening tools for you to use that will slow your mind instead of getting judgmental or shutting down during a conversation. These tools will help you pause before you react with harsh words of prejudice. Put simply, you save face and get more of what you desire.

💬 Parrot-Phrasing: Paraphrasing Proves You're Listening

It's time for a story. Riley and her childhood friend, Sarah, went on many adventures. Occasionally, they returned home with an assortment of animal friends, including a rainbow turtle they rescued from the road and Checkers, the bunny, who turned out to be Tinkerbelle, the pregnant bunny. The groundhog? Parents delivered it immediately to a nearby animal hospital.

One day, Sarah brought home a parrot. Surprisingly, when Chirpie's owner found out his bird had been found, he told Sarah's family they could keep him. Chirpie often repeated what he heard, and because Sarah's family loved theater and singing, Chirpie began whistling show tunes. He could never quite get the hang of *"If I Only Had a Brain"* from *"The Wizard of Oz,"* so he would trail off or start freestyling. A bit of a jokester, Chirpie frequently enjoyed "wolf whistling" at his beloved owners for a hearty laugh. Chirpie was a listening sponge.

In workshops, we instruct participants to periodically "parrot back" what was said. Why is that? Because the goal of intentional paraphrasing is to prove you're listening so well you are able to repeat back the main message almost verbatim on the spot.

Doing so proves that listening is an attitude and a choice you make. You decide to listen...or not. Although listening and tuning in when emotions are roaring is an advanced skill, paraphrasing works well to slow the train that is veering off the tracks.

Challenge yourself to do this listening practice on your own. Simply say to the speaker "Let me see if I'm hearing what you're saying." Then repeat back what you think you heard in your words that accurately reflect the speaker's views without distortion.

You'll often find that what you *think* you heard isn't what was actually said. Words are so easy to misinterpret, and meanings are easy to mangle. Negative emotions can become magnified, and positive emotions can be minimized. Instigators especially are vulnerable when they struggle to listen to hear. But you can't learn anything new if you don't listen with an open mind.

Good times to paraphrase are:

- When your mind is receiving tons of new information.
- When your mind has begun to wander.
- When your mind is being challenged by information or viewpoints you don't want to hear.
- When you are judging what the speaker is saying as unworthy of your time.
- Any old time when you want to give the speaker a deep experience of being encountered and heard.

Paraphrasing doesn't mean agreeing or debating. It's simply making sure you heard the message without adding or forgetting any part of it. It slows down your spinning mind. It helps you confirm what you're hearing. It checks your tendency to read into a situation and distort what is really being said.

Simply repeating back what you hear will make the speaker open up and say more. Why? People like hearing themselves speak. Active paraphrasing will make people like you more. In fact, the FBI uses this tool in investigative interviews to get people to open up and divulge information. You can use this tool to keep lines of communication open when temperatures are rising. It's a negotiation technique that doesn't require manipulation or coercion.

Interrupting shoots the messenger and blows up the relationship bridge. It's the main complaint of everyone engaged in an escalating conflict. Interrupting shuts down the open flow of ideas.

So, how do you interrupt in a way that doesn't cause resentment or close down listening and creative problem-solving? Instigators can interrupt less, and Empathizers can repeat their points when interruptions occur.

⌬ Can I Interrupt You for a Minute?

Think back to your childhood. As a child, did you ever try to interrupt a parent who was focused on a television program? It didn't go well. You heard, "Uh-huh. Whatever." Similar patterns emerged during training whenever an Empathizer employee interrupted the Instigator supervisor without asking for permission.

At the robotics company client, satisfaction with management was in the tank. For five years, according to the vice president of human resources, the company had tried a variety of popular programs to fix the problem, but nothing was working and satisfaction scores fell even lower.

TALK2ME© training revealed a source of employee dissatisfaction: when someone would enter their workspace to relay information or ask a question, Instigators would continue to work instead of giving their full attention to the person speaking. E-Types and I-Types alike took this to be a huge sign of disrespect.

A better way to get attention from the supervisor is to simply ask, "Can I interrupt you for a minute?" Alternatively, you can ask, "Is this (still) a good time?" Then wait for a response and an indication of the supervisor's attention and proceed accordingly. He or she may be too busy and might ask you to come back at a specified time. Their mind might be focused on other things.

Time crunches are inevitable and understandable. Although most people think they can multitask, chances are you can't do it effectively. Take for example texting and driving, or listening to the news and hearing your partner. You can only do one thing well at a time. Concentration and attentive listening are compromised when you multitask. Instigators especially get peeved being interrupted when they're focused on their computer screen, television, or cell phone.

Let's examine a case example from the workplace.

We taught Instigator manager-supervisors two simple, respectful response tools. The result: The independent research team urgently called HR asking why company communication scores shot up so dramatically in one quarter.

Asking to interrupt is a simple courtesy that recognizes that everyone has short attention spans. It also conveys the understanding that passing information along in a timely fashion is crucial to complex task accomplishment. It's like passing a hot potato.

Here's what to say when you're breaking into someone's mental space and interrupting their focused concentration:

- *Ask Permission: Can I interrupt you for a minute?*

That's it. Respect the time of your co-workers. Examples: "I need five minutes of your time. Are you free now?" Or, "I see you're busy. When is a better time to pass along some information?" But the key is to ask, not command, another person's time.

Time is a very personal matter for most people. Instigators especially are performance-driven time crunching machines.

Co-communicators take steps to do what works well for both parties. Selecting a better time to talk is important even when you just need a quick question answered.

These steps only take 15 seconds to do. Whenever you're interrupted by a co-worker who is seeking to pass along information to you:

- Look up from what you're doing, if safe to do so.
- Turn to face the person who is asking the question.
- Smile warmly.
- Let yourself feel mildly irritated about the interruption.
- Don't fear losing your concentration on your work.
- If you can be interrupted, say: "How can I help?"
- If you can't be interrupted, say: "Can I get back to you in 10 minutes?"
- Keep your promise: Go find the person and finish the conversation.

Is it impolite to interrupt someone's workflow or weak to seek permission to speak? The answer depends on how impatient you are. Being respectful makes all the difference.

RULE: Ask permission to talk in order to activate listener attention and accountability. That way, you won't appear rude or disrespectful.

- *"Is this a good time? I'd like to discuss X. Are you free now?"*

REASON: Informative conversations need to be pre-planned and well-timed for the best results.

💬 Listen a Minute Longer

If you're an Instigator, how do you talk to yourself to prime the pump of the listening mind? As an Instigator, it's only natural to have the urge to interrupt to solve a problem speedily.

As you already know, I-Types often ask, "How can I get more people to listen to me?" What I-Types want is for people to do as they say, quickly and without question. But Empathizers often have a better way if you take time to seek out and listen to their input.

Our solution: "Take a minute longer to listen!" Why? In workshops, Instigators often cite this tool as most helpful in developing the patience to hear new ideas and hidden solutions. Often, the solution appears right after the interruption occurs.

> **PRO Rule:** Talking to yourself isn't listening.

Give yourself permission to just listen and not rush to solve a problem. In fact, in many cases listening *is* the solution. Empathizers know this because they listen with three ears.

This self-coaching technique can be used to focus your mind before and during a conversation. Here is an example of encouraging self-dialogue to get yourself focused and to listen a minute longer:

OK. I choose to listen now. This is a good time to practice my listening skills. I will have fewer problems later on by listening now. I'm going to clear my mind of this day's troubles and struggles.

I turn over my entire attention to the speaker. I have one mouth and two ears for a reason. I'm not going to pre-judge. I don't have to solve any problems or say anything wise or witty. I don't have to be right or prove my point.

I'm going to listen with three ears. Completely. Intently. Caringly. Just listening. That's all I have to do. Just listening is what most people need to feel OK about whatever they're going through. I will seek first to understand before being understood. I'll listen to what's being said and what's being implied. I will encourage the speaker by nodding my head, keeping steady eye contact, and having a slight smile on my face.

Here are several things you can say to yourself when you are feeling the itch to interrupt:

- When there's a pause or my mind is getting overwhelmed, I will say, "Let me catch up with you here and make sure I'm understanding what you're saying. You're saying _____."
- I also won't be too proud to say, "Could you repeat what you just said? I think I missed that."
- I will show my humility by asking "what" questions. I will actively

clarify what's being said, "What do you think would be helpful for us to do?

Fix your attention on becoming a better listener. You're not there to fix the other person's problems. Your listening will be the solution to help them fix their own problems.

🗨 Do You Have a Short Attention Span?

Listening is the key technique used to refocus the busy mind during a fast or complex conversation. You take charge of your mood and stay calm by focusing your mind on the speaker instead of the little old you.

During most of a conversation, you are holding your own conversation in your own head. You often think about what to say next. You wonder how the conversation is going. You question if you are doing a good job in the conversation. You wonder if the other person likes or respects you.

The mind wanders within 60 seconds of a topic. Don't hassle yourself about your short attention span. It's natural to go from focusing on the conversation to focusing back on yourself, your thoughts, and what you will say next. This is the mental default. Your mind is naturally self-focused. That's okay. It doesn't matter that you drift off. Just catch yourself. And get back on the listening track.

The mind is over-stimulated in this era of information bites. Expect and monitor distraction. Just gently bring your mind back to focus on the conversation at hand, similar to how you might refocus your mind on your breathing during meditation. That way, you are able to refocus your mind on the other person when you start drifting off during a conversation.

Here's how to bring your mind back to focus:

OK. My mind is wandering. What did they just say? This is natural. It doesn't mean I'm a bad listener.

How can I get curious about what's being said? What question can I ask to get reengaged? Breathe. What's the main message here?

I need to stop judging and censoring and keep focused on listening.

Listening creates change. That's why it's tempting not to listen. Your mind will naturally drift back to focusing on your inner world instead of what's going on in the outer world. Communication is wanting to be heard and the willingness to listen.

There's no end to the distractions that assault the senses. Listening prejudices and disruptions abound. It's especially tempting to drift off when you don't like the speaker. Or they might look funny or have a voice tone that grates on your nerves, like fingernails on a chalkboard. Or, they're too young or too old. You might question if they know anything that will be useful to you. Don't allow yourself to get distracted or judgmental. It's just the externals.

Be kind to your mind. Focusing on listening gets you into the internal reality of a person rather than judging them by social stigmas and personal prejudices.

Bringing It on Home

Here is a final listening tool that gauges your communication. Let's make this a real encounter in your life now. Think of a loved one, a partner whose life is impacted by yours, and ask this one simple question:

- **The Listening Question:** "What one thing could I do differently to improve our communication?"

But before you ask the question, decide if you are willing to commit to doing what's suggested of you, with no strings attached. You can bet this a big stretch for all of you "nobody's going to tell me what to do" stubborn ego-driven mules.

I (Dennis) asked the Listening Question to Riley when she was a junior as I dropped her off at Centerville High School. "Riley, what one thing could I do differently that would make me a better dad to you?"

Riley looked me in the eye while holding the Honda Pilot door half-open with her foot ready to jump out, and replied: "Dad, you could be less sarcastic." Then off she went to school leaving me to ponder this blunt feedback.

It was a very humbling experience for me. Here was the so-called communication guru being honestly told that I was too negative and snarky. Even though I asked for it, I could have gotten mad about listening to the feedback. I could have used many factual excuses to ignore or fight off Riley's point of view. And, frankly, it stung my gargantuan ego more than a little bit.

But Riley was right. Spoken from the trusting mouth of a child. I really did need to up both my leadership game and improve my role model as a single parent.

Children take on the views of their parents. It's only natural. "Do as I say, not as I do!" just won't cut it anymore. Do you want your children to turn out like you? If you do, good. If you don't, listen to the changes you need to make and do everything in your power to follow through on these changes.

Intentional Listening Checklist

In this chapter, you learned the differences between Empathizer and Instigator listening styles and how to sharpen your listening skills. Use this checklist to amplify your listening:

- *Be Intentional:* Set your intention to listen.
- *Be Present:* Let go of your "to-do" list and be present.
- *Be Open:* Listen openly to the message. Allow your view to change.
- *Be Here Now:* Dedicate your full attention to the person. Half-listening isn't listening.
- *Be Nonjudgmental:* Listen without judging. Embrace comments open-mindedly.
- *Be Curious:* Ask questions and get inquisitive.

- *Be Focused:* Pay attention to when your mind drifts off and refocus. The mind can only do one thing at a time.
- *Be Compassionate:* Nod your head, have a "warm" face, and don't look away.
- *Be Grateful:* Be thankful for the speaker's gift to you.
- *Be Clear:* When confused, summarize, and ask if you're on the right track by clarifying and confirming what you heard.
- *Be Without Tech:* Remove environmental distractions, such as technology.
- *Do Not Problem Solve:* Unless asked to do so.

Listening is "the fix" if you don't like having problems to fix.

💬 Key Takeaways: Listen to Hear

- Apply Law 3: Pretending to listen isn't really listening.
- Listening is the fix.
- Intentional listening is the greatest gift you can give another human being.
- The #1 skill associated with effective interpersonal communication is listening.
- Listening creates change. You resist listening because you resist change.
- As an Instigator, you earn Empathizer respect when you listen well and don't interrupt.
- As an Empathizer, you earn Instigator trust when you don't beat around the bush.
- Listen to what's in your head instead of what's being said.
- Be aware of what's not being said and shift flexibly between I-E mindsets. It's a sign of Level 3 Listening.
- The main listening mistake Instigators make is not listening a minute longer.
- The main listening mistake Empathizers make is not speaking up.

- Problems can't get solved until hot emotions cool off.
- Conversational coercion works in the short run but not over the long haul.
- Listening does not mean condoning or agreeing.
- Respect and trust are demonstrated through the intentional act of listening.
- Listening does not occur until hot emotions cool off.
- Careful listening is indicated when you can paraphrase what's being said.
- Your concentration and attentive listening are compromised when you multitask.
- If you need to interrupt, ask for permission: *Can I interrupt you for a minute?*
- Listen a minute longer. Coach yourself to listen deeply and completely.
- You learn when you listen; you don't learn when you don't listen.

In a nutshell, active intentional listening solves many problems because people feel a sense of connection, belonging, and shared caring.

💬 Law 3: Sharpen Your *TALK2ME©* Skills

Activity 1- Practice Paraphrasing: Rather than offering advice, set your goal to simply listen to what people are saying to you. Reflect their words and see what reaction you get to your show of focused interest and empathy.

Activity 2- Listen a Minute Longer: As an Instigator, when you reach a point that you feel you have to interrupt, listen a minute longer. In that listening space, you will hear things that will blow your mind. Just listen. See what you hear that ordinarily, you wouldn't have learned because you cut off talks in mid-stream.

Activity 3- Don't Get Off Track When Interrupted: As an Empathizer, pause when you're interrupted mid-sentence but don't get off the main track of your point. Restate your point calmly but firmly. Don't give up making your point due to Conversational Coercion. Ask the interrupter: "Will you repeat what I just said?" See what reaction you get to your show of assertiveness.

Activity 4- Ask Curious Questions to Test Your Listening Skills: Make it your mission today to ask curious "what vs. why" questions to inquire about the inner views of another. "What was that like for you?" "What did you think about that?" "How did that make you feel?" "What surprised and delighted you?" "What would you have done differently?" See what reaction you get to your show of active interest.

Activity 5- Ask for Feedback: Ask your spouse or children how you could be a better listener to better hear what you might be missing. Jot down notes to show you're serious about changing. See what reaction you get when you show tolerance.

FOUR

YOUR MOOD DICTATES YOUR REPUTATION

"If you change the way you look at things, the things you look at change."

—Dr. Wayne Dyer

TALK2ME© Mood Rules

1. Your mood is your choice.	7. Healthy mood habits help you bounce back from stress.
2. You have the power to change a bad mood.	8. Empathizers take in the moods of others that don't belong to them.
3. Bad moods spread like a virus.	9. Instigators influence moods in others to get their way.
4. Better moods equal better outcomes.	10. Positive moods are installed by adopting Instigator and Empathizer strengths.
5. You are a mood maker or a mood breaker.	11. You can control your insides even when you can't control your outsides.
6. You have the final say on how long a bad mood lasts.	12. The moods you send out come back to you like a boomerang.

💬 Blindspots

Moods are invisible and can distort your reality. That's what makes them so difficult to understand and counteract. Just because you can't see something doesn't mean that it doesn't have a huge impact on you and your relationships. It's similar to driving and trying to change lanes when someone is in your blindspot. The problem is there, it's just outside your perceptual field.

Approaching 70 years of age, I (Dennis) had noticed for years that my eyesight was getting worse bit by bit. I made adjustments. I got better glasses. Although I adapted, driving at night became a real challenge. My mood became quite anxious. Signs and lights became magnified blurred images as if I were hallucinating. My depth perception was off. I had difficulty staying in the middle of a traffic lane. I missed turns. I couldn't read the dials very well on my dashboard when it was dark.

Prior to cataract surgery, my most anxious times were pitch-black nights with hard rain and heavy traffic. I felt like I was driving blind and couldn't clearly read signs to navigate turns on unfamiliar turf. I felt mad, inadequate, vulnerable, and old. "Getting old ain't for sissies," I would joke with clients. Although I struggled with getting old, I didn't fear dying. I feared being useless and alone.

One night in particular scared me straight. While driving in fog and heavy rain on narrow roads in the back country to reach the home of my fellow psychologists and board members for a holiday celebration, I was in a near-miss accident that would have been my fault because of compromised vision and blind spots. I finally made it to the event, but made darn sure going home that I followed another board member's car.

What does this aging-and-eyesight experience have to do with your mood and how it dictates your reputation?

- First, anxiety is a normal mood asking you to make a change to help you cope.
- Second, dark rainy moods restrict your self-confidence.

- Third, blind spots of perception will cause accidents in your relationships.
- Fourth, being too stubborn to get help doesn't help.
- Fifth, the attitude you take toward unwanted people, places, and things will dictate your mood reputation.

💬 What Is Your Mood Reputation?

Others evaluate how you handle difficult situations and moods. Your mood reputation is determined by how others view your ability to handle pressure in tough talks and tense situations. What is your mood reputation? Are you too easily set off or put off?

Let's be real. If you gave Riley and me permission to survey your loved ones, children, colleagues and friends, how would they honestly describe you? Give that a minute of your thought right now. How are you viewed when talks are tough, and times are hard, and your anxiety is high?

- Stubborn or open minded?
- Approachable or avoidant?
- Optimistic or pessimistic?
- Likeable or unlikeable?
- Effective or ineffective as a communicator?
- Complimentary or critical toward others?
- Short-fused or long-fused when frustrated?

Your mood matters. Don't leave it up to chance or say there's nothing you can do to feel or act differently. Bad moods are big fat excuses.

Everyone you touch is touched by your mood. Your mood infects the mood of every person you encounter. Expert communicators pay attention to their own moods and how others' moods impact their motivation, performance, and personal outcomes.

🗩 Front Desk Mood Setters

It was a warmer-than-usual Dayton January morning that I had scheduled for my cataract surgery. I had been stressed about it for weeks. But as is my style, I was pretty calm by the time I went into action. I was reluctant to ask Riley to be my chauffeur even though it would give us an opportunity to discuss what shape this chapter would take. But Riley, always ready to go and in a pretty good mood, volunteered to help out.

When we hit the front desk at 7 a.m. sharp, we met Jennifer, the surgery receptionist. She sat erect at the front desk, obviously in full command of this surgery center ship. Jennifer was in her late 50s, with a faint smell of tobacco, and greeted me with a broad welcoming smile and a little mischief in her eye.

The small waiting room was quiet, full of patients awaiting their turn to see better. I could feel the quiet tension and fear that older people feel when they face surgery's unknowns. Riley settled in for a two-hour wait.

"You must be Dennis," a blue-coated Jennifer said in a loud and friendly voice.

"You must be a mind reader," I joked. I looked into her Instigator eyes and saw them sparkle ready for a verbal dance or duel.

"I can tell you're glad to be here," Jennifer teased, appreciating the nervousness patients feel. "I just talked to the doctor and he's in a pretty good mood this morning."

"I'm glad he's not grumpy and that he's in a good mood," I shot back. "No one wants a grumpy doctor or surgeon cutting on their eyes."

We both laughed. We chatted for several minutes as I filled out the necessary paperwork. We talked back-and-forth about all sorts of things, including which pizza was the best slice in town. I could tell Riley was taking it all in, watching and listening intently. Since I can remember, she's been an excellent observer, almost spooky sometimes.

⌕ Be a Mood Leader

Let's examine this example regarding mood management dynamics. It shows how moods set the tone at work and home and spread quickly. Here's how:

- First, the frontline worker sets the mood tone for your entire business or family.
- Second, the front-line person is the organization to the customer.
- Third, the front-line professional sets the mood tone of warm or cold, personal or impersonal, caring or detached, careful listening or preoccupied.
- Fourth, the front-line representative sells the effectiveness of the service or product to customers.
- Fifth, customers will buy more and talk more about the company and make more referrals when the front-desk person is positive not negative.

Setting a reliable and upbeat mood tone is the key to success in a marriage or a company. The moods you send out come circling back to you and your company like a boomerang.

⌕ Law 4: Your Mood Dictates Your Reputation

Communication of your mood dictates your reputation, personal credibility, and likability.

Just like Jennifer, you have hundreds of people you deal with every day. During interactions, especially high-stress situations such as surgery, every person depends on you to reduce their fear and add cheer.

Do you dependably leave people in a better mood as a result of interacting with you? Or do you act standoffish, snap, or get self-involved and leave others feeling resentful? The choice is yours, including how well you treat yourself when you're in a crummy mood.

Moods are like weather patterns. A third of the time you won't feel so hot, a third of the time you will feel sort of neutral, and a third of the time you will feel happy to be alive. An attitude of gratitude helps put salve on moods that feel like wounds. You don't want your reputation to be the tornado or hurricane that tears people down as you blow through town.

Because you choose your mood, you can change your mood. To access your mood power, keep reminding yourself of the tangible links between your mood and your life.

- Bad moods spread like the flu.
- Empathizers take on the moods of others.
- Instigators transfer their moods to others.
- Angry moods poison relationships and create loss.
- Your mood is your choice. You can change your mood.
- Better moods equal better productivity, longevity, peace of mind, and happiness.
- In a traffic jam, you're in the driver's seat when it comes to your mood.
- Your mood dictates your professional reputation, personal likability, and credibility whether you're aware of it or not.

Always remember: Your mood is transferred in the form of positive or negative energy that rubs off on you and others. Your first job, therefore, is to be your own responsible and responsive mood manager and set the tone in your mental home. You have full control of what dread goes on inside your head. Communication of your mood dictates your reputation, personal credibility, and likability.

Moods travel along a pipeline between home and work and back again. People are happy who work daily on improving their mood attitudes. When you strive to be in a genuinely good mood, people will notice you and want to work with you.

In this chapter, we will be examining the distinctly different reactions E-Types vs. I-Types have when flooded with stress. We also will give you practical tools you can use to feel calm in the midst of a workplace crisis or home chaos. But first, let's summarize the teachings from our case study.

💬 The Doctor Is Out

As effective communication trainers, Riley and I always like to analyze the mood mojo of every family business, office culture, school classroom, team, and any company that we interact with. Kunesh Eye Surgery Center in Oakwood was no exception. Dr. Michael Kunesh held the reputation of being the best in the business, according to my personal physician, Dr. Stephen Robbe, who I trust deeply. So, I was eager as his patient to get an eyeful of his communication style.

His was a family business. When I first met "Dr. Michael," as his staff called him, he was efficient and all business without being brusque. He sounded pretty chipper when he greeted me, but he operated on a tight schedule. I tried to banter a bit during my evaluation session, and although he was polite, he stuck to business as he dictated the medical findings to his assistant. And then he was gone.

> **PRO Rule:** You will prosper by putting yourself and others in an upbeat mood.

As a fellow doctor who was fairly recognizable in our community, I could have elected to feel miffed or put off. But I decided not to be because I just figured he wanted to stay focused on the mission of restoring eyesight to all his patients. And I wanted him to be in a good mood when he set his laser to my eye. How do you feel when you put your mental or physical health in the hands of a stranger? That's when professional reputation and credibility really matter. Likability is nice but not always necessary.

The surgery on my right eye was successful. I could see again. Instead of 20-70 in my blurry right eye, I had returned to my normal 20-20 eyesight. Plus, colors were far more vivid and bright; I could see shadings again and depth was restored. And this from just the right eye. The left eye was still to come. I was jumping for joy and thanking higher powers and scientists and medical communities everywhere.

💬 Mood-Altering Feedback

On my next-day follow-up eye surgery visit, I decided to give Dr. Michael, who wasn't cold but still all business, some heartfelt mood-driven feedback. Why? Critical feedback is critical to your growth, and the growth of others with whom you interact. Feedback needs to be a fair balance of positives and negatives. One of the best ways to improve your mood when feeling upset is to improve the mood of others by using genuine positive feedback.

Although I still wasn't sure of Dr. Michael's type, and because he appeared to be an Instigator, I decided to find out. Because I know professionals can be one type at home and a different type at work, I decided to use our feedback approach. Empathizers like positive feedback, while Instigators are suspicious of it. So, I looked the good doctor in the eye and with an assertive voice tone, I said:

"Dr. Kunesh, I know you do hundreds and even thousands of these surgeries every year. And I'm sure all of your patients are very grateful for you and your expertise. I just wanted to make sure that you know that I am grateful for you. I am grateful for your restoring my eyesight. And I am very grateful that you've given me a second life."

The cool Dr. K. smiled a huge broad all-teeth smile, seemed genuinely happy with this feedback, and heartily slapped me on the back. "I appreciate you saying that," he said. "We try to please. The outcome of each patient is important to me." Then in a flash he exited the office and was gone.

Let's apply this situation to your reputation as you determine how you would like to be known at work and home in the future. Some things to know about your mood and reputation:

- Your reputation is your business and leads to losses or profits at home and work.

- Your reputation is independent of your degree, status, role, hierarchy, age, or other considerations.
- Your mood is monitored by all those you interact with, consciously or subconsciously, and it fashions your reputation.
- Your positive mood helps create positive results, while a negative mood can create negative results.
- Your mood rubs off on others and is how people remember you.
- Your mood is taken more personally by Empathizers, so take time to connect personally.
- Your mood is taken less personally by Instigators, so get right down to business.

There may be a disconnect between how positive or negative you view yourself, compared to how others view you. In an ideal world, you want to have 20/20 vision when it comes to how well you see others and how well others see you.

By flexibly using Empathizer eyeglasses or Instigator eyeglasses, you will clearly see hidden instructions to resolve a conflict.

Empathizer and Instigator Moods

Your mood is created right away as you start your day. The challenge:

- If you're an Empathizer, you will allow fearful moods to stick to you and weigh down your enthusiasm.
- If you're an Instigator, you will allow frustrated moods to control you and limit your happiness.

When times are stressful, your moody side might start to show. It's only human.

Empathizers and Instigators have different reactions when feeling vulnerable; a strength can turn into a weakness with the flip of a mood switch.

For example, Empathizers have soft hearts and are devout people pleasers. Under pressure, this trait can turn into self-criticism by taking everything people say too seriously. Instigators, on the other hand, are hard-driving passionate leaders who can be hypersensitive. This trait can turn into a combative or angry reaction when Instigators are under pressure.

Life is like a two-sided coin. One side is your strengths, the other side your corresponding weaknesses. You can turn around negative thinking. You can flip off negative thoughts. Not totally, but enough to change the mood music of your life.

- As a group, Empathizers will focus their mood on a few negative things and ignore positives, which can make an Empathizer *feel* everything is bad.
- As a group, Instigators will focus their mood on a few positive things and ignore negatives that can make an Instigator *think* everything is good.

Both extremes can be disastrous. Moods contaminate clear thinking and healthy decision making. They are the leading cause of the communication mistakes you make.

Empathizers and Instigators display their moods in different ways. Understanding your own mood triggers, and the triggers of your opposite type, can help you save face. Understanding these mood differences can also help you know when it's time to give someone else space or when it's time to diffuse a situation before it goes nuclear.

In the next few sections, we will discuss these mood riptides that exist in the Empathizer-Instigator worlds. Each type is vulnerable to trigger certain habitual moods and to be misperceived. Fighting against strong mood currents will wear you out and cause even the strongest swimmer to drown. Letting the energy of moods work for you instead of against you is life-saving.

Standard subconscious Empathizer-Instigator prejudices are distorted perceptions that cause blurred perspectives and cycles of conflict. The triggered conflict escalates unhelpful and hurtful critical feedback. Anger blocks needed seeds of change from taking root and growing. Then everyone blames everyone else for everything and nothing good is achieved.

⨀ Moody Empathizers

If you're an Empathizer, these are standard negative perceptions of you when you're moody:

- Sad
- Indecisive
- Weak
- Beats around bush
- Too sensitive about little things
- Rambles
- Offers no opinion
- Non-confrontational
- Blames everything else
- Has no backbone
- Passive-aggressive
- Cries too much
- Easy pushover
- Sneaky
- Scaredy cat

⨀ Moody Instigators

If you're an Instigator, these are standard negative perceptions of you when you're moody:

- Mad
- Bossy
- Bully

- Loud
- Mean
- Never wrong
- Narcissistic
- Argumentative
- Selfish
- Arrogant
- Quick to judge
- Cold
- Proud
- Overly competitive
- Condescending

⌬ Are You Sad or Mad?

Instigators traditionally default to anger when upset. Empathizers traditionally default to sadness when upset. Intense moods interfere with clear thinking and flexible problem-solving.

When Instigators and Empathizers collaborate as a team of "different but equal" partners, their combined energies help each other climb to new heights. This is accomplished when Instigators don't automatically default to a mad mood as their defense habit.

Likewise, Empathizers don't automatically default to a sad mood as their defense habit. Truth be told: Mad moods intimidate Empathizers, while sad moods intimate Instigators. When these two defensive habits clash, the result is fault-finding instead of solutions.

⌬ Sad Empathizers

Empathizers default to feeling depressed when they're emotionally depleted. In our workshops, Instigators like to know the answers to these questions about the softer feeling side of Empathizers:

- How do you want to be treated when your mood is off?
- How can you always sacrifice to please people?
- Why do you dwell on past hurts when you can't do anything about them?
- Why do you care what people think?
- Why do you seem to be laid back? Are you really?
- Why are you so slow to respond or defend your ideas in a debate?
- Why are you so slow in making decisions or saying what you want?
- Why do you perceive Instigators as offensive, aggressive bullies?
- How would you like me to approach you with criticism?
- Do you use silence to get your way when talking isn't working?
- What can I do to become a more attentive listener to you?
- How do you deal with conflict with your spouse and family members?
- Do you think you're weak?

These are all excellent questions that are intertwined in the mind and mood of Empathizers. If your significant other is an Empathizer, and if you're up for an insightful duologue as an Instigator, then consider asking your partner some of these questions.

Bottom line, sad bouts make Empathizers doubt themselves and resist needed personal changes. Empathizers excel by giving more positive feedback to themselves. Stop expecting your opponent to change. Start expecting yourself to take charge of your own assertive actions when your mood is compromised.

Going From Sad to Confident

If you are in a tough situation as an Empathizer, you can feel less sad and more confident by being like an Instigator:

- Not caring what others think about you.
- Focus on the positives; what's going well.

- Pat yourself on the back for a job well done.
- Let go of wanting to be liked by everyone.
- Stand up and speak up more.
- Be decisive and move on.
- Confront the situation instead of stuffing your feelings or self-blaming.

🗫 Mad Instigators

Instigators default to feeling mad when anxious. In our workshops, Empathizers would like to know the answers to these questions about the short anger fuse of Instigators:

- How do you want to be approached when you're in a bad mood?
- Why is it always your way or the highway?
- Does talking about your anger make you mad?
- Where does your burst of anger come from?
- Why do you have such a short fuse?
- When you blurt out hurtful words, do you regret them later on?
- Why are you so demanding?
- After you've gone off on someone, why do you act like nothing happened the next day?
- Do you consider your anger habit an addiction that you can't change?
- Do you use anger to get your way when nothing else is working?
- What impact do your anger outbursts have on your physical health?
- Do you fear how your anger might impact sensitive members of your family?
- Do you think you're tough?

These are all excellent questions that are intertwined in the mind and mood of Instigators. If your significant other is an Instigator, and if you're up for an insightful duologue as an Empathizer, then consider asking them some of these questions.

Bottom line, anger outbursts steal your joy and peace of mind right from under your nose. Balanced Instigators excel by listening to negative feedback so they can improve. Stop bulldozing. Start expecting yourself to take charge of how your moods affect your outcomes and the moods and motivation of those around you.

💬 Going from Angry to Calm

If you are in a tough situation as an Instigator, you can feel less angry and calmer by being like an Empathizer:

- Let go of needing to control or fix everything.
- Listen more and speak less.
- Be receptive; paraphrase negative feedback you don't want to hear.
- Step back and take a deep breath when you feel mad.
- Come across with more empathy in a conversation before confronting.
- Reveal "I feel vulnerable" before lashing out in frustration.
- Take accountability for the power of your words.

Every day we see the miracle of communication take place in our counseling offices.

💬 Meet in the Middle

It's normal for the people that we love to make us the gladdest and the maddest. An Air Force pilot who was an extreme alpha Instigator had in my (Dennis) estimation about a 5% chance, if that, of turning around his marriage. By learning how to talk calmly and effectively when he felt mad, he brought his marriage to an Empathizer wife back from the brink of divorce.

Here are the top tools that can help Alpha Instigators rekindle their love lives by defusing unhelpful anger episodes with Beta Empathizers:

- Start soft, not hard.
- Focus on the other's viewpoint...their feelings.
- Ask "Do you have any input?"
- Stop snapping...don't escalate.
- Everyone has to feel safe and comfortable.
- Take a step back...don't holler.
- Accept I can't change you. You have to change yourself.
- Sometimes you have to let it go. The juice isn't worth the squeeze.

What does meeting in the middle mean to you? To us, it means being a more balanced communicator. This is done by moving toward the middle of the communicator spectrum by approaching the color zone of your opposite type.

As my I-client liked to quip, "You have to bring the blue into the orange." This was his way to remind himself to meet in the middle of the E-I spectrum of Empathizer (blue) and Instigator (burnt orange) views. When you do this, you will unleash creative problem-solving energies with your partner.

Luckily, my client beat the odds stacked against himself and saved his marriage. His transformational personal growth journey had begun.

You can do the same. If you take anything from this book, remember that balancing E and I strengths and energies, and knowing who you are talking to and what that matters, are the master keys to your success. Oh, and one other small thing. Choose to grow continuously by being a flexible and open communicator who is willing to change old attitude habits and unhelpful moods.

While it can seem like Empathizers and Instigators are not meant for one another, the opposite is true. When both forces are brought together in relationships or in the workforce, extraordinary things can occur.

💬 Yin and Yang

Yin and Yang is a concept of dualism, describing how pairs of opposites often attract and need one another to experience life fully. Introvert and Extrovert are two of these universal pairs that highly impact you and all of your relationships.

My (Riley) best childhood friends were often Instigator Extroverts. In contrast, I am an Empathizer Introvert. According to our leadership studies, I am an "Intuiter" (Empathizer Introvert) leader who is able to radar in on solutions to fix vexing problems. In contrast, one of my gal pal friends, Amber, is an "Adventurer" (Instigator Extrovert) leader who can find back-up routes when roadblocks crop up. It created a yin and yang dynamic. In fact, people would comment on this invisible power that connected us. This synergy took us both to higher levels of performance.

Amber and I were complete opposites on the communication spectrum: Opposite communicator types of Empathizer vs. Instigator, and opposite personality types of Introvert vs. Extrovert. All of your relationships exist along these invisible dimensions, too. It just goes to show opposites can attract and don't have to clash.

During one week-long summer encampment for teens 12-21 at WPAFB (Wright Patterson Air Force Base), the Instigator Commander mentioned that Amber, my Instigator partner in crime, made an interesting observation. Normally, we were always together. Amber was "out there" and boisterous, which made me worry less about my performance. We were different, but our strengths intertwined, and people noticed.

After conducting a leadership training exercise, the Instigator Commander said, "It's strange not having you and Amber together. You were such a great team. It was like yin and yang. I've seen a lot of young people lead together but you two were something else."

I truly believe that Instigators and Empathizers are made for each other. They were designed to be a yin and yang that combines to create the fiercest friendships, strongest relationships, and unstoppable teams. What matters is that we don't allow mood prejudices to cloud our judgment.

When we stop judging our opposite type as the enemy, we can cultivate the strongest relationships that last for years that are mutually beneficial.

Empathizers and Instigators were designed to be liberating forces, not polar power struggles. Harnessing these energies will empower you to reach higher levels of personal and professional performance.

Before this can occur, though, it's important to identify a key trait difference in E's vs. I's in addition to the types of moods they have. Empathizers are what we call "mood catchers," while Instigators are "mood pitchers."

💬 Mood Pitchers and Mood Catchers

Your reputation as a positive or negative person depends on how you infuse moods in others, and how you productively deal with your own changing moods.

Instigators, in particular, know how to pitch moods around. That's why in the ballgame of life Instigators can fondly be called mood pitchers. Instigators also know how to make you feel guilty, scared, or intimidated with as little as a slight sideways glance.

> **PRO Rule:** Instigators are Mood Pitchers, while Empathizers are Mood Catchers.

If you're an Empathizer in the batter's box facing the steely-eyed focus of an Instigator pitcher, you had better be ready for a 98-mph fastball that can strike you out and make you feel like a loser. If you're an Empathizer who lives or works with an Instigator, you've no doubt experienced the impact of being in the charismatic Instigator mood zone.

In order to be the most skilled baseball player, you need to learn how to bat and catch. Mood Catcher Empathizers can't play ball well with two catcher's mitts on both hands. Likewise, Mood Pitcher Instigators need to do more than wield a big bat; they need a glove to play a well-balanced ballgame.

Competing in the game of life means becoming a balanced Mood Pitcher and Mood Catcher. Becoming a balanced communicator requires a balanced mood.

E-Mood Catchers: If you're an Empathizer, you don't have to catch every mood thrown at you, especially when it's BS.

> **PRO Rule:** Empathizers who don't absorb others' moods feel more confident.

Empathizer Self-Coaching Example: "It's not always about being nice. What others think of me is none of my business. Their mood and attitude is not my issue. It's not my circus, not my monkeys. I'll be direct so I won't be taken advantage of."

I-Mood Pitchers: If you're an Instigator, you can feel the relief of releasing a bad mood without setting it loose on those around you.

> **PRO Rule:** Instigators who set a positive mood tone at home feel calmer.

Instigator Self-Coaching Example: "It's not always about competition. Enjoying others is as important as getting things done. That starts with me keeping my word and being more open about my feelings."

Become a translator of mixed signals so you will be able to choose to pitch or catch depending on the situation at hand. Soon you will have all the tools at your disposal to play major league ball like a highly paid PRO. When you change your thinking, your outlook and mood will change.

At work, good vs. bad moods are a primary factor in employee retention, workplace satisfaction, relationship longevity, and overall quality of life. A Gallup Poll found employees are 62% less likely to be burned out at work when mood-boosting feedback is given on a regular basis.

Always keep in mind this sobering message: M-O-O-D spelled backward is DOOM. Most employee turnovers are due to bad manager moods. The same holds true for failed couples or family relationships. Moods form your destiny.

The truth is that moods spread like viruses, and worst of all, toxic people don't realize how highly contagious they are.

💬 Moods Spread like a Virus

"Bad moods spread like a virus," I (Riley) had explained to a group of fourth- and fifth-graders during an after school enrichment program to develop social-emotional learning. I learned the virus metaphor as a child. Eerily, the lesson became all too real three weeks later when the elementary school hosting this enrichment program closed during the COVID-19 pandemic.

During the winter of 2020, the second year of writing this book, COVID-19 emerged out of the blue. Soon, all Ohio schools and restaurants shut down, businesses sent their employees to work from home, or worse, laid them off, and the economy took a plunge. Toilet paper and hand sanitizer were in short supply, while fear and paranoia were in huge surplus.

No doubt moods are contagious. Numerous psychology, sociology, and business research studies back up the science behind viral moods. The social contagion theory, for example, predicts how humans can "infect" one another with their moods. Moods are transferred to you if you allow them to be. For example, you can pick up how others feel. If you listen to someone who is angry, you might start to feel a ping of anger yourself. If someone is laughing, you might have an uncontrollable urge to giggle. Lastly, you know from your practical experience that certain people and relationships conduit certain moods.

When someone feels "a certain way" it's contagious and spreads among the group or family. Continuing the virus mood metaphor, you could say we all come equipped with our own strain of mood virus. When we go about our daily lives, we pick up and pass moods around, our own or others' moods, loaded either positive or negative.

It can be argued that Instigators who are "mood pitchers" have a higher "immunity" against picking up moods, and they also host more contagious strains that can infect others. Alternatively, Empathizers who are "mood catchers" most likely have a lower "immunity" against picking up moods, and they also host less contagious mood strains.

Maybe though, it doesn't have to do with immunity at all, it has to do with our communication habits. Reflect on how people suddenly became far more conscientious of cleanliness and disinfection routines during the COVID-19 pandemic. People finally realized the importance of washing their hands and not touching their faces. They became aware and mindful of how their actions, such as wearing a face mask, equally impacted themselves and others.

One NBA player's news video went viral, pun intended, when he made fun of the virus by touching all the reporters' microphones; later that day he tested positive for COVID-19. Could this be analogous to Instigators who unknowingly spread their moods around? Instigators don't realize how contagious they are. Then when others get ill, well, it's sometimes too late. Empathizers say Instigators have the habit of not containing their moods and "coughing" all over those they care about. Instigators counter that they're just pushing hard for results and mean no harm.

Instigators, on the other hand, say Empathizers need to be more responsible and guard themselves against picking up the moods of others. This is the same as not washing your hands, touching your face, or practicing social distancing, especially from the ill. Of course, they come down with a bad mood! A weakness of Empathizers is that they will absorb and wear the bad moods of others that aren't their own.

In short, if you're an Empathizer, you need to guard yourself more closely from mood viruses. And if you're an Instigator, you need to gain awareness and stop casually spreading around ill moods. Could you imagine the change? Empathizers would become chronically ill less often from others' bad moods. Instigators would practice small healthy habits, such as smiling and complimenting, instead of scowling or complaining about being exhausted.

Moods are invisible but powerful, and they determine your relationship destiny. When stressed, what mood would people closest to you say you purvey? How does that mood reputation work for or against you?

How contagious are your moods? Do you honestly know how loved ones react to your moods? Do you try to shake off a bad mood on your way home from an exhausting day at work? Do people at work give you helpful accurate feedback about how your moods impact them? Do you demonstrate a good mood at work but a bad mood when you come home and let down? Do kids learn from their parents which moods are OK to pitch around? These are important life-changing questions.

When it comes to moods, "what goes around comes around." What you do to another is brought back on yourself. The aim of the remainder of this chapter is to discuss how you can protect yourself and others from viral moods.

⤺ The Manure Mood Ball

We purposely use a variety of visual emotional metaphors to make our mood management ideas stick. First up: you can change your mood and drop a bad mood at the door when you come home. We're not messing around with the concept of throwing manure moods around. It's a concept thousands of our trainees have benefited from.

When I (Dennis) worked in forensic psychology, I co-led group therapy with Dr. Jimmy Johnson, an African American psychologist. We became fast friends. Because I was white, and Jimmy was black, we were known as the "salt and pepper" team. No one quite knew what to make of us because we got along so well. Every week, 12 black inmates participated in our anger management program. Initially, you could cut the atmosphere of fear with a knife. Needless to say, these weren't men who were accustomed to talking about their feelings. Also, it was a bit intimidating for me, as a young psychologist, knowing that many of the inmates had been charged with violent crimes and had been determined not guilty by the courts by reason of insanity.

I learned from this deep experience that anger is often a defense or barrier to walls of hurt, fear, or grief. One time, an inmate was talking about getting revenge on another inmate for a disrespectful slight. "I'll make him pay and throw back at him three times what he did to me," the inmate bellowed threateningly. That's when Jimmy told us the story of the manure ball. The simple story is this: If you throw a ball of manure back at someone else, it just runs down your arm and gets your clothes all dirty and nobody wants to be around you because you stink to high heaven. It was a vivid visual reminder that revenge boomerangs, that instead of "getting even," you actually fall behind. After a lengthy discussion, the inmate cried as he described the hurt he had felt as a child who was abandoned by his father. The current event had triggered those past memories.

Riley and I have adopted this mood management concept in our corporate training classes. We call it The Manure Ball Exercise. It's an effective way to visually demonstrate how fast bad moods spread around and how reactionary we all are to our own and others' bad moods. We don't think, we just react with prejudice without pausing, and throw the mood ball. In a class, we use a hacky sack. There's a twist. We ask the participants to imagine it's a squishy ball of manure that stinks to high heaven. This usually gets everyone's attention.

The instructions are simple. "Imagine this is a ball of manure. I will throw it to one of you. Then I will stop the action and ask you how you feel and what you want to do with it. Ready to play ball?" We then throw the hacky sack to one of the group members, who inevitably catches the ball with a cool attitude. Stop action is called and the tantalizing question is popped, "What would you like to do with the ball of manure now?" Invariably, the person wants to immediately throw it to someone else without stepping back and thinking about it.

⤺ Catching and Throwing Bad Moods Around

Hundreds of workshops show a pattern with people. The biggest pattern: The manure ball is always caught, never dropped, and always thrown to someone else. Do you catch bad moods and pass them on?

This interactive exercise creates "aha moments" that we hope will be useful for your daily mood management efforts:

- Mood pitchers squish the ball passionately between their hands. Do you make bad moods worse by focusing your thoughts on them?
- Mood pitchers take a second to decide who next to throw it to. Do you realize how your mood impacts others at home?
- Mood catchers typically feel resentful for being dumped on. Do you view bad moods thrown at you as impersonal due to venting or dumping?
- Mood catchers smile and laugh nervously, pretending hurt isn't happening. Do you realize the amount of stink attached to your mean words, grumpy faces, failed promises, and tendency to ignore loved ones?
- Mood pitchers will pick up the manure ball if they drop it. Do you go out of your way to make yourself upset, mad, or down?
- Mood catchers rarely drop the ball, or duck and let it go sailing past them. Do you feel free to drop the manure ball?

When I was a kid, we had rock wars. Rocks are another good metaphor for resentments. Stoning someone doesn't improve your relationships. People will want to avoid you when they can. Drop that rock. Instead, use rocks to build a solid foundation for a new home filled with love and hope.

Bottom line: What is your mood reputation when you're hit with shit?

You encounter many bad moods every day. But for a lack of a better term, negative moods can feel really shitty. Resentment toward others for what they are or aren't doing right according to your expectations will rob you of joy.

⤬ Pause and Think Before You Spread a Bad Mood Around

Think before you speak! This has inevitably been drilled into your head by parents, teachers, and probably anyone who became a victim or witness to one of your mood manure balls.

Ironically though, you don't think when you feel the intensity of a bad mood. It's a well-known fact that the neural circuits responsible for conscious self-control are highly vulnerable to stress. Primal impulses go unchecked and mental paralysis sets in when executive functioning takes a back seat, strapping in for the rollercoaster ride controlled by the emotional centers of your brain. Put simply, you're more like a thoughtless reptile when you are upset than the thoughtful lifeform you like to think of yourself to be. You bite before you think.

So, what can your thoughtless reptile brain do? The answer is not, "I didn't intend to do it so I'm off the hook." Or, "Well, I guess it's not my fault because it's out of my control." Not so fast! Take responsibility. Instead of exploding blindly, step back and pause until you become the calm thoughtful human you are. Then, respond.

This especially goes for emails, texts, and posts that you will regret later on. It's just all too easy to press "send" without thinking. What to do when you're in a frustrated mood, feeling reactionary, and ready to fire off a text?

- Pause! Take a step back before you react with prejudice.
- Take a deep breath. Take another breath. Accuracy matters here.
- Decide if you're allowing yourself to feel frustrated by an Empathizer or Instigator.
- Don't make things up. Accept the flaws and strengths of the offending type.
- Review how your opposite type listens and prefers feedback.
- Take more deep breaths.
- Imagine reading the text out loud to the receiver's face. Still like the message's tone?
- Don't give feedback when you're frustrated.
- Write your response in a draft but do not send it. Sleep on it for 24-hours, if possible. THEN decide whether to send.
- Say exactly what you mean without being mean.
- Whether you send the message or not, get your happy mood back.
- Keep being ever mindful of the moods you send and receive.

Now you know your mood is under your control. You also understand the mood patterns of your opposite partner. And now we are going to focus on what to do when you're angry or depressed.

🗫 Case Study: Angry Mood Habits

The Greek god Achilles was invincible to attack except for a small spot on the heel of his foot. If an enemy shot an arrow piercing that spot, Achilles was toast. Whether an Instigator man or an Instigator woman, anger is the Achilles heel that hides grief for most tough-charging I-Types.

Instigators are known for their anger attacks and short fuses. Instigators default to mad whenever they feel vulnerable. Anger often covers up sad or fearful feelings with a show of bravado. They have "out of mouth" experiences and say things they later regret.

Instigators know how to win arguments and influence minds, but they can lose friends. Empathizers aren't perfect. They will feel mad but will hide feelings until the anger builds up inside. Then they explode like a volcano, spewing hot lava and shocking their Instigator partners.

Moods don't have to determine what you say and do. You can be responsible for and grow up about moods. Like combining paint colors, your moods are a blend of emotional and attitude states. Moods and how to handle them are first learned in the family culture. Moods become everyday habits that you default to when stressed, distressed or facing conflict. You modeled moods after your parents during childhood.

For many years, I (Dennis) would be in a grumpy mood at the start of my day. I also would become angry at any driver who drove slow in the passing lane on the highway or violated my space by nudging too close to my back fender in crowded traffic. I remember a time when my quiet father, an ordinarily excellent driver, would slam on his brakes to scare the driver behind him for pushing too close.

"Grandpa O'Grady" was an Instigator. He believed when you were in the right it was only right to say so. Being right requires you to make your point forcefully and stick to it. When my Instigator mother was in the car, she would shush my dad for swearing. Like me, you have absorbed attitudes and moods about what is kosher in any given situation from your parents. You can break a habit chain. It took me a while, but now I drive very calmly; I consider my vehicle to be a meditation chamber. I don't believe Riley has seen me react in "road rage" all these years. And all three of my daughters are excellent and careful drivers.

Angry moods cause heart attacks and shorten lives. Anger kills. "Road rage" is a misnomer for mad moods chosen by you while driving instead of choosing joy. Anger while driving can be changed in three practice sessions using our tools. Get help before you blow a blood vessel, have a heart attack, or cause an accident that puts others at risk. Is it really worth it to blow a gasket about something you cannot control?

Always remember: You have the most control of your mood and least control over what other people think, say, or do in relation to their moods.

Defusing anger begins with calming down. When you feel calm, your mind is open to intuitive solutions, and other people will feel safe around you. By spreading around a contented mood, new opportunities will be presented to you. As a daily practice, pause and focus on your breath going in and out when your mind is spinning to feel calmer.

A good balance of being aware of your mood and passively experiencing feelings allows calmness to flow through you. The urge to explode in rage can dissipate like a falling tide.

Letting Go of Mad Moods

Here are some emotionally responsible mental steps you can take to choose a new mood on a bad day:

1. Take ownership of the mood.
2. Go into the mood. Be aware of how it distorts your thinking and impacts your body.

3. Accept the fact that you can change your mood. You are in charge of your mood.
4. Allow the mood to be there without giving it attention, acting on it, or spreading it. When you stop fueling it, your mood will dissipate.
5. Increase the positive things you are thinking and saying.
6. Predict and prepare yourself for upcoming mood landmines.
7. Enjoy your new mood.
8. Rinse and repeat as needed.

The fundamental thing to remember when life feels out of control is that you *can* change the mood channel if you don't like what's playing.

Getting Feedback About Your Mood Reputation

Pick a truth-or-dare friend and ask them for feedback about your mood reputation. These questions are designed to tap how your moods are viewed by others and what you can do to improve.

1. If I were an animal, how would you describe my everyday mood?
2. What is one word you would use to describe my bad moods?
3. How do I behave when I'm in a good mood?
4. Which moods of mine make you feel unsafe or uncomfortable?
5. How do you see me putting energy into helping other people be in an upbeat mood?
6. When I'm super-stressed, do I come across as mad, sad, or unapproachable to you?
7. Do you view me as an optimist, pessimist, or a realist when times are tough?
8. What mood would you like to see me in more often? Less often? Why?
9. In your experience, do I give you good feedback free of anger?

10. Overall, do I appear to be in control of my mood and set a positive mood tone at home?

Challenge yourself to be mood savvy and use the power of your mood to make good things happen that last.

🗩 Case Study: Depressed Mood Habits

Empathizers default to a sad mood when stressed. They feel down and blue. Empathizers are more likely to experience intense sadness instead of anger. They then become self-critical, more prone to drowning in a sewer of self-pity.

As a mood habit, Empathizers magnify negatives and minimize positives. In reverse, Instigators magnify positives and minimize negatives.

An example of depressed mood habits comes from a 33-year-old Empathizer client named Shane. He was in treatment with me (Dennis) for severe depression that he labeled as an addiction. Shane would depress himself by focusing on these six mood attitudes, described to me in woeful detail:

1-Defeated: "I can't stick to anything. I'm a failure. What's wrong with me?"

2-Resigned: "Nothing works out for me. Why should I even try?"

3-Joyless: "It's such a drag getting up in the morning. My escape is sleep."

4-Resentful: "I don't make enough money. My partner nags me about what I spend."

5-Fearful: "I'm afraid of what I might do. What if I can't get out of this dark place?"

6-Scattered: "I don't feel centered. I jump around from one thing to another and don't finish anything."

One of the most common self-shredding questions in therapy I receive is, "What's wrong with me, Dr. O'Grady?" Nothing's usually wrong with the person at their core. It's just a bad-mood wave crashing on the beach of life. It's a shame that we are told to feel shameful about having intense moods.

In truth, there aren't good or bad moods; moods are just energy. For example, anxiety is the flip side of excitement. What matters is how you frame or view the mood. Change your view and you change your mood.

Empathizers are especially hard on themselves for experiencing moods. Moods are a healthy and normal part of the human experience. What will harm you is when you choose to ignore or dramatize your moods. Instead of fighting against a mood, change your mood by naming it, claiming it, and allowing it to "just be." This starts by being aware of how your thoughts shape your moods.

💬 Your Thoughts Create Your Moods

Change your thoughts and you change your mood. Allow your negative thoughts to move across the stage of your mind without putting on a big dramatic show.

Shane didn't believe he could change his thoughts. They were so familiar. Even negative thoughts are a weird sort of comfort zone. Shane egged me on:

"But how do you change your thoughts to change your mood?" Shane asked.

I replied, "Do you really want to change your mood? It's a pretty big change. Bad moods are pretty addictive, and kicking them is pretty tough, like quitting alcohol or cigarettes. Be honest with yourself. Are you really ready to change? Are you willing to go into the unknown of fully enjoying your life?"

Cynicism is at the core of bad moods. Shane listened half-heartedly, and shot back, "Yeah, I want to change. But isn't that a lot like trying to *will* yourself to grow taller? It won't work. It's dumb. Why should I even try? I tried writing in my gratitude journal but that only lasted a week."

I kindly replied, "Shane, a pessimistic or optimistic mood is up to you. But your mood, whether mad or sad or somewhere in-between, needs to serve you. Can you imagine how your life would take off if you were in an average or pleasant mood 50 percent of the time?"

That did it. Shane responded, "I'm sick and tired of being sick and tired. Really good things are happening in my life, but I act like someone died. What do I have to do to break out of this bad mood cycle that is addictive?"

"Change your mind," I replied.

You are not the servant of your mood. Your mood serves you. And try not to psych yourself out about your change potential. You can teach old dogs new tricks when the master is patient. Rightly claim you are the master of your mind and mood right now.

Accept the mood that you are feeling and the thoughts you might have. They aren't bad. Giving them weight and viewing them negatively is what makes them "bad." Allow negative thoughts to flow through instead of damning them up. Then, be mindful of what you are thinking and start consciously generating more positive thoughts. It might feel a bit forced at first, but what starts as a conscious exercise will eventually become an unconscious way of living. Just like the mental habit of being in a bad mood, you can develop a new mental habit of a positive mood.

🗩 What You Focus on Expands

What you focus on expands. Positive begets positive, and negative begets negative.

Because Empathizer Shane was focusing on negatives, his negative thinking expanded, and so did his self-depressing mood. I'm not blaming Shane. As an Empathizer, Shane naturally put all blame on himself. Although he was very, very successful in his personal and professional life, he couldn't experience being pleased with himself because he didn't equally own his own strengths. Focusing on what you don't have depresses your mood and motivation. That's why we say Empathizers are humble to a fault.

In fact, Empathizers chronically question themselves and upsize or magnify the negatives while downsizing the positives. That's why Empathizers need regular and ongoing doses of positive feedback. It's their brain vitamin.

Shane was addicted to drinking the poison of a bad mood. I needed to help him flip off the negatives if he wanted to, to be more balanced. Shane needed to fight back and get back up when negativity knocked him down. It's a huge change, but one most of my clients are willing to make.

⤫ Flip over Your Mood Coin

How can you shake off a bad mood? By flipping around your Mood Coin. Let us explain.

On paper, I asked Shane to write down what he perceived to be his six major weaknesses and come up with a corresponding list of his six major strengths. This goal was to upstage each weakness with a corresponding reality strength.

To entertain a more balanced view of life all you need do is flip your Mood Coin over and take a closer look at the strengths etched there. What does this mean? How can you inspect your Mood Coin to become a more balanced communicator?

- *If you're an Empathizer, you need to look at the positive side of your Mood Coin more closely and own it.*
- *If you're an Instigator, you need to look at the negative side of your Mood Coin more closely and own it.*

For now, we're focusing on the Empathizer style for now. Activating your own strengths and adopting the "dormant" strengths you admire about your opposite communicator type will help change your negative mood to neutral or positive. Balancing your mood helps you control what you can and let go of, who and what you can't control.

💬 Empathizers Who Think like Instigators

Shane wanted to feel better and entertain a more balanced view of his life. In essence, I taught Shane how to think like an Instigator when he was putting himself down.

- Empathizers who become more decisive promote good moods.
- Instigators who become more empathetic promote good moods.

Shane wrote the matching strengths on the opposite side of his mood coin. Together we flipped around the negatives to highlight the opposite matching positive traits. These six strengths would "be" what he would embrace when stress hit. Examples are:

1-Resilient is the flip side of the Defeated Coin. "I would like to be more resilient."

2-Hopeful is the flip side of the Resigned Coin. "I would like to be more hopeful."

3-Joyful is the flip side of the Joyless Coin. "I would like to be more joyful."

4-Grateful is the flip side of the Resentful Coin. "I would like to be more grateful."

5-Confident is the flip side of the Fearful Coin. "I would like to be more confident."

6-Focused is the flip side of the Scattered Coin. "I would like to be more focused."

I explained to Shane how his mind was dumping negatives into his brain like a bad habit to please him. He had to redirect his thinking in believable ways.

Shane then shared how he grew up watching and listening to his father, a diehard pessimist. Familiarity is comforting. We often do what we saw done by our parent figures. That being said, you can let go of old ways of doing things that no longer suit you, just like tossing out an old pair of jeans that no longer fit your current style. Name your new mood to change your old mood.

💬 You Are in Charge of Your Mood

You can impact your mood proactively to stay in a good mood throughout the day. If you view your inside mood as being manipulated or impacted by outside events or players, you will feel resentful and mistrustful. You have the power to change your mood at will.

If you continually find yourself in a bad mood, try this easy tip. Start your day with a phone reminder, such as: "I am in charge of my mood." Or, "My attitude today is up to me to choose." Or, "Everything's OK even though I don't know it right now." Record and use the good mood reminders that come your way.

Moods spread out from you as energy waves like ripples in a pond. You don't have to believe it to see it. Put it in your phone right now, read it aloud each day as it appears on your screen, and your positive experience will be all the scientific proof you will need to keep pumping up your mood with positives.

Negative thinking is like drinking poison. What you think and speak internally affects your relationships, results, and overall health and wellbeing.

Being pessimistic to protect yourself from hurt won't work in close relationships. Be mindful of your mood. Choose your mood carefully. As anger or bad moods go down, your joy of life will go up. When times are tumultuous, an attitude of gratitude will save the day. Being grateful brings you more to be grateful for.

Small things net big results. In our case, we share a daily positive affirmation calendar by Louise Hay or Dr. Wayne Dyer. Each day when we awake in different locations, we still share a simple positive message about possibilities that impact our combined moods. To some, daily affirmations might seem corny, but by doing something small daily to center your mood is an easy technique that can make a difference. This could take the form of short meditations, working out, yoga, watching a motivational video, or whatever you find easy and effective.

By claiming your mood, you can preemptively pump up your mood with positive thinking.

Cynical moods can make a "mountain out of a molehill." Next time you are in a situation where you feel unconfident or off, spend time pumping yourself up. This balances negativity, especially negativity outside your control, so you can courageously conquer the challenges of today.

We aren't suggesting that you blindly tell yourself that your marriage is great when it's on the brink of divorce or that you love your job when you hate it. You might be able to fool others, but you can't lie to yourself. The takeaway is not to fake positivity.

If you are on social media, you have likely noticed that many people will selectively post the highlights of their lives. Everything seems great on social media. They might use hashtags like #blessed...more like #barf. Everyone finds fake positivity to be obnoxious.

You don't have to sugarcoat or ignore the negative things going on in your life. Instead, acknowledge the reality of the uncomfortable, frustrating, or dissatisfying aspects of yourself and control what's within your control, and let go of what's not.

Here are a few things that you can do to calm yourself when you are feeling off:

- Monitor self-shaming words you say to yourself.
- Track compulsive complaining.
- Say negative thoughts out loud to hear how stupid put-downs sound.
- Talk with a friend who will listen to you without babying you.
- Have a safe peaceful place in your home to get centered and go there.
- Let yourself pout and spout off but put a limit on your "poor me" pity-party time.

- Be strict about what media messages you allow to come into your head.
- Get serious. Spend 15 minutes in the morning listening and reading hopeful messages.
- Be kind to yourself. "It's all going to turn out OK. I've got this. I've been through this before and survived."
- Feed your head a steady diet of positives before you get sick.

Showing yourself empathy requires a "dare to care" attitude.

💬 Choose a New Mood

You can change your mood with good old-fashioned elbow grease. Think of your mood as a bicycle wheel or chain that's grown a bit rusty from lack of use. It will take a larger effort to get rolling at first, and you will feel like you're struggling uphill, but soon you will be cruising along with less effort.

Practice "day at a time" mood management tools. Pick a mood attitude from this list to try on for size today. Say the strength out loud when you harshly judge yourself or others:

- "I am choosing today to be the mood of HONESTY."
- "I am choosing today to be the mood of HOPE."
- "I am choosing today to be the mood of COURAGE."
- "I am choosing today to be the mood of INTEGRITY."
- "I am choosing today to be the mood of WILLINGNESS."
- "I am choosing today to be the mood of HUMILITY."
- "I am choosing today to be the mood of LOVE."
- "I am choosing today to be the mood of FORGIVENESS."
- "I am choosing today to be the mood of PERSEVERANCE."
- "I am choosing today to be the mood of GIVING."
- "I am choosing today to be the mood of GRATITUDE."

Mood tools are everywhere to use. This is only one tool. By activating your combined Instigator-Empathizer mind, you will attract other tools to you that will fit your unique circumstances.

Changing a bad mood habit is slow going at first. Although it will feel like you're walking in wet concrete that's up to your knees, you will pick up momentum as you keep on going to get on solid pavement. Warning: Your negative mind will focus on how slow things are going in your first efforts to beguile you to give up and quit. Don't quit, be patient, and keep moving forward.

Yes, it's the first step but a big one to get honest about how you are the maker of your own moods.

⌕ How Not to Let Mean Words Get to You

"Mean words can cut like a knife," I (Riley) explained to the same group of fourth- and fifth-grade students mentioned earlier. This came after an incident where one student whispered something mean to another student. I'd already spoken to both students privately, but this was also a great opportunity to reinforce our group lessons on viral mood.

With tears in his eyes, the student who was hurt asked, "How can I not let mean things hurt me when I already feel hurt?" This led to a thoughtful group discussion on techniques to overcome the negative things others say to us. We talked about how moods are like viruses. One student chimed in saying, "Be a virus protector, not a virus spreader."

When words do cut and hurt you, what can you do?

⌕ Minimizing Bad Moods: Talking Kindly to Yourself

Use these tools to treat and prevent the scrapes or cuts caused by mean words. How do you stop repeating mean words said to you that ruin your mood?

Ways to show empathy to yourself when you're hurting to counteract negativity:

- This is a good opportunity to practice my mood management tools.
- Opinions are like assholes. Everyone's got one.
- Even though I feel vulnerable and kicked down, I'm still worthwhile.
- Because my feelings can lie, I'm going to take a step back and think before reacting.
- I'll prove I can change my mood with some elbow grease and practice.
- Hurtful words don't hurt me unless I agree with them. Was their intention to help or hurt?
- I can't control what people say, but I can control how much I let it bother me.
- No one can use harsh words against me as effectively as I can. I choose to let hurt go.
- Is it true of me? If it's not true of me, I need to stop upsetting myself about this.
- Because words have power, I will magnify the positives I see in others without minimizing the negatives.
- My mood and calm confidence is my choice.

Brainstorm a list of your own favorite self-acceptance sayings when you are hurting and your energy is sinking. Begin the habit of making the subject of moods part of your everyday self-analysis.

Why Can't People Be More like Dogs?

As we close this chapter, we'd like to praise our furry friends.

When Riley was 7, she was terribly fond of her Doberman pinscher pal, Sydney. Riley and her sisters, Erin and Kasey, learned to walk with Sydney's help and would dress her up all frilly while pulling on her pointy ears. They tried to ride her like a horse, but Sydney would gently sit down and a little O'Grady girl would slide off. Sydney watched over my children like a guardian angel. It was a mutual love affair.

One day Riley asked me, "Dad, why can't people be more like dogs? Dogs are friendly and always glad to see you." Isn't that a great question?

Here are the questions to answer honestly to rate if you're as loving as your canine friends:

- Dogs don't care what you look like. (Are you non-judging?)
- Dogs are always there for you. (Are you emotionally available?)
- Dogs are glad to see you, whatever mood you're in. (Are you approachable?)
- Dogs will wait for you. (Are you patient?)
- Dogs don't watch TV when you're trying to talk with them. (Are you an attentive listener?)
- Dogs are cuddly. (Are you warm and affectionate?)
- Dogs make you happy when you're sad. (Are you a mood-uplifter?)
- Dogs go with the flow. (Are you flexible when things don't go your way?)
- Dogs are only mean when threatened. (Are you a mood manager?)

That's why people should be more like dogs. The world's best anti-depressant has a cold nose, four legs, a wagging tail, and all the time in the world just for you.

In your view, is this a dog-eat-dog world or a human-help-human world? It all depends on your 20/20 view of moods, and what you know to do to change your mood. Are you as loyal, forgiving, and unconditionally loving as your dog? For example, do you always come out to greet others in a good mood? Or do you bark orders when you get home and leave your partner alone in a cage for long periods of time?

Your mood is a choice you make every second of every day. Fred Rogers, a famous children's TV icon known for spreading a message of kindness, put it well, "There's no 'should' or 'should not' when it comes to having feelings. They're part of who we are and their origins are beyond our control. When we can believe that, we may find it easier to make constructive choices about what to do with those feelings."

One time Mr. Rogers was asked how he could be in such a good mood all of the time. He replied honestly that he wasn't always in a good mood. Although he had moods like everyone else, Mr. Rogers made a conscientious decision not to take his bad moods out on others. His wife added that he would swim every morning which was a great form of stress relief. What's great about this famous example is that he knew the secret: *Because we are in control of our moods, we have the ability to change them.*

As we close this chapter, let's all remind ourselves to be more like our cold-nosed friends, change our mood habits that aren't serving our highest interests, and adopt the feedback strengths of our opposite type.

What mood will you choose to fuel your future success and happiness? You will reliably boost your mood when you mirror the views and respect the customs of the Instigator or Empathizer person you're talking to. The good news is that you can become a master of your moods over time with practice.

💬 A Call to Action: Mood Training Tips

In summary, it's up to you to commit to being responsible for your moods and demonstrating a mood that you can be proud of. Mood tips and tricks to remember when the going gets tough in your relationship life that will help you:

- "I am in charge of my mood."
- If you don't know your mood reputation, just ask someone who's close to you and they will surely let you know.
- When Empathizers are moody, they will be self-critical and unsure of themselves.
- When Instigators are moody, they will be critical of others and too certain that they're right.

- If you're an Instigator, you don't have to routinely default to a mad mood during anxious times to feel in control.
- If you're an Empathizer, you don't have to routinely default to a sad mood during anxious times to feel in control.
- Feedback-wise: Empathizers don't hear compliments when in a sad mood.
- Feedback-wise: Instigators don't hear complaints when in a mad mood.
- You will have a standard "favorite" mood that is your home base or comfort zone during hard times. It fashions your reputation. You can adopt a new better-fitting mood.
- Fiery moods in relationships are a minefield that spells doom.
- Managing your mood will set you up for success in every area of your life.
- Your willingness to promote a good mood at the start of your day will impact your entire day.

Commit to using mood management tools every day. That way, when you're in a tight spot or when your back is up against a wall your response will be calmer.

PRO Rule: What you say and do in a high-pressure situation forms your reputation.

Life still won't be perfect, but you will be more in control of your feelings and reactions than ever before.

You will be a responsive, positive, and accurate communicator who gives and receives critical feedback well without getting tripped up by a bad mood.

💬 Key Takeaways: Better Communication= Better Moods=Better Outcomes

- Apply Law 4: Your mood dictates your reputation.
- You will prosper by putting yourself and others in an upbeat mood.
- Moods are contagious and spread like a virus.
- Bad moods boomerang back to hurt you.
- Your negative or positive thoughts create your moods.
- Empathizers default to a sad mood, while Instigators default to a mad mood.
- Empathizers and Instigators were meant to be liberating, not polarizing forces.
- Instigators are Mood Pitchers, while Empathizers are Mood Catchers.
- Empathizers who don't absorb others' moods feel more confident.
- Instigators who set a positive mood tone at home feel calmer.
- Dodge the mood manure ball when it's thrown at you.
- Your mood isn't chosen for you. You choose your own mood.
- Unresolved conflicts, internal or external, wreck moods. Flip over your Mood Coin.
- Trying too hard to fight off a bad mood will make a bad mood worse.
- Trying too hard to hang onto a good mood will make it vanish.
- Acting like you're in a good mood eventually puts you in a good mood.
- By being in a genuinely good mood, people will notice you and want to work with you.
- One of the best ways to improve your mood is to improve the mood of others.
- What you say and do in a high-pressure situation forms your reputation.

Positive moods make you live longer and laugh harder. For the contrarians among us: Shitty Communication = Shitty Moods = Shitty

Outcomes. Let's laugh instead of weep. Your opposite is not necessarily your opponent.

As a PRO parent, sibling, partner, boss, or co-worker, you will want to be known as a likable person who spreads positive moods around during trying times and tense talks.

💬 Law 4: Sharpen Your *TALK2ME©* Skills

Activity 1- Viral Moods: Fearful moods spread faster than a virus. When times are crazy, and fear is getting the upper hand over facts, what can you do to keep the faith? Friends over fear! By staying in touch with your positive relationships, you reduce fear.

Empathy puts a healing salve on fears. The message: "I hear you. I see you. I am with you." To fight off the toll isolation takes, answer these questions:

- Who can you talk to?
- Who do you need to get together with?
- How do you find support? Where and with whom?
- What can you still enjoy although your favorite places are closed?
- What new ways can you invest your personal growth time? With whom?
- How can you still maintain your social bonds?
- How can you limit toxic information that triggers you?
- What alternative ways can you gather facts from more than one source to fight fear?
- How can you talk more deeply with your life partner?
- How can you joke more to keep a sense of humor and know "This too shall pass...?"

Be in charge of your mood. Reach out to your mentors and friends. Don't let fear make you sick. It's up to you to keep a cool head when anxious moods are rising.

Activity 2- Partner Moods: This activity is for an Instigator partner to talk with their sensitive partner. During a quiet time, share with your partner your goal to create a positive mood tone in the home.

Then ask your Empathizer partner this simple question: "What can I do in our relationship this week that will impact your mood in positive ways?" Then listen to the answers. If you must say something, simply add, "That's a valid point."

Here is a checklist that can help keep the train of the conversation on track:

- Use soft eyes. Don't interrupt. Summarize and clarify the concern of your partner in a caring mood tone.
- Quietly ask your partner if they have a fix or solution to the concern. Tell them you're willing to do the new thing even if it doesn't make sense to you.
- Give your Empathizer's concern the same weight you would give your own Instigator opinion.
- Don't immediately refute the solution offered. Do not say, "Yes, but what about you..." Or, "I can't because there's no time to...." And, "That's just not true..." or other change resisting excuses. E-Types hear this as they're not important or worthy.
- STOP arguing and debating why your Empathizer partner should just get past the past and shouldn't be hurt or feeling what they do. They just do!
- Thank your partner for sharing a complaint and not shutting up or shutting down for fear of your reaction.
- Don't feel bossed around, resentful or pressured. You have the power to change but no one can make you.

As an Instigator, you have the power to change the mood thermostat in your home. Start by being in a good mood yourself as an Instigator when you come home. Listen to E-suggestions with an open mind, and refuse to get defensive or feel like a failure if there's a problem you haven't yet resolved. Uplifting your relationship is possible.

Activity 3- Mood Badges: Mood mastery is a defining hallmark of the mature person. By naming and claiming your mood, you will move from a negative mood to a more neutral mood and then on to a positive mood. Color your mood. This will prove to you that you can change the mood state you're in by following a few simple steps.

Use one week for this daily Mood Identification practice. Imagine you and everyone else wearing a cell phone-sized badge on their shirt or blouse. The badge shows the color of the wearer's mood and changes colors as their mood changes. Orange for agitation and purple for happiness, as examples. This device would give a mood sender immediate feedback about how their words were impacting your mood.

Being conscious of mood states without shaming or blaming shifts moods to a higher level. By naming and claiming your mood instead of fighting it, your bad moods will last half as long. Here are colors and moods for you to use in your Mood Mastery steps.

Name your color to improve your mood:

- Elated (Yellow)
- Happy (Purple)
- Pleasant feeling (Green)
- Neutral (White)
- Unpleasant feeling (Red)
- Agitated, hyperactive (Orange)
- Worried; depressed (Black)

Fear magnetizes negativity and makes it stick to your self-esteem like a leech. Both Empathizers and Instigators alike feel quite powerless when powerful mood shifts create verbal conflict and relationship resentment.

Oh, the calmer places we would all go if we knew one another's moods before trying to talk together.

Activity 4- Planting Mood Seeds: After accepting that you're in a bad mood, what can you do to change mood channels besides blaming someone or something else for your troubles and woes? Say out loud, "I can choose a new mood attitude." Come on! Who's in charge of your mind and mood if not you?

Your moods are combined with thought-feeling memories. Like rooms in the mansion of your mind, they can be renovated and changed. Print out a list of these new mood attitudes, or create your own, to remind yourself that your mood is not your master:

- I can change my mood.
- I won't spread my mood around like the flu.
- I can act like I'm in a good mood instead of grumping around and scowling.
- I will let go of who and what I can't control.
- I won't let fear push me around into making bad, cowardly decisions.
- I will stay the right course and be true to myself.
- I am going to be my own best friend instead of my own worst enemy.
- I will take this opportunity to learn more about how mood changes impact me.
- I will remember that everyone matters (including me!)
- I will accept that dark times are an opportunity to showcase my *Talk2Me©* leadership communication skills.
- I will never forget that hope is alive.

Being brave of heart means having the courage to live in times of uncertainty. To live means feeling safe risking failure so you can march into unknown regions of creative personal growth.

Let's skip the doubt so you can find out that even during deeply troubling times, you are far stronger than you think.

FIVE

IN A CONFLICT, PAUSE BEFORE YOU REACT WITH A COMMUNICATOR PREJUDICE

"Life is very short, and there's no time...for fussing and fighting, my friend."
—We Can Work It Out by The Beatles

TALK2ME© Creative Conflict Management

Step 1—Identify Who's Talking
Step 2—Pause Before Reacting
Step 3—Accept Their View
Step 4—Match Their Feedback Style
Step 5—Measure the Results

💬 Invisible Prejudices

Predator is a 1987 American science fiction action film directed by John McTiernan. It stars Arnold Schwarzenegger as the leader of an elite military rescue team deployed to save hostages in the guerrilla-held territory in Central America. A technologically advanced alien called the Predator hunts, stalks, and kills members of the elite team... until the epic showdown between Schwarzenegger and the Predator.

If you have seen the film, you know the Predator's most lethal ability was invisibility.

Invisibility is also a primary perpetrator of prejudices. If you don't see it; it can't be changed. The first step in overcoming prejudice roadblocks is to be alert to what they are.

> **PRO Rule:** You can't fight the predators of invisible prejudices when you can't see how they're stalking you.

The person you have a conflict with isn't the core problem. The real problem is prejudices have been activated in your subconscious mind, altering your mood and controlling how you react. "They" aren't the problem and "you" aren't the problem. Your invisible hidden prejudices that form relationship patterns are making you react ineffectively to an invisible enemy.

In the movie, frightened, fierce warriors are picked off by a force they can't see. In one scene, they all just open fire with all they have, shredding trees and lighting up the jungle as the invisible predator safely looks on overhead from a high tree. Due to fear-driven prejudices, you will react irrationally instead of calmly to conflict.

In this chapter, you'll begin moving toward the middle of the Instigator-Empathizer spectrum.

We'll show you how to stop making the other person the problem so you have a fighting chance of solving problems peacefully. We'll show how to go on pause and take a step back instead of reacting in a conflict. Lastly, we'll show you how to put your mind over your mood during high-pressure plays.

What It's Like Growing Up As an Empathizer in an Instigator World

Everyone needs to get along with people who are different or people we dislike. If you were an Instigator child, what was it like growing up in your family? If you were an Empathizer child, what was it like growing up in your family? As a child, did you naturally gravitate toward the parent or caregiver who was your identical communicator type? What is it like growing up as an Empathizer in an Instigator world, or the reverse? Interesting family dynamics to ponder, aren't they?

The next story is told through Riley's perspective as a six-year-old Empathizer child. She had the advantage of knowing that two different communication styles roamed in her world:

When I was an Empathizer child, I would retreat and avoid "difficult" Instigators. Their energy, mood, insecurity, and loudness would hit "little Riley" like a ton of bricks. Often, I would not speak to them. Instead, I would hide behind my dad, and look away.

On numerous occasions, an extreme Instigator would approach my father and me. They would often approach with a sarcastic joke, a loud hello, or a strong handshake with my father. Like other kids in preschool or kindergarten, I was inherently cute. This, of course, drew their attention to me, but it was the type of attention I preferred not to attract. They would lean down and speak in a high-pitched, sing-songy way. It sent the impression of "I'm speaking to a child who doesn't understand much."

The conversation went off about the same each time. "Hi, Riley. How are you doing?" They would give me a fake smile that quickly became a frown when I would turn my head and hide behind my dad's leg. I never understood why adults would talk to me in a different voice. I found it creepy and ingenuine.

I always hated it when people would say "What's wrong with her?" I would defensively think in my own head, "What's wrong with me? What's wrong with YOU! You're the one with the negative mood and weird voice, pretending to fake some interest in me." It also felt strange to me that they would say critical things about me, as if I were invisible, although I was standing right there and could overhear them. That's not a great way to get an Empathizer kid to warm up to you. Plus, I didn't totally understand why I needed to reply to Instigator adults who were busy talking in competitive ways. For the longest time, I always wondered why adults talked so much. Without words, I intuitively felt people were saying much more about who they were in between their speaking lines.

At this early age, I strongly disliked how "pushy" Instigators seemed. They came across so intense and would spread their bad moods to others if they felt like it. I didn't realize at the time that it was their customary way to try and connect to me. From my view, it seemed rude and disrespectful of me. Often, Instigator adults disliked and disapproved of me as a result. Or at least that was my view at the time. From their view, I would react to them with a look of distress or disgust, backed by purposeful silence. They actually thought there was something wrong with me that needed correction. I lived by "It's not how you meant the message that matters, but how it was received."

It often disturbed me as a young Empathizer how easily I could sense and "radar in" on the emotions and moods of others. Adults seemed fake, troubled, and tense. The only way I felt I could protect myself was to back away and not engage. To hide or look away soothed me. All my senses seemed turned on to maximum intensity. For example, looking at people always seemed to cause a visceral reaction. As a kid, I didn't see the point in faking how they were making me feel. My natural sensitivity caused interpersonal intensity.

One thing that helped me validate my feelings was validation from my dad. He encouraged me to develop my intuition and not let other people make me feel insecure or upset. That it was *their* mood, not mine, and I could let bad moods pass me by. That I wasn't crazy for picking up people's moods like a sponge. I learned that I could put a shield or a bubble around me to reflect people's moods so they wouldn't stick to me. I could choose what moods I picked up.

PRO Rule: Emotional safety during a conflict is of utmost importance to Empathizers.

This example demonstrates both an inner-personal conflict as well as an interpersonal conflict. Conflicts can be inside or outside of us, or both. The positive purpose of conflicts is to promote personal growth and change.

When the relationship stage feels uncertain, a person feels unsafe to be who they are. Often children are unintentionally discouraged from developing their intuitive sense of people and situations. "Now, you don't really feel that way, do you?" is an Instigator's way of trying to make you feel better. In reality? Seeing the "inner world" of your opposite type frees you up to be your balanced self.

Having a dual perceptive sense of other people means you can see someone through your perception while simultaneously seeing them as they see themselves. I'm glad my dad helped me feel more confident and to always trust my intuition. He taught me I didn't have to absorb others' moods and that I could protect my own mood in a conflict.

Sometimes I still have trouble not absorbing the mood of a negative Instigator, or Empathizers for that matter. What helps me is knowing that their mood isn't my mood. I have trained myself to almost switch off or turn down my radar when I am around negative people. It's like a fire alarm that goes off in my head. Instead of looking for an escape, I turn down the volume and put on some "mood deflective" mental armor. This allows me to talk confidently, look them in the eye, and show that I understand them. I can understand them and am able to respond effectively to them because I know that they are reacting the way Instigators act. They want respect just as much as the next person.

Overall, I've found that the moods or "extreme" characteristics of my opposite type have been inherently triggering ever since I was young. As an Empathizer, I've found bad moods will bounce off of me when I put on my mood deflective mental armor.

Between the ages of 3-6, children start developing a stereotype catalog, one that solidifies over time. Maybe that's why one of my greatest hopes is that this book can create insights that reverse these hidden judgments so we can love each other instead of hiding from or stigmatizing our opposite communicator type or anyone for that matter.

Reflecting on your childhood, can you recall an invisible communication prejudice that you started to develop? For example, that a quiet voice indicates the person is uncomfortable or a loud voice indicates confidence? Or that crossed arms mean defensiveness instead of relaxation?

Interestingly, interpretations of behavior are colored and distorted by the I-E lens you're looking through.

I count myself lucky to have grown up understanding Empathizer and Instigator Communicator preferences from an early age. As an Empathizer, I still have to be mindful so I don't discriminate against Instigators when I'm feeling triggered. I find that early detection and awareness have helped me to be open-minded and fluid in my communication style. I've built my confidence in dealing with, and acceptance of, my invisible prejudices once they were pointed out to me. I adapted and became the communicator that I am today.

While negativity from both Empathizers and Instigators is not acceptable to spread to one another, bad moods often are the result of invisible prejudices that are just outside of your perceptual field. This chapter is focused on breaking down tall walls of invisible communication prejudices. You will feel less triggered and more at ease when speaking with someone who is your opposite.

Instigators who regularly give more positive feedback produce better outcomes. Empathizers who regularly give more corrective feedback produce better outcomes. Instead of viewing your opposite as the opposition, you will be able to redirect the dynamic back to something positive instead of getting stuck in a rut of miscommunication.

⬭ Law 5: In a Conflict, Pause Before You React With a Communicator Prejudice

Subconscious prejudices make up most of your communication problems.

Our workshop participants view the "Communicator Prejudices" portion of our workshops as eye-opening and relationship-changing. This training is an opportunity to look at the enemy within–Communicator Prejudices; an ideal way to "see and hear" the "classic view" of Instigator and Empathizer customs, preferences, and misperceptions.

The activity works in this way. Each team faces off across the room. The Empathizer team is seated on the left side of the room, and the Instigator team is seated on the right side of the room. Each team huddles up to answer "How would you ding your opposite type? What do you honestly dislike about them, and why?" Then each side writes their answers on a whiteboard with Negative Instigator or Negative Empathizer written across the top of the ledger.

Each side gets to present their responses. The other side does their best to hear honestly—for better or worse—how they're perceived by the other side. Laughter and challenges ensue. Heels turn as responses are applied to spouses and children at home, too. Sincere questions are asked and answered about what each type thinks and feels in certain situations and why.

What's so mind-altering about this exercise? Basically the same list of prejudices is recited in every class, proving that these are universally subconscious prejudices that are impacting your decisions and mood. Once you bring them safely to the surface, they will never again hold the same kind of power over you.

By acknowledging the prejudices, you don't have to fix people, or feel wrong for being who you are.

⤬ Prejudices Instigators Possess About Empathizers

If you're an Instigator, these hidden prejudices will be triggered when you get into a conflict with an Empathizer. Each distortion changes your view of what to say or do. For example, the Empathizer is too...

- Too sensitive
- No backbone
- Sissy
- Weak
- Sulks
- Won't push back
- Always wants to talk

- Brings me down
- Backs off from disputes, debates, conflicts
- Too thin-skinned
- Pushover
- Takes crap when shouldn't
- Too indirect; wishy-washy
- Whiner
- Can't get past the past
- Slow reacting
- Acts nice when ticked
- Sucker
- Can't handle criticism

💬 Prejudices Empathizers Possess About Instigators

If you're an Empathizer, these hidden prejudices will be triggered when you get into a conflict with an Instigator. Each distortion changes your view of what to say or do. For example, the Instigator is too...

- Too insensitive
- Bossy
- Impatient
- Rude
- Pushy
- Steamroller
- Angry
- Ticks people off
- Bully
- Cocky: "It's all about me!"
- Cold logic
- Short fuse
- Stubborn and hard-headed

- Impatient
- Too harsh: Hurts others without remorse
- Critical
- Fast-reacting
- Hot tempered
- Robotic
- Selfish: Too wrapped up in work or raising kids
- Criticizes others but won't take criticism

The Instigator-Empathizer Wrestling Match

Here are a few standard ways distorted Instigator vs. Empathizer views can clash, a reaction that causes unintended losses for both teams:

- As the Instigator judges an Empathizer as too wordy and beating around the bush…

    …The Empathizer judges the Instigator as not listening and too close-minded.
- As the Instigator rudely talks over and debates…

    …The Empathizer shuts up and shuts down.
- As the Instigator doesn't tune in and paraphrase what's being said…

    …The Empathizer gives up trying to get their point across.
- As the Instigator gets louder to make a passionate point…

    …The Empathizer feels intimidated and pressured to go along quietly.
- As the Instigator thinks everything is OK…

    …The Empathizer increasingly feels very NOT OK.

This spiralling resentment dynamic ejects from your life the helpful feedback that can lead to greater happiness.

💬 Fight Loop

Let's enact an extreme example of escalating conflict between an Instigator and an Empathizer couple. These prejudices and false assumptions mirror what you might hear:

Instigator: You're too sensitive. **Empathizer:** You're too insensitive.
Instigator: You're a sissy. **Empathizer:** You're a bully.
Instigator: You're too agreeable. **Empathizer:** You can't agree to disagree.
Instigator: You worry too much. **Empathizer:** You couldn't care less.
Instigator: You're too touchy-feely. **Empathizer:** You don't feel a thing.
Instigator: You can't let go of fear. **Empathizer:** You make me feel afraid.
Instigator: You're depressing. **Empathizer:** You avoid and ignore me.
Instigator: You're too timid to talk back. **Empathizer:** You talk over me and shut me down.
Instigator: You don't take good care of yourself. **Empathizer:** You take care of only yourself.
Instigator: You're too laid back. **Empathizer:** You're too pushy.
Instigator: You're too wishy-washy. **Empathizer:** You're stubborn.
Instigator: You're a rule follower. **Empathizer:** You break the rules when it suits you.
Instigator: You stuff your anger. **Empathizer:** You spew your anger.

Communicate Like a PRO

Instigator: You have no backbone.
Empathizer: You have to win at all costs.
Instigator: Why can't you let go of the past?
Empathizer: Why can't we talk it through to resolve it?
Instigator: Why don't you look me in the eye when we talk?
Empathizer: Why do you look down on me?
Instigator: You're too patient.
Empathizer: You're too impatient.
Instigator: You're afraid of failure.
Empathizer: You're afraid of closeness.
Instigator: You're afraid of conflict.
Empathizer: You love conflict.
Instigator: You're a guilt magnet.
Empathizer: You're a guilt pusher.
Instigator: You're too moody.
Empathizer: You're too moody.

Well, at least there's one thing our I-E couple can agree on. Everyone's too moody! Does this argument have a familiar ring to it? Tame your tongue. Words have power. Prejudices rob you of the integrity of principled living.

💬 Learning From Critical Feedback Without Throwing Daggers

You can learn from critical feedback without your pride getting in the way. But it requires that you don't look through the distorted lens of subconscious prejudices.

A 68-year-old cynical Instigator female client was being coached to exhibit more positive attitudes in her personal life. She was instructed to listen carefully to critical feedback from loved ones instead of raising her voice. She sarcastically said this about her listening skills, "I can't help that, at my age, I suffer ear fatigue after a hard day's work."

On one occasion, she was again loudly complaining to her married, older brother that her dating life was terrible and she was ticked off at men ever since her divorce. Her Empathizer brother finally snapped, and said, "Well, that's because you don't talk 'to' people, you talk 'at' them. You don't give good guys a chance. And your cynical attitude and griping turn people off."

Instead of firing back that her Instigator brother was an insensitive jerk who's always bossing her around, the client took a step back and calmly considered the feedback. She considered the validity of her anger as a force field that keeps men out of her life. She decided to show more warmth and sincere appreciation toward men she would meet...and her dating life improved. She no longer was a loner walking around with a big boulder-sized chip on her shoulder.

Continual learning is a process of listening to and applying helpful feedback without defensiveness. Not easy, to be sure. Although this feedback was difficult for her to hear, it improved her attitude about men. By changing her attitude, she changed her life, and now she is happier personally and in her relationships, including with her brother.

Positive communication leads to better moods, improved attitudes, and physical benefits as well. For example, your body and blood pressure will thank you. As you argue less with others *and* yourself, you will grin more and feel a deep sense of gratitude. You will feel fit and more youthful. Your mind will slow down instead of heading to the races when you wake up in the morning.

In summary, both Instigators and Empathizers are born with a shared set of prejudices. These universal subconscious prejudices are the root cause of most conflicts. Hidden from view, these invisible sources of conflict do enormous damage. You and most people are largely ignorant of the pressures prejudices put on your relationships.

It's time to change that.

Communicate Like a PRO

🗨 Communication Crashes Between Instigators and Empathizers

Tense moods trigger prejudices, and prejudices fuel conflicts.

Let's keep it real: Relationship conflicts in your life are fueled by hidden universal prejudices. These invisible resentments fuel discord. For example, if you're an Empathizer, you believe Instigators are too blunt and harsh. In contrast, if you're an Instigator, you believe Empathizers beat around the bush too much and are soft.

Much of your behavior under stress is driven by these invisible prejudices that fuel conflict and war. When you "see" what's been hidden from your view, you will spontaneously see new options to solve stale problems. You will respond flexibly and respectfully, not punch back blindly.

Prejudices are roadblocks and barriers to productive communication. They pop up when moods are heightened by misunderstandings and feelings are hurt. It helps to think of these prejudices as invisible cement blocks strewn along your local highway. Learning to drive around these invisible cement prejudice blocks will dramatically reduce expensive crashes that require repairs. Wouldn't you agree? But if your speeding car slams into an invisible cement block, you can't blame anyone (including yourself) because no one could see the real cause of the crash.

Prejudices are a sensitive topic, but instead of turning a blind eye, we've found that it's most impactful to discuss prejudices honestly in our workshop exercises or couple therapy. Instigators and Empathizers vouch for the importance of knowing how they're viewed negatively by their opposite type so they can learn how to change their behaviors. The blindfold comes off.

How you view someone determines how you act toward them. A pushy Instigator can get his or her way by using a loud debating voice with an Empathizer. As you know by now, Instigators take pride in "telling it like it is" but can hurt feelings unnecessarily. Instigators have a strong drive to be right, which can trigger anxious thinking when their pride gets hurt.

When Instigators push, Empathizers take a step back to center themselves. Empathizers feel shot in the chest by an arrow. That's because the E-Type needs to process what's gone wrong and what they've done wrong. Silence, however, doesn't mean condoning or agreeing. In fact, E's who over-accommodate and keep silent will resentfully stew about how, "They're so rude and disrespectful toward me. They are such a jerk!"

Cycles of conflict take on a life of their own. For example, Instigators initially get their way, only to pay for it down the line when the Empathizer brings up the previous incident. Instigators get irked. "Why didn't you say something at the time? You're always so sensitive about everything. Geez." And that's how two well-meaning people can veer sideways and slide into a ditch.

A conflict is anything (including another person) that bothers you and makes you dwell on it. You paste your internal prejudices on the difficult antagonist who has disappointed your expectations. Everyone does it. Much world conflict is caused by people who do not behave as you think they should.

Empathizers think, "Why aren't they acting like me? Something's wrong with them." And Instigators think, "Why aren't they acting like me? Something's wrong with them." How you view someone dictates how you act toward them and how they react back. Are you the main cause of difficulty in your life? Of course you are. Seek to view things from a new point of view.

"It's not me, it's them!" is a blame game fueled by subconscious prejudices. We blame the other party instead of putting the responsibility squarely on where it belongs: internal prejudices. The enemy is within and we will go without peaceful co-existence until we realize this fact. Work with the I-E prejudices that threaten to run your relationships off the road and into a ditch.

For now, though, be aware that specific universal subconscious prejudices exist that stalk you and when triggered defeat you.

🗨 A Mother-Adult Son Case Study

The most challenging conflicts are those in our closest relationships. Conflicts between generations, such as parent-adult child conflicts, can hurt feelings deeply and can cause stand offs or end relationships. A lot is at stake.

In conflict, how do you turn your "opposer" into your "co-communicator?" By stepping back to pause and compose your mind before reacting. Let's take a look at a single mother-adult son example.

In a fierce email blast, an Instigator mother forcefully criticized her adult Instigator son for failing to bring the grandchildren to see her because he was bowing to his wife's will. He fired back that interstate travel with little kids was a chore, and they wanted to visit her but preferred to stay at a nearby hotel. She fired back that raising him as a single mother wasn't easy either, but she managed it and he owed her respect; if they didn't stay with her, then they could just stay home.

Mother and son were both hard-charging Instigators who were like two mountain rams, banging horns and knocking each other senselessly. Neither mother nor son felt good about the stand-off. What to do? Listening to the other person's view builds bridges while invisible prejudices builds tall walls. The trained communicator needs to change. The PRO has the courage to change when others are making idle threats or twiddling their thumbs.

After learning about I-prejudice threats, Mom wrote back in E-language to appeal to the heart of the matter:

> *After thinking about what you said to me, I think you're right to take this stand. As the father of your family, you need to protect the children and respect your wife's wishes. You didn't have a dad, and I'm proud of how you're being a dad. I don't like how I came across to you. You don't owe me anything. You're a great man, husband, and father. I will enjoy all of you whatever you decide. I hope you will come. I do agree that staying in a hotel is probably much easier for all of you to manage. Because your kids live seven hours away, I was just*

trying to get every single second in. Maybe we could compromise. I could take the grandkids overnight so the two of you could have some couple time, which you probably don't get much of. Anyway, let's find a way that we all can enjoy the time we have together. Thank you for listening to me, and please know that I heard your objections and am sincerely trying to address them.

Love, Mom

Our kids are our best teachers. To combat emotionally escalating relationship issues, start with disarming yourself.

To finish the story, the son responded back enthusiastically, and the mother-son bond was strengthened. Also, the son's wife wasn't put in the middle of the strife or used as a scapegoat. The Instigator mom felt her position of authority was respected. Instead of continued conflict, mom and son generated a novel solution. The children would stay overnight with grandma and parents could enjoy couples time.

When you know the real cause of a communication problem, you can fix it. Don't let prejudices take you hostage.

⮒ Power Plays: How Do You React Defensively in a Conflict?

Empathizers and Instigators react to conflict in predictable ways that don't have to throw either type. Being aware of Instigator vs. Empathizer pain points will help you and your co-communicator avoid tense talks that go to hell.

Instigators in Defensive Conflict Mode

- You wear people down until they say 'yes.'
- You argue to get your way.
- You push others to do what they don't want to do.
- You listen to argue, not to hear.

- You are uncomfortable letting others make decisions.
- You turn conversations into competitions.
- You attack back when you feel attacked.
- You feel angry when dismissed.
- Failing makes you feel worthless.

Empathizers in Defensive Conflict Mode

- You don't push back and say "no" quickly enough.
- You are submissive when someone argues with you.
- You discourage yourself and give in.
- You listen to harmful statements.
- You are uncomfortable making decisions yourself.
- You always try to find a middle ground, even when there isn't one.
- You give up when you feel attacked.
- You feel sad and quietly resentful when rejected.
- Failing makes you believe you're not good enough.

How do you react in a conflict? What triggers you? Reflect on a recent time of conflict or grievance. Write down and identify your typical traits. Then, preselect new PRO traits you would like to adopt for the next dispute.

🗩 TALK2ME© Creative Conflict Management (CCM)

What's the secret recipe to communicate effectively during a conflict? You pause and take a step back before you mindlessly react with a slight or prejudice that offends your partner. When you're in a conflict, use these five *TALK2ME©* Creative Conflict Management steps to slow down the speeding train of your mind.

> **Step 1-** Identify Who's Talking
> **Step 2-** Pause Before Reacting

Step 3- Accept Their View

Step 4- Match Their Feedback Style

Step 5- Measure the Results

Next we'll show you how to do just that when the heat is on and your nerves are frayed.

⤵ Calming Your Moody Reactionary Mind

Use the CCM mental steps to calm your moody reactionary mind so you think clearly before you speak:

1. **Who's the Talker?** First, identify whether an Instigator or Empathizer Type is triggering you. Make a vow to respond, not react. What annoying prejudices cause them to react poorly under pressure?
2. **Push the Pause Button?** Second, put your mood on pause to think clearly. Take a step back, breathe, and view the incident in a calm state of mind. What is your goal in the situation?
3. **What's Their View?** Third, tune into how your partner views the struggle. Let go of judging them as wrong. Instead, can you accept their point of view as a valid one?
4. **Respond in Their Feedback Style?** Fourth, use a feedback approach that will match the language style of your conflict partner. How can you creatively tweak what you have to say so it will have the best chance of being heard?
5. **Measure the Results?** Fifth, track how well your new approach is working. How are these little changes working to the benefit of all parties?

This problem-solving structure opens up the prejudiced mind to think of creative alternatives that lead to win-win solutions. It fosters a mindful give-and-take dialogue within yourself.

🗫 Feeling Better Fast

Small conflicts can spin out of control fast. For example, take disputes about money. We trip on the stupid small stuff.

Let's look at an example of a small misunderstanding that could build into an unnecessary conflict.

I (Dennis) sent an invoice by email to a client for family coaching services. The client zapped back a stern email questioning a charge for a session that couldn't have occurred. It was a particularly "hard" day in the life of this psychologist, so I was on guard not to shoot from the lip. This is the "internal work" I did to keep calm and carry on when I was feeling exhausted:

1. **Who's the Talker?** *First step:* Identify who you're talking to to create empathy.

   My client was an example of an Alpha female Instigator who takes pride in telling it like it is and solving problems fast, without the feelings. However, when I'm stressed out, I prefer a softer-gentler-easier Empathizer approach so that my response doesn't come across as a character critique. In fact, I would have preferred a phone call to chat about it. But in her Instigator style, that "touchy feely" approach would have been an unnecessarily huge waste of time.

2. **Push the Pause Button?** *Second step:* Think rationally first to calm your runaway mood.

   I knew my judgment was compromised by the difficult demands of the day. Instead of firing something back, I had to put my mind on pause. I needed some time to reflect quietly on the matter. I reminded myself about our strong relationship and her gratitude for my help in her email response. Then a light bulb came on: I recalled this tough-charging, no-nonsense client had recently lost her beloved husband of five decades. That changed my view of what to do! I also recalled how sad I felt at her husband's funeral because I admired and enjoyed him so much. Here I was stewing about a stupid little thing as a bill, while she was mourning the loss of her husband and their lifetime of love.

3. **What's Their View?** *Third step:* Look through the lens of your antagonist to show respect and build trust.

In her Instigator view, this was simply a question about a bill. It was in fact being respectful of my time. She just wanted to "check off" another box on her "to do" list to feel a sense of worth. My prejudiced view was that I was being falsely accused of making a stupid mistake and I ought to set the record straight.

4. **Respond in Their Feedback Style?** *Fourth step:* Manage the conflict by talking in their preferred language style so they can hear what you're saying through walls of fear or misunderstanding.

Because I know Instigators like quick action, I sent a one-line email back saying I would check into the invoice first thing the next day and correct the item. As an Instigator, I knew she simply wanted an answer but would grow impatient without some response. After some digging, I discovered she was right and that in a hurry I had mislabeled by one month the session date with her husband. No wonder she had a question. The session couldn't have taken place. The session date I had listed on the invoice occurred after her husband's death. Instigators pride themselves on being strong; they aren't fans of grief. Had I unintentionally poked the wound of her grief? I think so. And Instigators who say "I feel vulnerable because…." get their messages heard when they're hurting.

5. **Measure the Results?** *Fifth step:* Honor yourself by monitoring the impact of your creative conflict management.

Although emotional work takes work, it repairs the relationship bridge between yourself and those you care for. As expected, I didn't hear back from my esteemed I-client but soon received a check in the mail. Given the freshness of her grief, I vowed to keep in touch. I respected that she didn't want to be seen as weak or needy. I knew her Instigator husband would have agreed.

Who-Pause-What-Respond-Results...You will use these steps time and again to calm down before responding during an emotional conflict or interpersonal crisis. This approach will save you untold pain, sorrow, and aggravation.

It's Not How You Meant the Message that Matters, But How It Was Received

A common defense of hurtful behavior is, "But that's not what I meant. You're twisting what I said and taking it way out of context. You're not hearing what I'm really saying. You're putting your own spin on it. Look, I'm sorry if you took it that way, but I didn't mean it."

> **PRO RULE:** Combatting relationship issues first starts with disarming yourself.

"I didn't mean it!" excuses are true, but they stifle empathetic listening and creative problem solving. Next time a conflict is brewing, step into the view of the other person to understand their inner anxieties.

What causes anxiety to escalate in Instigators during a conflict with Empathizers? From the Instigator view, the Empathizer...

- Complains too much, doesn't offer solution.
- Acts too nice, is vague or rambling.
- Poor eye contact, soft speech, hard to hear.
- Won't express opinions bluntly, too indirect.
- Wishy-washy, won't defend opinions, stews.
- Intimidates easily, won't push back, can't trust.
- Won't get straight to the bottom of what's wrong.

- Tells you what you want to hear but later resents you.
- Non-confrontational, too sensitive, beats around the bush.
- Expects hand-holding, manipulative, cries.
- A huge people pleaser, no self-confidence.
- Too apologetic when not at fault.
- Won't stand up for own opinions or beliefs.

What causes anxiety to escalate in Empathizers during a conflict with Instigators? From the Empathizer view, the Instigator...

- Doesn't listen, jumps to conclusions.
- Gets mad easy, talks over you, bullies.
- Speaks before thinks, runs mouth, makes snide remarks.
- Thinks knows everything to be done, lectures.
- No negotiation or meeting in the middle.
- Prove they're right to prove others wrong.
- Unable to maintain relationships, won't pull weight at home.
- Will show themselves as an Empathizer around authority.
- Not approachable, always in a rush, no time.
- Dominates, stubborn, abrasive, mean when mad.
- Grim-faced, acts grumpy, unhappy.
- Stomps around and acts mad when doesn't get way.
- Interrupts, argumentative, fierce debater.
- Can't tell if they're listening or just waiting for their chance to jump in.
- Points out wrong then walks away, cold-like robot.
- If you ask a question, gives the impression that you're stupid.

How you view someone determines how you act toward them and how they react toward you.

💬 It Was So Stupid

Couples who fight unfairly rarely fight about big stuff. They fight about stupid little stuff. Distressed couples will be the first to tell you so. It's not the big issues that will kill you and make you split up; the thousand little cuts to tender flesh will. As a marriage counselor, I often ask couples to recount an example of a recent fight. They almost always say: "It's kind of embarrassing, Dr. O. It was over something small, something really stupid."

Think of little resentments as sharp pebbles in your shoe. Over time, a single sharp stone in your shoe will hobble you. If you don't take time to pause and empty your shoe, these unresolved little resentments will stop you in your tracks and steal your peace of mind. In this chapter, we will teach you a single powerful *TALK2ME©* tool to help you handle internal and external conflicts creatively to stay on the happiness track.

Let's use the metaphor of the sharp pebble in your shoe to show how resentments impact your mental health. What's happening to you? You feel something's off, something's wrong. Something in your left shoe is pricking your heel. Although you can ignore the small sharp pain in your heel for a bit, the ignored pain will intensify and spread to your foot. The harder the road you have to walk, the greater likelihood the pain will spread to your ankle, then the calf, then up your entire left leg until your good mood is drained and your gait is hobbled.

All this pain could have been avoided by making a little upfront change when you felt that first pain in your heel. You could have paused to think calmly about what's going on. If you act strong and unbothered, or if you ignore the pain signals to avoid looking weak to your partner, the conflict will grow larger. During a conflict, little changes you make will help both of you resolve the conflict.

Think small when it comes to conflicts. You define conflict as all those collected little hurts and resentments that you dwell on in your mind that impact your wellness. This includes disappointing expectations or stewing about what someone has or hasn't done to and for you. These unaddressed little aggravations, hurts, and irritations build the

Plexiglass wall of resentment that separates the two of you. A failure to hear your partner's view then creates distancing patterns or repetitive fight loops.

PRO Rule: Tense moods trigger prejudices that fuel conflicts.

Worse yet, feelings run stronger in your personal relationships. Thus, conflicts feel bigger because the stakes are higher. Some examples of relationship conflicts that are draining:

- Sharp words that stick in your self-esteem like a harpoon.
- Harsh insensitive texts that blame or invalidate your view.
- Being ignored or scolded, making you feel invisible and crazy.
- A big circle of lashing out instead of listening.
- Being lectured to like you're 5, making you feel "less than" you are.
- Mad Attack: "Don't tell me what to do. I'll get to it when I get to it."
- A forgotten event that makes you feel like lowly mud on a partner's shoes.
- A conversation that turns into verbal slams, single-finger salutes, and sore feelings.

You want to feel supported in your most important relationships. Why do little things have to be made into such a big deal? Because they are in your partner's view. And as you know, volatile moods fuel misunderstandings.

A tiny pebble in you or your partner's shoe can turn into a catastrophic avalanche of rocks and boulders that bury both of you and make you feel hollow and empty. Because we all have insecurity issues, conflicts drain a couple's self-esteem. As human beings, we feel a deep need to be connected and valued, not discounted and lonely. We seek to find meaning and growth in the field of our relationships and dreams.

💬 Case Study: A Text-Caused Escalating Conflict

Let's apply your new insights to the world of texting. Texts are easy to misinterpret and misuse. They prove trust is easy to lose and slow to regain.

This is a tragic case of texting with prejudice. Two friends had known each other and worked together for 10 years. They celebrated milestones, birthdays, graduations, babies, and generally being there for each other. Both were equally invested and supportive of the other. They were living proof that men and women can get along and be friends.

The male Empathizer friend rented a house from his female Instigator friend. Their relationship easily expanded to a tenant-landlord arrangement. The conflict began when the Instigator friend needed to move back into her rental home because of a nasty divorce. As an Instigator, she abruptly and unilaterally texted her tenant friend to announce the housing change. Due to time pressures, she didn't discuss this major life change face-to-face with her friend.

This was mistake #1. A text fight ensued. Important changes, new directions, and relationship decisions are best relayed in person to avoid escalating conflicts.

Following is the text trail that blew up their relationship, perhaps beyond repair, and activated many prejudices and resentments. Next, we will share how to avoid escalating text anxieties and crises in both Instigator and Empathizer partners.

I-Landlord: My husband is getting our house in the divorce. You need to move out of the rental so I can move into it. It would be easier for you to find a new place as opposed to me.

E-Tenant: But I still have a lease. I know things are hard for you right now. I've painted every room in the house, floored the kitchen, and just loved and cared for the place. You've always said I've been an amazing tenant.

I-Landlord: I had a meeting with the divorce lawyer, and due to lack of finances, I have to refinance the house. I will not be able to renew your contract. I'm giving you as much notice as I have been given. If you find a place before the contract ends, I won't hold you to it.

E-Tenant: (Angrily) Then I'll be completely out by the end of this month, that is, if I can find something. I did a lot to this place, fixing it up and painting and now you're pushing me out.

I-Landlord: (Angrily) Look, I didn't want this to happen. It's not my fault. It's only business. Enough of giving me attitude and making a big deal out of something I don't have control over. Stop taking this so personal. You'll find an even better place to live. So, are we no longer friends?

E-Tenant: (Escalating not listening) Stop telling me how I should feel or think. I don't know what I'm going to do. How would it make you feel getting kicked out all of a sudden? You just don't understand. I figured when you started giving me the cold shoulder and abruptly stopped talking to me you were done with me. The next thing was telling me to move. You pulled your friendship from me without consulting me.

I-Landlord: (Talking, not paraphrasing) OK, I was broken from all the divorce crap that was going on and how everything was handled. I wasn't holding it together very well but didn't want to vomit my crap on you. But this isn't all my fault and you could have spoken up to me sooner about how hurt you were feeling and why. How am I supposed to read your mind? How can I fix anything if you don't tell me what's wrong?

E-Tenant: (Resentfully) You're not hearing a word I'm saying. Glad your life is in a better place. I'm working two jobs, and this is coming at a really bad time. But now soon you can be back in your precious house. I'm sad having to leave the house, but losing your friendship hurts more. I'll be out of your life soon. I need to protect myself because you can't be trusted, and I don't feel emotionally safe around you.

I-Landlord: (Resigned) I've never stopped being your friend. Can you let me know what day you'll be finished at 5:45? I have set up a time with the plumber. Does anything else need repaired?

Right or wrong, the Empathizer tenant decided to move out quickly before his lease ended and move on without his Instigator friend. Could this debacle have been averted?

Words have power. What you say in words has enormous impact, for better or worse.

💬 Be Proactive: Respond Instead of React

Text messages are going to be received with more intensity because they arrive without non-verbal cues. Texted words have a memory that can wound a relationship beyond repair.

According to practicing psychotherapists, eighty-two percent (82%) of communication is in your own head. You talking to you. Everyone is prone to thinking about fake negative things when prejudices have been triggered. Talking sensibly to yourself is a key skill to still your fears.

Emotions dictate outcomes. The point of the next exercise is to show you how to slow down your rising emotions so you will pause during a conflict instead of reacting with prejudice. Let's return to our texting case example and apply the 5 Steps of Creative Conflict Management. What would the saner "inner talk" of each friend sound like? How might it produce a better outcome?

Instigator Landlord Pre-Meeting Internal Dialogue

Landlord Coaches Self: "I'm really emotionally reeling from all this divorce legal craziness. I feel vulnerable. I need to slow down my mind. I know that when I feel anxious, I'm much more likely to make quick but poor decisions. I don't want to hurt my friend. We've been through so much together these past 10 years.

I know my tenant Empathizer friend isn't wired like me. So, I'm going to approach him and speak to him in his preferred way of talking. He's not going to like this, and although I don't blame him, I don't see another alternative right now. So, I'm going to set up a person-to-person meeting. I'm going to script what I'm going to say to him. I'll use his feedback preferences. I'm going to give a detailed backstory explanation of why this change needs to occur, from my view.

I'm not going to just blurt out the message or give a command. I'm going to ask for his input to show caring and respect. He loves the house and has made it his home. I'm going to have compassion that my friend is going to feel shocked and that his sense of safety and security have been threatened by me. He has no idea how brutal and nasty this divorce was. I just want to get out of there.

He has enough stress of his own, working extra hours to pay off his debts. I'm going to give him time to get his arms around this. I'm even going to ask if he can see a better solution to our situation. Who knows, maybe I don't see all the alternatives and a better way we can move forward. I'm going to reassure him by emphasizing that our friendship won't get lost in the process.

I'm afraid he's not going to understand no matter what I say or do. He had no idea this was ever a possibility. I really need to think like an Empathizer. I need to adopt Empathizer ways, so I don't blow up our friendship."

Each party is 50% co-responsible for enacting a new solution. Let's turn now to how the Empathizer friend could have calmed fears of change and loss.

Empathizer-Tenant Self-Talk

Tenant Coaches Self: "This makes me feel kicked in the gut. Where's this coming from? Why is she doing this to me now? This is crazy. I've got to slow my mind and step back from reacting with more emotion. I've got to keep my mind positive about this change.

I'm feeling really anxious. What am I so afraid of? I'm losing my home. My friend is concerned and doesn't want to hurt me, but I can't see it right now. What I can do right now is take a deep breath, step back, and be calm as I can be. Change is scary but I can cope.

What do I know to be true? I know she can be too blunt when she's afraid to say things. I know I felt happy and settled here. I know that I assumed I would be here for years until I paid off my loans. I've got to go easy here. I can't blame her for this unexpected change. She doesn't owe me anything and I don't have to be mean about this. Here's another chance for me to flow with change and trust the process that something better is waiting around the corner.

Her bad break-up is rippling into my life, and I resent that. Both of us are at a disadvantage. She's probably feeling guilty for kicking me out after all the work and effort I put into redoing this place. I am grateful for our friendship and for the amount of time I had to live in this place. I know things will turn out all right. I need to have faith and confidence that I will find a place soon. I need to pull back on snarky comments that will make me feel better but make my friend feel guilty."

Empathetic Self-Correction: How the Message Was Received Isn't How It Was Meant

What does the E-friend in the example need to remember to keep calm and move things forward?

- My friend is an Instigator. I can't expect her to be like me or approach me in ways that make me less anxious.
- She's anxious, too. I know when I-Types are anxious they are blunt, blurt out the decision, get straight to the point, and want to move on because it's so emotional.
- I know she likes and respects me and must feel terrible about this, even if she is coming off as unempathetic. I need to keep a cool head and not yell at her.

- I need to think like an Instigator. I need to speak up now, be assertive and directive, and say what I want to see happen.
- I might even suggest we consider living together through the winter, so I have a sense of slower transition.
- In any case, our friendship needs to be mended and I'm willing to do my part. I'll write out notes about what I need to say honestly.

Most people are good and have your best interests at heart. Invisible prejudices fuel fears that result in hurtful decisions, and hurtful decisions can further escalate painful conversations.

⌕ Feedback Styles: How to Help Your Opposite Type Calm Down

Honesty solves problems. Match the talking style of your opponent during a conflict. Here are shortcuts each type can take to show respect and signal trust:

Biggest I-Help During a Conflict:

- Get to the point.
- Speak up.
- Act driven to solve a problem.
- Be direct and directive.
- Speak up louder.
- Don't be so intimidated.
- Let I-speaker know where you stand.
- Be decisive.
- Focus on finding a solution.
- Do something now and don't worry about making mistakes.

Biggest E-Help During a Conflict:

- Listen.
- Don't interrupt or prejudge.
- Ask open-ended questions.
- Use caring nonverbal forms of communication.
- Paraphrase the last point.
- Don't wear your displeasure on your face.
- Give reassurances that the E-speaker is making sense.
- Nurture relationships by making time.
- Be approachable, show warmth.
- Show who you really are around authority figures.
- Self-disclose vulnerable feelings when the answer isn't known.

Ironically, when people become anxious, they tend to do more of what doesn't work. They interrupt or become passive-aggressive. This, of course, ramps up spoken and unspoken friction.

- If you're an Instigator: The best conflict management tool is to listen a minute longer and paraphrase what you're hearing.
- If you're an Empathizer: The best conflict management tool is to speak up assertively and stick to one point.

During disputes, polarization occurs. People drift apart and feel pushed away. Insecurities cause talking over one another because they're tearful of loss. Loss of the relationship, loss of progress, loss of respect. So, defensively they come across too strong. Slow down, be attentive to your fears, and resolve to be more attentive to your communication tactics.

The Minefield Game

Communication that's littered with Empathizer and Instigator (E-I) perceptual prejudices can be like walking blindfolded through a minefield. You can get your legs blown off at the knee without knowing exactly why.

In workshops, this threat is simulated by having teams of two instruct a blindfolded teammate through a fake "minefield." The mines are red paper picnic plates with a party popper placed underneath. Twenty of these "live" mines are scattered in a 10x12 minefield. You can also use mouse traps as a nod to the 1997 comedy *Mouse Hunt* with Nathan Lane and Lee Evans.

The objective is for the non-blind or "sighted" teammate to verbally guide the blindfolded teammate through the fake minefield. A blindfolded teammate who steps on an explosive mine is required to start over since they blew it and "blew up."

Can you imagine being verbally guided blindfolded through this scary scene? Fear could cause you to step too fast or too slow and not clarify and confirm what you are hearing. You have to listen very carefully. You have to step gingerly, one small step at a time. You have to trust the feedback of your guide. You have to keep the faith that your communication is effective.

Is your mind overloaded with stress? Not good. When you're agitated or angry, you can't calm your mind. When you can't calm your mind, you can't listen. When you can't listen, you can't hear feedback to accomplish what you desire.

When you can't process helpful critical feedback, you won't understand what to do next. And when you don't know what to do, chances grow higher that you will blow it by stepping on a landmine. Then a relationship resentment loop will start playing in your head. To create a safe way ahead, you need to use a better view of where you are in a relationship and what to do next.

This fun activity highlights key concepts of communication, teamwork, and navigating such barriers as Empathizer-Instigator perceptual prejudices. Distorted views stuff cotton in your ears so you don't hear constructive feedback. In your daily communications, start to look ahead to notice the "mines" in front of you. Notice what has been blocking your communication and what causes your relationships to become explosive.

💬 Equality: The Damage Prejudice Can Cause

In social psychology, "confirmation bias" is when you don't view people or events objectively but think you do. Your mind zeroes in on "proof" that the prejudice is true and closes out contradictory input that would challenge the bias.

Prejudices divide and conquer the rational mind, making you think you're right in a relationship and don't need to change when you're wrong and need to evolve.

The effects of confirmation bias and the invisibility of prejudices can damage even your most cherished relationships.

A millennial Instigator business owner was managing his mood at work far better than at home. "She's pregnant and I snapped at her after she criticized me for not taking out the garbage after my 15-hour day." His Empathizer wife exploded like a volcano and snapped back, "If I lose this baby taking out the garbage because you didn't have time to, then the fault is all yours." She ended up taking out the trash in a huff and felt angry and uncared for.

- If you're an Instigator: Freely give praise to boost your reputation with Empathizers.
- If you're an Empathizer: Freely give constructive criticism to boost your reputation with Instigators.

To be happy at home, the client decided that his #1 customer was his wife. His mood reputation with his wife became even more important than how his customers rated him. As he did chores without needing reminders and found ways to enjoy it, romance in the bedroom bloomed.

People who know you just want to know they matter to you. Patient listening will transfer a positive mood to others.

Your best behavior is needed both at home and work because a mood pipeline runs between both of these important places. Many of us work out of a sense of love for our partner and family. Just because your family is a captive audience doesn't justify taking out your bad mood on them.

Displaced moods are like kicking the dog who ends up biting you in defense. Finding fault doesn't fix anything.

💬 Suspending Instigator-Empathizer Conflicts

Clearly, not everything is rainbows and butterflies between Empathizers and Instigators. Here are some of the most common prejudices each type secretly resents about the other type.

If you're an Instigator, as a habit you will fail to listen and cause conflict by...

- Not tuning in.
- Prejudging the Empathizer as too wordy.
- Assuming you know what the Empathizer is going to say.
- Rudely interrupting or talking over.
- Getting all "huffy."
- Loudly repeating your point like a broken record.
- Being a solutions pusher but dismissive of people.

If you're an Empathizer, as a habit you will fail to be heard and cause conflict by...

- Giving up trying to get your point across.
- Prejudging the Instigator as too close-minded.
- Assuming the Instigator will disapprove of you or your view.
- Getting all intimidated.
- Not requiring what you said to be paraphrased.
- Quietly going along but fiercely disagreeing.
- Not pushing your solutions so you won't upset people.

These behaviors escalate the situation and reinforce communication prejudice.

🗨 Universal Communicators in Harmony

Disappointing expectations cause you to feel slighted, ignored, not seen, disrespectfully treated, unfairly criticized, or rebuked. But by acquiring and demonstrating the strengths of your opposite type, you become multilingual and far more effective and happy.

> **PRO Rule:** See *yourself* the way your I-E opponent *fears you*.

This will change your perception of what next to say or do. Adopt these rules of "proper behavior" and "good conduct" that each respective type firmly believes is the correct way to do things and show respect.

If You're an Empathizer	If You're an Instigator
Be confident	Be calm
Be blunt	Be caring
Speak up	Listen closely
Strong body language	Welcoming body language
Be a go-getter	Go with the flow
Keep it brief	Take time to connect personally
Shorter texts and emails	Longer texts and emails
Use an affirmative sounding voice	Don't ever raise your voice

Which of the traits above will you adopt to turn your "opponent" into your co-communicator?

🗨 Positive Attitude Is Everything

We get it. Ego and false pride muck up the works. It takes courage to admit vulnerability, be assertive, and refrain from being rude or sarcastic when you feel hurt or anxious.

Instigators need to be more approachable and receptive when anxious. In contrast, Empathizers need to be more assertive and direct when anxious.

Now you know what and who triggers your negative emotional responses. This gives you more control over cranky emotions. Naming the problem pattern will help you predict an upcoming stressful situation so you can make new communication moves.

For example, you know that every time you get into a team meeting with your I-Type coworker, they will irritate you with interruptions and talk over you. In the past, you've shut down, ruminated on it, and gossiped with your coworkers for sympathy instead of fixing the problem.

Because you can now predict the future, you can pre-determine what you'll do to make life easier in a crisis. If you're an E-Type, this makes it far easier to start your new communication habits of speaking up for yourself and not allowing yourself to shut down or doubt yourself when you've been interrupted. This permits you to share the remainder of what you have to say.

By understanding your previous mood-hijacking triggers, you will instead trigger inner strengths while blending the blunt vs. caring team roles. When hurt happens, you'll rebuild the communication bridge instead of escalating fears of failure or loss.

In summary, you've learned that you can expect a prejudice to be at the root of any conflict. The best way to resolve things is to be aware of the triggering event and choose to change the script. In the next chapter, you will learn about the crucial role of balanced feedback and how to tailor your feedback for your opposite type to encourage change.

💬 Key Takeaways: Defuse the Ticking Time Bomb of Communicator Prejudices

- Apply Law 5: In a conflict, pause before you react with a Communicator Prejudice.
- You can't fight the predators of invisible prejudices when you can't see how they're stalking you.
- Prejudices, not difficult run-ins with people, are the problem.
- Subconscious prejudices make up most of your communication problems.

- Emotional safety during a conflict is of utmost importance to Empathizers.
- Viewing Instigators as pushy or rude, and Empathizers as weak or wishy-washy, provokes conflict.
- Tense moods trigger prejudices that fuel conflicts.
- Rewriting your I-E Conflict Script improves your listening and leadership skills.
- Combatting relationship issues first starts with disarming yourself.
- Calm brewing conflicts by using *TALK2ME©* Creative Conflict Management steps.
- Hearing and understanding the anxiety of a partner de-escalates conflict.
- Select the best medium for a tough conversation: Text, videoconference, email, or voice. Ideally, meet in person when emotions run high.
- Tense moods trigger prejudices that fuel conflicts.
- Determine the outcome you seek. Mentally practice having a difficult conversation. Decide how you will measure satisfactory results.
- If you're an Instigator: The best conflict management tool is to listen a minute longer and paraphrase what you're hearing.
- If you're an Empathizer: The best conflict management tool is to speak up assertively and stick to one point.
- If you're an Instigator: Freely give praise to boost your reputation with Empathizers.
- If you're an Empathizer: Freely give constructive criticism to boost your reputation with Instigators.
- Instigators need to be more approachable and receptive when anxious, while Empathizers need to be more assertive and direct when anxious.
- See *yourself* the way your I-E opponent *fears you*.

When what you're doing isn't working, do something different, including the opposite of what you're doing.

💬 Law 5: Sharpen Your *TALK2ME©* Skills

Activity 1- Rewriting Your Conflict Script: Many Instigators and Empathizers aren't fans of conflict because the conflicts in their childhood home were not managed well. Conflict-avoidant or conflict-aggressive extremes create more problems than they resolve. Also, knee-jerk reactions make you look and sound like a jerk or a wuss.

Let's take a look at the script you were handed as a child. Explore these Conflict Script questions with a companion:

- How were conflicts handled in your family growing up? How were differences settled?
- How did you feel about the style of conflict management used by your parents?
- How were conflicts handled between siblings? Who managed conflict well, and why?
- What was your role during a family conflict? To be silent, be a moderator, speak out, go away, create a distraction, or what?
- How might your childhood script impact how you confront or avoid relationship conflicts today?
- What do you fear the most about conflict? Being abandoned, ridiculed, rejected, looked down on, or what?

Next, rewrite your Conflict Script to create emotional safety, honesty, and creative problem solving. Which one of these "push the pause button" rules might you use to calm the spinning mind?

- Review the Empathizer-Instigator anxiety arousing prejudice lists in this chapter. How might they apply to the current situation?
- Disallow shouting, pouting, bullying, using empty threats, or character assassination.
- Pre-plan a thoughtful response. Write out or type your response and review it. Patience and slowing down your mind will pay off.

- Don't defer to text or phone what needs to be done eyeball-to-eyeball and kneecap-to-kneecap.
- Wait to speak until you are less emotionally charged. Draft the text or email instead of sending it. Revisit it in 24-hours.
- Think through how your co-communicator doesn't handle conflict well and anticipate those mistakes.

Calm your fears to hear better. Take time to cool off and reflect before you act out and do or say something you won't be able to take back. The next time you're caught up in a fight, make an effort to include these tips you ordinarily would skip. This tactic slows your mind and gives you enough time to think.

Activity 2- Resigning from the Fixer Role: Much conflict is self-generated by trying too hard to solve the complaints or grievances of others. What if you were off the hook for fixing the problems of a mate, co-worker, child, girlfriend, boyfriend, partner, or anyone else? Would you relax more and feel more at peace? Less embroiled in conflict? You can't change other people, but you can change yourself. Perhaps it's time to feel less frustrated and focus on your life's work.

Tender your letter of resignation. It will reduce by half your levels of self-caused anger.

To Whom It May Concern: "I resign from fixing others. I focus solely on fixing myself. I listen to problems without the urgency to fix anything. I don't stick my nose into other people's business. I don't give any advice or suggestions to others unless I am repeatedly asked to. I don't berate others, or bring torment and turmoil into my life by seeking to control who and what I cannot control."

Write your own letter and read it to a counselor or confidant. Keep your feet within your own life hula hoop. Stop calling out people on issues they need to self-manage.

Activity 3- "WHAT IF..." Mind Racing: Imagine standing on the ground holding the reins of a bucking horse that is ready to crash its hooves onto your head. Worries are wild horses. Your job is to calm the horses instead of feeling small and out of control.

"What If..." catastrophic thinking magnifies fears over external events that have a very low probability of occurring in your life. These can be fears about illness or death, divorce, job loss, financial collapse, etc. They have about as much chance of occurring today as seeing a camel walking through your front yard. Possible, but not likely.

Make a list of your "What if..." worries. Examples: "What if I get the virus?" "What if I never get control of my anxieties and emotions?" "What if I made a mistake in switching my major or career?" "What if we break up?" "What if I never find a romantic relationship?" "What if I'm going crazy?" (Too late because I've already gone there.)

Try this self-correction: "Whatever happens, I know that I will have the necessary support to cope with it."

Mind Racers will push back with, "Yeah, but, what if I'm that one case in a million? You can't deny that it could happen. I could be the unlucky one!" Just because something could occur doesn't mean that it will happen. Let go of conflicts you no longer need in your life.

Anxiety and How to Cope With It

Do you fear getting the coronavirus? "What if ..." triggering and anxiety-provoking thoughts magnify fears. Here are seven "Even if ..." self-corrections to use:

- Even if I worry, I am still safe and okay.
- Even if my body gets worked up, I can still take it off alert mode.
- Even if there are changes beyond my control, I can adapt and control my attitude.
- Even if I start to feel sick, my body is still healthy and strong.
- Even if the virus spreads easily, that doesn't mean I'm going to get it.
- Even if I am at risk, I am taking the necessary precautions to protect me and my family.
- Even if I get the virus, I will be OK.

The mood of fear doesn't have to spread like a virus in your mind.

Activity 4- Couple Prejudices: Prejudices will try to divide you and keep you from talking honestly about ways to keep growing. As a couple, sit across from each other and take turns answering these questions to showcase changes you can make.

1. What is our mission or purpose as a couple? What are we seeking to co-create?
2. How can I be helpful to you when there's strife between us?
3. What do you fear most when we're at odds?
4. What would you like to explore in our relationship?
5. What would cause you to fire me as your partner?
6. What would cause you to give me a raise as your partner?
7. How can I show you more compassion as a partner?
8. What are you afraid of to ask for from me?
9. On a grading scale of A, B, C, D, F what grade would you give our conflict management skills?
10. What three little things could I do to take our grade up one level? What could you do?

Prejudices are like termites that try to eat away at the home of your love. Giving voice to silent tensions frees you and your partner to love more deeply and completely.

SIX

CRITICAL FEEDBACK IS CRITICAL TO YOUR GROWTH

"Feedback is the breakfast of champions."

—Ken Blanchard

TALK2ME© CRITICAL FEEDBACK ZONES	
Controlling Inaccurate Feedback (-)	**Constructive Accurate Feedback (+)**
Is my aim to coerce and control?	Is my aim to reach and teach?
Outcome: Stunts Growth (*Shame*)	Outcome: Promotes Growth (*Change*)

🗩 The Talking Stick

It was a true delight watching Riley and her two sisters grow up. All four of us loved the outdoors. We would often go hiking, shelling on the beach, and wading down rocky creeks to catch crawdads. As you might know, the wildness of nature teems with healing hugs and messages.

Many Ohio hikes in muggy, hot August weather found us cooling off in streams shaded by overhanging tree limbs that sheltered us from the sweltering summer sun and heat. We took refuge as a family and found peace in these places of Mother Nature. My mind could release the cares of psychotherapy work and refocus on the joys of fathering.

Little Riley would fill my cargo hiking short pockets with prized fossils and rocks to cart home. Before I knew it, my pockets would be bulging at the seams and poking me in the leg. With amazing stealth, she would slide smoothly in beside me for a quick second to drop off a new found prized rock in my pocket. I still have some of these rocks, fossils and stones in my office and home. I've always felt at home outside, safe and protected, in the wide open skies.

Our love for the outdoors also inspired another invention: Our family Talking Stick. In Native American lore, various tribes used a Talking Stick in group pow wows to ensure conversations didn't get out of control. The rule or custom was to listen to the person who held the Talking Stick. When that person was done talking, the Talking Stick was passed to the next talker. This practice slowed tempers, encouraged careful listening and provided time to cool off, if needed. When there's a conflict or emotionally sticky issue, the Talking Stick keeps talking to one person at a time.

My daughters loved playing in the woods. They built a teepee, made bows out of tree branches, and one day Riley created a Talking Stick. Riley's "Talking Stick" was a 6-foot ash-tree branch that she found by the river in the woods. She meticulously sanded it until it was smooth to the touch and she decorated it. Old shoe laces tied on an assortment of snazzy ornaments, shells, pine cones, different shapes and sizes of wood that looked like whistles, feathers and fake fur. Rawhide twine wound around the pole for good gripping. The Talking Stick was really inventive and occupied Riley's creative play time.

Today, the Talking Stick leans in a corner of my office, right underneath the "How Are You Feeling Today" poster of emoji faces. When I begin to feel frustrated with a client who interrupts me, the Talking Stick reminds me that I must not be delivering my feedback correctly for their ears to hear. Ultimately, it's up to each one of us to give feedback that is helpful and balanced, and teaches new skills that can be applied in daily life. Getting mad and getting even put you behind.

How does the Talking Stick apply to you? Before you enter into tense talks, imagine the "Talking Stick" in your hand. Feedback sessions are smoother when you slow the mind and cool overheated emotions. Be aware as you manage your escalating mood. And you know why feedback sessions will go better, right?

- Valid balanced feedback packaged specifically for your communicator type challenges you and nurtures your growth in unexpected ways.
- Because Empathizers are their own worst critics, you give them a more balanced diet of positive verbal feedback to access their strengths.
- Because Instigators are their own best cheerleading squad, you give them a more balanced diet of constructive criticism to alter their weaknesses.
- As a PRO, you choose to listen to helpful feedback and block hurtful feedback.

If you are an Empathizer, you need to be careful not to overthink or over-analyze sharp feedback that feels cutting to you. In contrast, Instigators need to slow down their critical thoughts before they say rude things they'll regret later.

As a general rule, if you're an Empathizer, you need to hear more accurate positive feedback. If you're an Instigator, you need to hear more accurate negative feedback.

Hitting Someone With the Talking Stick Is Not Allowed

The Talking Stick metaphor grounds you. It reroutes knee-jerk reactions and fearful attitudes into open orderly talks that don't boss other people around.

Inappropriate feedback—too much or too little, too loud or too quiet—is harmful to personal and relationship growth. As Winston Churchill put it, "Criticism may not be agreeable, but it is necessary. It fulfills the same function as pain in the human body. It calls attention to an unhealthy state of things."

What does the Talking Stick have to do with your feedback life?

- No stick, no talk. (Taking quality time to talk improves listening.)
- No stick, no interrupting. (Interrupting with questions or arguments is disallowed.)
- No stick, no whining, complaining, or wearing a mad face. (Temper tantrums are discouraged.)
- No stick? Listen carefully and caringly. (Distractions are removed to improve concentration and problem solving.)
- Stick? Speak honestly, but not hurtfully. (Being honest solves problems and puts no one down.)
- No hitting someone with the Talking Stick. (Using raw aggression to get your way is a primitive act that wrecks your reputation.)
- Stick to the stick and that's no bull-stick. (Temptations will always come your way to wound with words; ignore the temptations.)

As much as Riley and her sisters might have wanted to, yelling and hitting someone with the Talking Stick were not allowed. The loudest voice often makes the least important point. Holding your tongue and listening instead of interrupting gives feedback a chance to be completely voiced and completely heard. Listening to feedback from the Empathizer or Instigator stylistic view of the sender works wonders.

Whenever you choose to use constructive criticism to improve, you will achieve more than you think yourself capable of.

Instead of actually holding the Talking Stick in order to be allowed to talk, use your inner self-calming talk to keep your mood in check and your mind open when times are tense and talks are tough. Keep on hearing the content of the message and thinking about it. The message sender and the message receiver have equally valid and valuable roles.

🗩 Law 6: Critical Feedback Is Critical to Your Growth

Most people function best when they give and receive a healthy balanced diet of feedback. The purpose and function of feedback is to improve personal communication performance. If you're a mature communicator, you voluntarily ask for and learn from feedback that differs from your self-view. You don't fight to be right; you strive to learn from times when things go wrong. Accurate feedback helps you to see clearly what part you played and what you can do differently to achieve the results desired.

Empathizers are prone to give too many positive compliments. Instigators are prone to give too many negative critiques. Neither tactic alone helps close the gap between where you are now and where you would like to be tomorrow. Too many sweet positives or too many salty negatives will stunt your growth. A balanced mixture of sweet and salty feedback is best.

PRO Rule: The master communicator has become proficient at giving accurate and helpful feedback.

Pre-planning, delivering, and packaging feedback designed to appeal to the specific Instigator or Empathizer brain you're talking to works best. Why walk upstream and frustrate yourself by fighting against the flow of the river? In today's workplace and home space, much feedback is unbalanced—too permissive or too restrictive. Giving credits and constructive criticisms speed up change and promote growth.

Here are quick tips for **Airing Feedback** that works well for both types:

1. Decide Type
2. Remove Feelings
3. Focus On One Key Point
4. Write It Out Before Talking
5. Package Feedback Delivery

Instigators give blunt feedback without being asked. Empathizers hold back critical feedback for fear of harming the relationship. Both of these fears must be faced and overcome to excel. Although it's true that sharp feedback can sting your ego, you are wise to continually strive to learn from feedback.

In this chapter, you are going to learn one of the most challenging communication skills. How do you give and hear helpful critical feedback that creates personal and professional growth? Let's first take a serious look at the obstacles that might be standing in your way.

Empathizer Feedback Obstacles

Empathizers become more balanced through hearing and reflecting upon helpful positive feedback while rejecting false critiques designed to manipulate the mind. One humble Empathzier put the challenge of listening to positive feedback this way, "I don't want to appear selfish, stuck up, or better than other people."

Most Common E-Type Feedback Obstacle: Sad Empathizer moods block giving and receiving accurate and helpful feedback.

If you're an Empathizer, use these clues to tell when you're in a feedback slump and need to pump up your mood:

- I brush off praise.
- I overthink criticisms.
- I magnify false feedback.
- I don't push back when I'm right.
- I lose confidence in a disagreement.
- I compromise instead of standing my ground.
- I try too hard to please others and it hurts me.

Empathizers take in and wear bad moods that don't belong to them. Negatalkers who want to hurt Empathizers know how to do so. A hit to the heart!

Hard Conversations for Empathizers: Here's what you need to say when tape is over your mouth but your point of view needs to be respected and reviewed:

- "I'm not sure you heard me. Would you repeat what I just said?"
- "You keep interrupting me. Can we agree to hear one another out?"
- "Let me be blunt. My main point that I need you to hear is _____."

If you're an Empathizer who wants to be at peace with yourself, you need to be self-approving, and behave in confident ways when disapproved of. Your self-esteem is not up for grabs. Being too humble for your own good does no one any good. Being too "sweet" causes cavities.

Remember that not all feedback is equal or accurate. It shouldn't be given equal weight. Negatalkers have agendas they are trying to push off on you. You've got to make up your own mind about the worth of feedback. Good feedback, including good constructive critique, won't make you feel shamed or blamed. Toxic feedback, on the other hand, makes your soul feel poisoned.

Instigator Feedback Obstacles

Instigators become more balanced by hearing and reflecting on helpful negative feedback. One proud Instigator put the challenge of listening to negative feedback this way, "I do nine attaboys and then get slammed for one 'oh, shit.' It's hard to listen to any of it."

Most Common I-Type Feedback Obstacle: Mad Instigator moods block giving and receiving accurate and helpful feedback.

If you're an Instigator, use these red flags as cues to stop debating and open your ears to listen and hear feedback:

- Mad attitude: "What you're saying is making me mad."
- Nitpicking about small details: "It happened one year ago, not two years ago."

- Interrupting to interject and deflect: "You're overreacting. It's nothing personal."
- Quick to invalidate the authenticity of the feedback: "That's not what other people I've talked to think is true."
- Focus on the exception to the behavior: "Really, I do it all the time? I didn't do it last week."
- Reject feedback: "I don't think that's true at all."
- Make excuses: "If it was such a big issue, why didn't you bring it up sooner?"

Hard Conversations for Instigators: What to do when you feel tongue-tied and don't know what to say? Here are three simple options:

- "I don't have the words. I don't know exactly what to tell you. But I do hear you."
- "I cut you off. I'm sorry that I interrupted you. Would you repeat what you were saying?"
- "Let me see if I'm accurately hearing what you're really saying. You're saying _____."

Hearing feedback is a "correction in direction" that makes your life journey more enjoyable. Just remember this: If getting feedback doesn't scare you just a little bit, then you're not getting enough quality feedback.

In a Conflict, Can You Spot a Fired-Up Instigator?

Instigators get hot under the collar fast and react rashly when they see something going off course. They have the compulsive need to fix problems fast.

When I (Dennis) moved my counseling practice into a new building, I parked in an end spot in the outdoor parking lot to protect my car doors from getting dinged. My kids used to tease me about this. As I hopped out of my car and grabbed my briefcase, I felt upbeat because I was looking forward to my brand new digs.

Before I could lock my car, a man I didn't know aggressively sandwiched his car into the spot next to me at 7:30 a.m. He jumped out of his car like a growling lion. I was stunned to see this strange sight at my new professional office building in an upscale neighborhood. As his whole body puffed up, I noticed his bulging neck veins and reddening face. Then he verbally unloaded on me:

"What do you think you're doing parking here!" he yelled menacingly.

"Oh, I didn't realize there's assigned parking here. I moved into my new office space over the weekend," I replied nervously.

"There isn't assigned parking, but you're parking in my spot!" he bellowed, unfazed by his irrational comeback.

"OK. No problem. Listen, I'll just move my car so there's not a problem," I replied, still a bit stunned.

"Don't make this mistake again!" he threatened as he jumped back into his Jaguar.

As I got back in my car and parked as far away from "his" spot as I could, I reflected on his fast anger attack. I wondered if he might have been carrying a gun. Luckily, I had learned to control my Irish temper by helping angry sociopathic and schizophrenic patients in forensic psychiatry. In the past, I would have allowed myself to "get my Irish up" and be provoked. I would have fired back out of stupid pride. But I have taught my kids, and have dutifully practiced, that it's best to get along with your neighbors and not crap where you eat.

Come to find out, this man's name was Denny, and he was my new office neighbor. Geez, fate sure has a way of educating and enlightening us. In fact, Denny worked as a very successful small family business owner of an equipment supplier, and his wife worked with him as his office manager.

Denny and I got to know each other better over time, and I chose not to bring up the parking-lot incident. But Denny, being an Extreme Instigator, apologized for his outburst and acknowledged that he was having a bad day. It sounded good, but I quickly learned that Denny had a pattern of getting into fights with many, many people, including vendors. He had the reputation of being a ticking time bomb but an expert in his field.

Denny was a tough-charging Instigator, a good guy who defaulted to anger, and a successful business professional. He let anger get the best of him, and he died a few years later of a massive heart attack.

The unfortunate reality is that anger is addictive and can cause black-outs and relationship destruction. I was saddened but not surprised. Anger kills. And outbursts of anger kill loving relationships. Over time, I came to like Denny, and I miss him.

You Don't Have to Go to Mood Extremes When Someone Else Does

Knowing how both types will go to predictable extremes when over-stimulated emotionally will greatly help you remain calm and confident when tempers rise. You won't be thrown off your game. It's nothing personal. It's only the business of favoring the communicator type you are.

Look at the predictable Plexiglass walls each type erects when fearful of being hurt. Expect those walls and don't let them block your journey to who and how you want to be. Although not every defensive distraction will apply to you, look for patterns in your behavior so you can recall them when next you find yourself in a tight spot fussing with your opposite.

Instigators set the mood temperature in every room they enter. They:

- Are mood pitchers
- Are less sensitive in relationships
- Like to debate
- Give blunt feedback fast without being asked
- Interrupt people so as not to lose their place in a conversation
- Admit to having a hard head
- Conceal feelings of not being good enough

- Shelve negatives by focusing on positives
- Will wear a mad face but feel unworthy when triggered.

Accept the defensive habits of both types without giving them too much credibility.

💬 How to Spot an Empathizer Caught in a Sticky Web of Conflict?

In *Lord of the Rings: The Twin Towers*, the two main hobbit characters, Frodo and Sam, are on an epic journey to destroy "the one ring to rule them all" in the fires of Mount Doom to save the realm. Before entering the evil lands of Mordor, they must traverse "the pass of the spider" where Shelob, a giant-spider demon, captures and eats those who try to navigate its tunnels. Frodo ends up getting caught in one of Shelob's many large and sticky webs; Sam fights the spider to the death.

As dramatic as it might sound, Empathizers can also feel caught in an Instigator web of sticky emotional manipulation. When they feel used or poisoned, Empathizers will perceive they are emotionally un-safe. That's because emotions get ramped up in Empathizers who believe that relationship conflict leads to disaster. This makes Empathizers feel like hostages. They shut down, lock up, and bottle up their frustration until they can't take it anymore.

If you're an Empathizer, you do have your breaking point. When you're in a conflict, you will appease and adjust your attitude to try and accommodate the other person, typically an Instigator, to mitigate the conflict. After a while, Empathizers who give and give and give will feel taken advantage of and explode. This shocks the Instigator partner, who typically doesn't perceive anything was ever wrong in the first place.

Case in point: Empathizer Carol and Instigator Steve came to me (Dennis) for marriage counseling because their golden retirement years were turning into a rusty disaster. Carol objected to Steve working part-time because his health wasn't the best and their bank account was fine. But soft-spoken Empathizer Carol would back off when Steve got grumpy and refused to give his notice to the company. Carol compromised for several years, but finally reached her limit. Carol felt taken advantage of because Steve had promised to stop working and repeatedly broke his promise to her.

In one session, Carol looked sadly at me while describing how she felt about the broken promises, "It took awhile but I reached my boiling point. This time I was done being taken advantage of. He didn't take my feelings into account, and didn't act like I was important to him. What I know about myself is that when I'm done as an Empathizer, I am done, and there's no going back. That's why I suggested we come to marriage counseling. I knew it was reaching the point of too little too late."

Steve loved Carol deeply. He replied, "I wish she would have spoken up sooner. Sometimes I need to be hit by a 2x4 in my thick head to hear what's being said. I didn't know that my unilateral one-sided decisions would hurt Carol so much. I had no idea. I know she's sensitive. But I swear that I didn't realize that not including her in my part-time work decisions would hit her so hard and make her feel invalidated."

Having a moderator who understood Empathizer vs. Instigator feedback styles helped Steve and Carol understand each other's views. They moved to the middle ground when Carol and Steve took turns holding the metaphorical "Talking Stick." Steve added, "Look. My marriage to Carol is far more important than my work." Carol had never heard Steve say that before, but it was his truth. Carol and Steve decided that retiring was the right choice to make for them both.

This client story captures the repetitive dynamic of "I'm not important!" and "My feelings aren't validated!" that destroy the happiness of many well meaning E-I couples. Carol learned how to speak up more to Steve when she felt unimportant but had an important point to make.

Empathizers are mood sponges who want to please because they:

- Are mood catchers
- Are more sensitive to others unhappiness
- Like to talk things through calmly

- Don't want to hurt anyone's feelings with critical feedback
- Listen longer at deeper levels but won't push back
- Admit having a big heart but being a pushover
- Trust gut feelings but second-guess their best decisions
- Are self-critical and will magnify negative feedback whether accurate or fake
- Will wear a sad face but feel inadequate when triggered

During a conflict, Instigators will talk bluntly and sound tough when they feel vulnerable. Empathizers will be too agreeable and not share their genuine views of what to do.

Our goal here is to help "desensitize" both types to behavioral cues that "trigger" subconscious prejudices. Experiencing these defensive postures as par for the course will equally help both types team up more successfully.

ᗰ Don't Tell Me What I Feel or Think

The Empathizer-Team can irritate the Instigator-Team without intending to, and the reverse. Red flags of hurt and anger get thrown on the field of competitive communication all over the place.

You might wonder why this happens so frequently at work and at home. To put it simply, you're misinterpreting the actions and motives of your opposite type. You "react vs. respond" to incidents, causing more misunderstanding and hurt.

For example, a female Empathizer partner said to her Instigator husband, "You tell me what to feel. You dominate me, talk down to me and you're loud and condescending. That's how it comes across to me. I want us to make things better in our relationship. But all I get from you is that I'm supposed to shut up and be silent."

It's easy to get frustrated when you don't understand or appreciate the view of your opposite type.

💬 Change Occurs When Feedback Is Heard

Much feedback is useless. Or let's put it another way. Most feedback is biased because it's contaminated with toxic emotions. You want your feedback to be helpful not hurtful, accurate not distorted, heard not ejected. For mental balance, if you're an Instigator you will require more constructive criticism. If you're an Empathizer you will require more regular praise, and that includes from yourself.

Crucial Feedback Question: "When I'm designing my feedback, is my true intention to be helpful or hurtful?"

Helpful doesn't hurt. A good feedback rule is to step back, take a deep breath, and stop and think before you speak out. Package your feedback by communicator type to help obtain superior results.

Use this insider view of how Instigators and Empathizers like their feedback cooked and delivered. Which of these two views do you use for giving or receiving positive and negative feedback?

- If you're an Empathizer, you take negative feedback more personally and give it more weight.
- If you're an Instigator, you take negative feedback more impersonally and give it less weight.

- If you're an Empathizer, you're a better self-criticizer after tough conversations.
- If you're an Instigator, you're a better self-promoter after tough conversations.

- If you're an Empathizer, you prefer multiple feedback streams that come at you slowly.
- If you're an Instigator, you prefer a single feedback stream that comes at you fast.

- If you're an Empathizer, you forget positive words spoken about you in a dispute.
- If you're an Instigator, you deflect negative words spoken about you in a dispute.

- If you're an Empathizer, you naturally give positive compliments during strife.
- If you're an Instigator, you naturally give constructive criticisms during strife.

• If you're an Empathizer, you are a better ego-booster when others hurt. • If you're an Instigator, you are a better ego-buster when others need to change.
• If you're an Empathizer, you magnify weaknesses seeing the glass as half empty. • If you're an Instigator, you magnify strengths seeing the glass as half full.
• If you're an Empathizer, you dwell on what you don't have. • If you're an Instigator, you dwell on what you're going to get.

Change occurs when feedback is heard. Package and deliver your feedback in the preferred Instigator-Empathizer talking style of your partner. It will have a better chance of being heard, and you'll be happier with the results. When what you're doing isn't working, do something different.

> **PRO Rule:** I-Types require more *constructive criticism* while E-Types require more *constructive recognition*.

Tough conversations don't have to crash into resentment walls. Feedback often gets jumbled between E and I-Types when fear hijacks the conversation. Let's take a look at this in our next diver story told by Riley as a new PADI Scuba Instructor.

🗨 Diver Communication Comedy

As a new dive instructor, I had several underwater comedic events where miscommunication was the culprit.

I spent one college summer on Catalina Island teaching scuba in the Pacific Ocean. Located in the Santa Monica Bay, off the coast of Los Angeles, the diving is known for kelp forests that are home to a multitude of marine mammal and fish species. Typically growing to 40 feet from the base to the tops, kelp forests are akin to the Amazon jungle—many different species live in these ocean forests.

On one occasion, several friends and I went weekend diving to Lion's Head, a popular kelp forest in a protected area where lobsters and fish could grow large, fat, and happy without getting hunted by spear fishermen. But after a dive excursion, I would walk by the grill area and see large fresh fish or lobsters being prepared to cook on the open barbeque spit. It made me wonder where they were caught but it was hush-hush if you wanted to eat dinner with the locals.

As a diver, I would see different things each time I ventured into the same 50 feet of kelp forest. This included harbor seals, sea lions (you stay away from those), great white sharks, star fish, eels, octopi, bat rays, and abalone. The orange garibaldi fish were native to the island. During one particular hot afternoon, one of my diving buddies got stuck in the kelp in the underwater forest off the shore near Lion's Head. He was starting to get a bit panicky, as he couldn't see how or why he was trapped or how to get out.

From my viewpoint there wasn't much of anything to panic about. Seeing that my fellow diver was caught up in kelp but that the situation wasn't serious, I wanted to have a little bit of fun with my friend. So as I was rapidly swimming towards him, I decided to dramatically pull out my large dive knife and wave it wildly as a bit of a joke.

His eyes went wide and he started to tug frantically. I hadn't thought about how my actions would impact someone who already felt trapped and cornered.

Then my training kicked in, like a warning alarm in my brain, I hand signaled to him "OK" and signed for him to slow down and take some deep breaths. Once I knew he was calm, I was able to confidently cut him free.

The way you change your communication pattern, when what you thought would work isn't working, often saves the day.

💬 That's Not Funny...But I Was Only Kidding

You might perceive as funny, something that your partner or teammate perceives as profane. Or perhaps you give feedback that is unintentionally taken as a harsh criticism. Your intentions matter little at that time of delivery; it's how your feedback is received that matters most. You need to keep in the center of your mind that the impact of your actions during a conflict matters a great deal. How you react can calm the situation...or cause panic.

When we surfaced, we were all laughing so much it hurt. "That wasn't funny," my laughing dive buddy exclaimed. "I thought something was seriously wrong."

Another dive companion chimed in, "I thought you were finally going to kill him!" We laughed so hard from comic relief that tears rolled down our red faces.

Apparently, when someone is afraid, it's not the best time to joke around. It's not funny! He clearly didn't understand the sharp blade of my joke. Could I blame him? No. I would have felt the same way in his shoes, ahem, fins.

Have you felt threatened or shut down by someone who was only joking? Mistakes can be mended right on the spot when you're aware of what communication moves to make to correct the situations. Even the extreme of abusive language can be stopped.

It's not what you say, but how the other person perceives what you say that really matters. Saying, "I was only kidding," isn't kosher when feelings have been hurt. Empathizers perceive the "kidder" to be making light of being a jerk instead of taking responsibility for their actions. When you see a startled Empathizer look, match where they're coming from emotionally, instead of brushing off their feelings.

Joking is only to be used with Empathizers who feel emotionally safe. You can't joke an Empathizer into feeling better. In contrast, Instigators believe that teasing helps people loosen up and feel less tense. These nuances matter. Bottom line, your carefully crafted feedback will help you and those you love grow.

💬 Drive the Fear Out of Feedback

Everyone has experienced feedback scenarios that went sideways, whether they were the sender or receiver. You will proactively address potential problems when you understand how Instigators and Empathizers prefer their feedback to be packaged.

The key reason people withhold accurate and helpful critical feedback from you is that they fear they will make matters worse. Often couple clients say, "We let conflicts fester for fear of things blowing up. It becomes an avoidance cycle. We need rules of how to argue. Time doesn't solve the problem."

But avoiding hurt today only compounds the problem tomorrow as relationship resentments grow. We need to know how to speak well to one another when emotions are welling up.

I (Riley) have worked with the Civil Air Patrol since I was a teen. My dad used to drive me to meetings. As a senior leader now, I still enjoy working with teenagers to build strong characters.

One summer while leading a week-long encampment at the Wright Patterson Air Force Base, I heard one of my Instigator cadets describe why he felt agitated with the feedback approach of another Empathizer cadet. This illustrates the importance of using and consciously choosing your tone of voice and feedback approach.

The Instigator Cadet said: "It's like when Empathizers talk, they are using commas instead of periods. The cadets won't take your commands seriously if you talk like, 'Sooo, if you could, ah, please…change that, that would be great. Alright?'"

Instead, they should just say: "Please change this. Understand?"

This illustrates how each Communicator Type likes to give the kind of feedback they prefer hearing, and they get irritated when it's not going their way. It's similar to how you like your steak cooked. Not understanding the feedback preferences of others causes unnecessary friction and frustration because you serve them the wrong meal.

You will reduce the fear of feedback and make fewer mistakes by using the feedback preferences of your opposite type. Start practicing your new I-E feedback tools in easy situations before you take them into the heat of a communication battle. In the next section, we are going to show you how to package your feedback according to the I-E type of the receiver you're talking to so you don't get caught up in feelings.

💬 Empathizers Giving Feedback to Instigators

If you're an Empathizer, respect the fact that Instigators will feel anxious and agitated if you don't stick to one concrete specific critique or subject. The Instigator brain likes one thing to concentrate on at a time, even though they will brag that multi-tasking comes easily to them. Stick to one point or topic area...then drill it home...and leave it alone.

How Instigators prefer their feedback served so you have a better chance of being heard:

- Don't sugar coat...no fluff.
- Get right to the point...no beating around the bush.
- Use a few short specific examples...no lengthy explanations.
- Use eyeball-to-eyeball and kneecap-to-kneecap concentration.
- Don't smile....use ferocious eyes...do not look down at the floor.
- Speak in a louder volume and confident tone...don't be hard to hear and don't sound wimpy.
- Answer questions quickly...don't clump feedback by opening up a new can of worms.

Remember, just pick one singular issue to focus on. Be direct and tell it like it is and don't fluff it up. For example, an Empathizer mate might say: "When you yell...I stop listening. Will you lower your voice so I can better hear you?" Singular Instigator Feedback: One problem = one fix.

One Instigator said this about critical feedback, "There's nothing super-positive or warm-and-fuzzy about spot on feedback. Your self-image and ego take a humbling. It's a shock seeing yourself in the mirror or the tape played back. It's a different perspective, but helpful."

As an Empathizer, it's perfectly fair to plan in advance how to package and simplify your critical feedback message and not fear pushback. As one E-wife put it, "I can let the lion roar and my hair fly back, and then I fearlessly repeat my point." Accurate feedback helps you stay engaged in a relationship that grows from feedback with less incidents of conversational coercion.

💬 Instigators Giving Feedback to Empathizers

If you're an Instigator, respect the fact that Empathizers prefer their feedback presented like a slow, home-cooked dinner, not a fast microwaved meal. E-Types are sensitive souls who listen carefully and take your words as gospel. So mean what you say and say what you mean without being mean. Empathizers will feel anxious and shut down if you come across too harsh or too forceful. Use the compliment sandwich approach: State a positive, insert a negative in the middle, and end on a positive note.

How Empathizers prefer their feedback served so you have a better chance of being heard:

- Use their first name first off.
- Smile and use a softer tone of voice.
- Lower the pitch of your voice...talk slowly.
- Don't fidget, look away, look at your watch/smartphone, or invade body space.
- Don't fly through feedback and then fly off....you will be seen as disrespectful and insincere.
- Listen and don't interrupt...then listen some more to quell listener anxiety.
- Use the compliment sandwich approach...sincere positive, insert correction, positive ending.
- Allow as many questions to be asked as needed for clarification.... do not show impatience.

- No finger pointing or arm waving...disrupts ability to focus on hearing the feedback.
- Say the positive obvious. For example, "I'm telling you this because I know you strive to improve at what you do every day, which I appreciate."
- End on a positive note or joke.
- Smile! No one ever died of a positive attitude.

Remember, feedback (unlike revenge) should *not* be served cold. Empathizers like the car to be warmed up on a cold winter day before taking off on a hard journey. E-Types are harder on themselves than other people are. And the compliment sandwich approach works well with Empathizers. For example: (+) "Dennis, you're one of the most efficient workers I know. (-) However, you didn't fill out the Q9120 form that's due. (+) I know you will take care of it today."

Different strokes for different folks. Use the customized feedback preferences of your I-E talk partner. There's no longer any reason to repeatedly run into invisible feedback barriers that frustrate you.

🗩 Let's Switch It Up in a Feedback Session

When you're in a feedback session, you now know to be flexible and use the Instigator or Empathizer style of the person that you're talking with. But what are some of these key attitudes you will use to harmonize like a tuning fork with your opposite type?

• If you're an Instigator, you will **Listen** a minute longer. • If you're an Empathizer, you will **Talk** a minute longer.
• If you're an Instigator, you will **Ask** more open-ended questions. • If you're an Empathizer, you will **Tell** exactly what's expected.
• If you're an Instigator, you will **Praise** more often. • If you're an Empathizer, you will **Critique** more often.

- If you're an Instigator, you will talk **Slower** and in a softer voice.
- If you're an Empathizer, you will talk **Faster** and in a louder voice.

Reversing these stereotypical roles for each type is a powerful way to "see the light" of the opposing type. It's with open hearts that we learn, love, grow, and change.

🗩 Don't Interrupt Me

Interrupting Chicken is a children's book written by David Ezra Stein about "Papa Chicken" attempting to read a bedtime story to Little Red Chicken. The cover of the book shows Chicken excitedly asking Papa Chicken, "This bedtime story is called *Interrupting Chicken* right, Papa?" with the Papa Chicken replying, "Yes. Now please don't interrupt the story."

This children's book holds wisdom not reserved solely for children. Even if interrupting is done out of excitement to make an unforgettable comment, it can still cause frustration in the storyteller and keep you from hearing valuable information. For example, if you're an Instigator, you will jump in and interrupt a speaker to dispute or debate a point or set the record straight. It's only natural for you. You're not shy about speaking up or disagreeing. You believe that mixing it up helps everyone come up with better solutions.

On the other hand, if you're an Empathizer, an interruption will throw you off your game, causing you to forget what you were about to say. This results in the Empathizer feeling frustrated and disrespected without the Instigator ever really knowing what happened. Worse yet, the Empathizer might shut down and think: "It's no use talking to them. It's always their way or the highway."

Emotions dictate outcomes for better or worse. For example, when tensions rise, Instigators are viewed as bullies who fight to be right. In reverse, Empathizers are viewed as sissies who won't stand up, speak up, and fight when their idea is the best way to go.

> **PRO Rule:** Interrupting defeats the reception of helpful feedback.

The solution to almost all human problems is to create open lines of communication between closed minds.

🗩 Interrupting: How to Get Things Back on Track When Talks Go Bad

Mid-sentence interruptions by Instigators make Empathizers feel invisible, inferior, unheard, and disrespected. You can avoid trouble by saying: "Can I interrupt you here?" Or "Whoops, I jumped in too fast. Sorry. Please continue what you were saying."

Interrupting is seen as a power play to get your way and will be met with listener resistance.

Even Empathizers won't listen seriously to what's being said when an I-partner or teammate fusses and interrupts. That's because intense passion disrupts clear factual reasoning.

Here are some examples of Instigator comments that disrupt the flow of good talks:

Instigator-interrupting-Empathizer: *"What is your reasoning? ...Why did you decide that? ...What exactly were you thinking? ...That's just not right! ...I don't agree with you. ...Give me some specific examples of why you have a problem with that?! ...I wouldn't have done it that way ...I think you're taking this way too personally ...You think I always do that, really?... That's not true ...I'll prove it to you because I didn't do it last month when..."*

The silent internal E-scream: *"Will you stop interrupting me? I can't hear myself think!"*

An aggressive Instigator approach makes Empathizers feel like they're sitting in the witness chair being cross-examined by a prosecuting attorney.

💬 Self-Correcting: Thoughts Instigators Use to Shut Up

Do you think Little Red Chicken was an Instigator or Empathizer? I-Types have great ideas, but blurting them out causes E-Types to shut down and become unreceptive. And if you're in an I-Type marriage, being too bossy or blunt also shuts down the Instigator partner who wears the Empathizer hat in the relationship.

The most costly critical feedback mistake I-Types make is not listening openly to alternative views. Instead of listening, Instigators strive too hard to solve problems fast. By interrupting the flow of talks, they pay a heavy price. Here's how to coach yourself to keep calm and listen more than you speak:

- I'll listen a minute longer, even when I think I am right.
- I'll look at things from the E side of the street and be sympathetic.
- I'll listen longer, and I won't interrupt.
- I'll chill out and let go of needing to solve the problem and listen actively.
- I'll slow down my mind to focus on the details of what's being said.
- I'll listen to what I might not like hearing without putting my spin on it.
- I'll paraphrase what's being said when there's a pause.
- I'll ask open-ended "what" or "how" questions to clarify what's being said.
- I'll be open to a different view of what is the right way to proceed.
- I'll use a warm, friendly even tone of voice and won't get hyperactive.

Are you able to attend an event or listen to a view that you typically judge and dismiss as wrong? For example, could you attend a religious service or political rally different from your own? Or, are you too chicken to go? Doing the new requires shutting up your internal self-talk and having the poise not to curse or throw a fit. If you are brave enough to try this, you will find out just how difficult it is to stay calm and listen to what your brain screams is crazy or wrong.

If you are an Instigator, you dominate a decision in the short run only to lose the respect and affection of your Empathizer or Instigator partner over the long haul. Genuine listening changes all that.

💬 Look Who's Talking: Our Differences Don't Have to Lead to Disputes

Awareness of Instigator vs. Empathizer habits and prejudices resolves most escalating conflicts and mood-driven power plays. Empathizers listen too much, and Instigators don't listen enough.

In our experience, undisputed "interrupting" is a leading cause of the failure to communicate. It's second only to not focusing your entire attention on the speaker to hear their unique point of view. We challenge you to practice using focused listening to hear the view of the speaker that differs from your favorite view. Knowing how to "interrupt interrupting" is a significant tool to use within yourself and with others.

Healthy disagreement yields better solutions. Interrupting a speaker frustrates this process. If you don't like to be interrupted, then you need to manage your mouth and not interrupt others.

• If you're an Instigator, tame your tongue because words have power.   • If you're an Empathizer, let go of false feedback instead of dwelling on it.
• If you're an Instigator, apologize when you interrupt a speaker's train of thought.   • If you're an Empathizer, repeat what you're saying when you've been interrupted.
• If you're an Instigator, be more comfortable giving genuine compliments.   • If you're an Empathizer, be more comfortable giving constructive criticisms.

> - If you're an Instigator, seek more input before making decisions.
> - If you're an Empathizer, make decisions quickly and stick to them.
> - If you're an Instigator, when you're in a dispute practice being patient.
> - If you're an Empathizer, when you're in a dispute practice being assertive.

You know what shuts down open lines of communication: Interrupting, nagging, bragging, criticizing, threatening, excuse-making, and not owning up to your part in the problem. In an ideal world, you would receive about an equal balance of helpful positive and negative feedback.

A Little Give Between the Generations

This next example is about a mutigeneral communication mishap that hit a gay couple with young children like a ton of bricks. Generational roles are ripe for unintended run ins.

Following *TALK2ME©* Laws, you know that Communication Types are not about gender, role, age, race, religion, or sexual preference. They're all about communication between Instigators and Empathizers.

Mishandled critical feedback is often at the root cause of intergenerational family conflict. And when fearful moods trigger distorted prejudices, boundaries get blurred and words you can't take back get spoken. Unresolved disagreements about appropriate discipline, safety issues such as wearing seatbelts and bicycle helmets, bedtimes, proper foods to eat, and religious observances, etc. can wreak havoc. Adult children often feel resentful that the grandparents aren't honoring their wishes or rules.

Grandparents have the unmatched opportunity to deeply enjoy both their adult children and grandchildren without the burden of carrying heavy responsibilities. But when there's an opinion or power dispute, cooperative moods crash fast. Because they have more experience, grandparents often take the position that their opinions ought to carry more weight. It takes real humility for older grandparents to be corrected by their own adult children and change.

In one case, I (Dennis) worked with a mixed Empathizer-Instigator lesbian couple with elementary school-age kids who felt strained by the grandparent's values. They had strong opinions about not texting while driving, but failed to use seatbelts for the children. When asked to use seatbelts, they responded, "Seatbelts weren't used in our day and we turned out OK. It's just for a short distance." Tensions were rising about a growing number of incidents. Both partners felt their preferences as parents were being dismissed. They even wondered if they were being dismissed and discounted because they were a female couple. Pebble-sized resentments grew into boulder-sized resentments that could no longer be swept under the carpet.

The Empathizer partner grew more hurt and angry, believing her Instigator partner was not standing up to the Alpha Instigator grandparents. She thought her partner could make them tow the line. The Instigator partner defended her older parents believing that trying to talk to them would prove fruitless. The couple disliked conflict and tended to steer clear of it. But the young parents were so frustrated that they decided to write and send to the grandparents a carefully written seven-page letter that stated their grievances and requested a sit-down family meeting.

PRO Rule: Don't give feedback when you're frustrated.

Their thoughtful letter wasn't received well. It was seen as disrespectful and taken as an insult. The family meeting turned out to be a two-hour disaster. The alpha grandparents scolded the couple, "We were blindsided by your letter. Why couldn't you just talk to us first? How are we supposed to know what's bothering you if you don't tell us? Family forgives and forgets and moves on. We're sorry you feel this way. This is ridiculous sitting down and talking about feelings. Don't take this personally, but we're just saying that you have to stop being so hypersensitive. Our conscience is clear. If you don't want us watching the kids, well, that's up to you."

Later that night, the Empathizer partner revealed to her beloved Instigator, "I feel put off and don't really want to be around your parents anymore. Their words have consequences." Tensions grew within the couple as the Instigator husband tried to explain to her Empathizer wife why the grandparents had made some valid points. "Oh, I get it. Now you're taking their side against me!" the Empathizer partner cried.

Granted, an apology wasn't enough. The damage had been done and both sides had made communication mistakes. How to put salve on the wounds? I asked the couple what could be done now to improve things moving forward. This is what they wanted to hear from the strong-willed grandparents to set things right:

- Thank you for the feedback.
- Your feelings are valid.
- You're right. This didn't need to turn into a dispute.
- We're sorry that I didn't make you feel important or respected.
- You're trying to protect your family by speaking up.
- We could have listened to and asked for your input earlier.
- You are the parents. We respect how you would like things to be done.
- We need more time to reflect on what you're telling us.

The issues got straightened out when all parties came to my office for an intensive consultation. I served as the translator for both parties. Tensions in relationships are released when honest feelings are shared and differing perceptions are carefully aired.

At the close of the two-hour meeting, the adult children said, "Thank you. All we really needed was a little give. A bit more give and a little less take." The grandparents solemnly replied, "And we just needed to know if we're still needed and our expiration date hasn't passed."

Empathy transforms relationship disputes into personal revelations.

💬 Feedback Practice: A Little More You— A Little Less Me

Balanced feedback, defined as giving and receiving a mixture of helpful and accurate negatives and positives, works best for the PRO who wants to keep growing and changing.

These practice exercises have been designed to bring out the strengths of your dormant opposite type. Check them out and measure the results you receive.

1-Compliments: If you're an Instigator, give positive feedback to everyone you come across this week. Make it a simple honest acknowledgement of little positive behaviors. Examples: "You've got a great smile." "Thanks for being on time." "You're fast getting my order out." "You've got a great sense of humor." "Your boss is sure lucky to have you on their team." "Your voice on the phone is very pleasant." You get the gist. Just say something nice and watch the reaction.

2-Critiques: If you're an Empathizer, give straightforward directive feedback in a calm voice this week. Examples: "Pick up a loaf of bread." "Let's go to Denny's for dinner." "Watch the kids for an hour so I can go out to exercise." "No, I won't do that." "Change your tone of voice if you want to talk to me." "Pick up the kids at 4 PM from school." "No more excuses. I won't tell you this again." Just say something direct and watch the reaction.

3-Getting Feedback: If you're an Instigator, ask for input before making a solo decision. For example, "How would it work for you if I go golfing with my buddies this weekend?" Or, "I'm looking at buying a new car, would you like to come along to the lot with me?" Or, "I'm thinking of putting 15% into savings for a rainy day. What do you think?" Just be available and approachable and watch the reaction.

4-Giving Feedback: If you're an Empathizer, directly say what you expect to be done and when. For example, "Let me be blunt. Take out the garbage before you go to bed." Or, "Let me cut to the chase. We're over the budget and need to eat at home the rest of the month."

Or, "Let me be perfectly clear. You need to stop cursing right now." Just set a boundary and watch the reaction.

5-Corrections in Direction: Just like an airplane uses an aileron wing flap to modify course, you can give a correction in relationship direction using this format.

- **Step 1:** When you _____ (describe behavior in few words without blaming attitude).
- **Step 2:** I feel _____ (use a feeling word such as vulnerable, sad, frustrated, upset, scared, confused, etc.).
- **Step 3:** Would you do _____ instead?" (Make a request in a caring tone of voice.)

Example: "When you drive and text ... I feel scared ... Would you please not text and drive when I'm in the car with you?"

6-Ask and You Shall Receive: Asking more "what or how" questions is an effective way to see through the viewfinder of your talk partner and walk in their shoes. Here are some gold standard examples.

- "How can I be more helpful?"
- "What can I do right now to reduce your stress?"
- "What roadblocks are you running into that I can remove?"
- "What did you enjoy most about your day?"
- "What would you like me to do more of?"
- "What would you like me to do less of?"
- "What kind of mood do you like me to be in?"

Now, don't take this wrong, but many of your requests will initially fall on deaf ears. The point is to *change your own mood on your own*. No one has to do what you want them to. But at the very least, relationship respect and abandonment of the resentment misery-go-round require you as a PRO to make your desires clear without pushing your partner into a corner.

It's no longer about "my way or the highway" or "your way or the highway" but "our way" on the two-way communicator highway.

💬 Translating Verbal and Non-Verbal Cues Accurately

"Watch your facial expressions," my (Riley's) drill-sergeant-like PADI Course Director bluntly bellowed as we surfaced from the pool's bottom. We had just undergone a relentless amount of mock-panicked diver response exercises.

It had been my turn to respond to a training exercise of a panicked diver, and apparently, I had the unfortunate tendency to act as a human mirror and reflect the panicked facial expression of my practice pupils.

When you are training to be a scuba diving instructor, you expect rigorous training, advanced dive theory, and long days out at sea. How you explain skills and how you communicate nonverbally are all critical to your students' learning and safety. You can't afford to keep making communication mistakes that compromise safety in extreme circumstances.

I had to tap into being aware of my *feelings* and my students' *feelings*. My facial expressions needed to display the calmness I needed my students to feel. When giving feedback I use this same technique: Instead of mirroring and heightening a scared emotional state, I focus on the emotional state I want to create in that setting. For example, if I want calm, I create a demeanor of calmness.

Let's check into the messages you are sending with your verbal and non-verbal actions, including facial cues and voice volume and tone. How Empathizer actions are perceived through Instigator eyes on a deep dive:

- When an Empathzier grins when feeling uncomfortable or ill at ease….This indicates personal dislike to an Instigator.
- When an Empathizer gushes too complimentary…This conveys incompetence to an Instigator.
- When an Empathizer is on time…This signals respect and competence to an Instigator.

- When an Empathizer has an urgent attitude and passionate energy…This implies motivation and commitment to an Instigator.
- When an Empathizer has shoulders back, head up and eyes locked on target…This denotes friendliness and confidence to an Instigator.
- When an Empathizer goes down one voice tone…This shows authority to the Instigator.
- When an Empathizer speaks with a louder voice volume…This indicates seriousness to an Instigator.
- When an Empathizer speaks crisply, is quick, and makes a brief point…This shows respect for time to an Instigator.
- When an Empathizer pushes back assertively…This signifies engaging in problem-solving to an Instigator.
- When an Empathizer uses a game face during a dispute…This implies composure and being in charge to an Instigator.

Constructive feedback is critical to task improvement but is not critical of the other person.

It's all in how you view what you do. Knowing these clues and alternative views of body language for both types will be helpful to get a grip on the nuances of giving and receiving critical feedback during crucial conversations.

Jealousy: Is It OK to Have Friends of the Opposite Sex?

Asking tough questions is critical for your growth as a communicator. Maybe you're too shy to ask tough questions because you might hear an answer you don't want to hear. But by clarifying and confirming, chances are you will resolve the inner conflict and clear your head of distorted thinking. Don't be fearful of necessary confrontations. From the ashes of conflict springs new growth.

This next client feedback story is about a college Instigator couple who were in a long-distance relationship. Lauren thought Ben was developing feelings for two of his female friends, but she didn't want to appear insecure and immature. Feelings of mistrust and suspicion grew. "He didn't tell me his female friends slept over. It triggered my insecurity and overthinking, both of which got out of my control. It would have been easy if I could have met them. I could see how they acted with him. I can tell with body language a lot if someone is flirting or put off that I am there."

Due to the physical distance, Lauren decided that approaching Ben directly on the phone in a caring tone was the wisest course of action to take. Feedback was an attempt to clarify for Lauren's sake that she had nothing to worry about, if that was the true story.

Text to Ben, "I just got done with my therapy session, and my therapist and I talked a lot about my overthinking and insecurity when you hang out with Karen and Katie. He said that I should ask you a question so I could move on and not overthink the situation any more. I'm curious if I can call and ask you that so I can clear my head of all the bad stuff and move forward."

Ben texted back: "Yeah, let's do it! I'll be out of class soon."

This is Lauren's description of the phone feedback session:

I was hesitant at first trying to pop the question. Ben said, "Don't be afraid. Just ask me the question." But I couldn't finish my sentences.

So I asked him the question I had in my phone, "Do you have any emotional or sexual connection with either Karen or Katie? And have they ever expressed if they have an emotional or sexual connection with you?"

He quickly said, "No. No, I don't. I have never felt that way toward them. I don't see them like that at all. I don't find them attractive in a romantic way to be honest."

I said "OK. Cool. That's what I wanted to ask you. I needed to ask you this to clear my over-thinking. It was overcontrolling my thinking when I was alone at home and you would hang out with your friends."

Ben said, "I understand, I want to make you comfortable. I would never lie to you."

Lauren described to me how their feedback session gave her a huge sense of relief, a tremendous weight lifted off her shoulders, "I felt teary.

I'm a strong independent woman. It was so much easier to get an answer in the first place instead of worrying about it. That one-word 'no' answer solidified my confidence. My question was direct. His answer wasn't wishy-washy. I felt a great sense of relief. I could trust the answer more. It stopped the flashbacks I was having about affairs from the past that had hurt me. Now I can officially move forward knowing that I have that answer in my head that can stop me from over-thinking."

> **PRO Rule:** If you're afraid to say something, that might be the very thing you need to say.

"When I'm away and not physically with him there's not a chance to see what's going on or receive physical signs of affection. His love language is showing me how he cares through touching. He doesn't express how he cares verbally, he shows me physically. I'm the exact same way. It's like looking in a mirror. As Instigators, we both need to evolve in our love languages from showing we care to sharing in words how we care."

The mood of jealousy ramps up many conflicts that crash loving relationships into a stone wall of resentment. But not this time.

⤸ Whose Rules Are We Following Anyway?

Feedback is like listening to a song on the radio in your Empathizer blue or Instigator burnt orange communicator car. You make the volume louder or softer as you tune to the Instigator or Empathizer channel frequency that sets a good mood tone.

But what can both types respectfully do when passions overtake reason? You can adopt and use the feedback strengths of your opposite type to promote and tap into the synergy of creative problem-solving.

What an Instigator caught in an emotional riptide during a feedback session needs to tone down:

- Tone down being too blunt and appearing harsh.
- Tone down competing too hard and pushing too hard to get your point across.
- Tone down taking credit or bragging instead of giving credit where credit is due.
- Tone down using implicit or explicit threats to force your view on a partner.
- Tone down throwing a fit or getting into a mad snit.

What an Empathizer caught in an emotional riptide during a feedback session needs to tone up:

- Tone up boldly by saying and going after what you want.
- Tone up taking credit and doing the right thing even when it hurts somebody.
- Tone up repeating your point and not backing down when others frown.
- Tone up making your case and making it again using as few words as possible.
- Tone up standing up tall and raising your voice loud to make your point heard.

Divisions are bridged and conflicts resolved by accepting your rules aren't used by everyone. In fact, what's perceived as fair for I-Types is perceived as unfair for E-Types, and the reverse. Most conflicts escalate from misunderstandings of what each type judges as "fair play" from their opposite type.

🗩 The Fine Art of Constructive Criticism

Winston Churchill once said, "Criticism may not be agreeable, but it is necessary. It fulfils the same function as pain in the human body. It calls attention to an unhealthy state of things." It is your duty to refine your constructive criticism skills in a way that cultivates insights without poisoning the relationship with resentment.

Criticism is a fine art. Better yet, it is like rain. It must be gentle enough to nourish personal growth, and not too hard that it damages the roots. Costly mistakes are made when E-Types and I-Types go to extremes when emotions take over. For example, I-Types who come across too strong cause resentment or pain instead of growth. E-Types who come across too gently stunt growth and wither relationships from the lack of feedback.

If you're an Empathizer challenging an Instigator, use respectful directive commands:

- I have some important feedback for you. Do you have a minute?
- This is the problem as I see it that needs to be solved...
- Here are the facts as I see them...
- I'm just going to be blunt and honest here and not hold anything back...
- Something's been eating at me that we need to discuss...
- I can't be responsible if something doesn't change....
- This is the bottom line of what needs to be done...
- What I'm expecting to happen here is....
- Will you repeat what I just said? What are you hearing me say?

A "directive commands" approach meshes well with the Instigator mind that's set on accomplishing tasks and solving problems quickly.

Delivering quality feedback is common sense but not commonly done. Improper feedback causes unneeded conflict. The "Inner Critic" of Empathizers and the "Inner Cynic" of Instigators create noisy communication channels that block the reception of healthy feedback.

Both types must do their fair share of work in the team canoe and paddle in the same direction to avoid going in circles. Riley and her younger I-Type sister, Kasey, experienced this principle rather literally on a family canoe trip. Starting downstream, they began playfully arguing about the fact they weren't paddling in the same rhythm. The result? The canoe went in only one direction...round and round.

If you're an Instigator confronting an Empathizer, use friendly "What/How" indirect questions:

- What are your thoughts?
- How do you feel about this solution?
- What are the options as you see them?
- How do you think we should handle this better?
- What can be done to make this work out more effectively for everyone?
- How can we change this with fresh ideas and novel approaches?
- What next steps do you recommend we take?
- How can I provide the resources you need to get the job done?

A "friendly questions" approach works extremely well with Empathizers who have creative solutions to vexing problems if you care enough to sincerely ask them.

A wise old owl of an Instigator put it this way: "Who-o-o's the problem? Whenever I want to see *who's* the problem, I look in the bathroom mirror." Funny but true.

We've seized upon the opportunity here of setting forth some "scripted responses" based on I-E talk technology that will work when other approaches fail. Moreover, by following the *TALK2ME©* Effective Communication Laws, we respect that you will develop your own language style and approach that works when nothing else will.

Instigator Actions that Drive Empathizer Reactions

If you're an Instigator, your moods are highly contagious to Empathizers. Consciously choose "softer" actions to leave sensitive souls better off as a result of rubbing elbows with you.

- When an Instigator shows a smiling face…The Empathizer perceives being approved of.
- When an Instigator looks with soft eyes…The Empathizer perceives being listened to.
- When an Instigator uses a soft voice tone…The Empathizer perceives being understood.
- When an Instigator expresses appreciation…The Empathizer perceives being valued.
- When an Instigator chit chats…The Empathizer perceives being respected.
- When an Instigator uses a calm pace and movements…The Empathizer perceives safety.
- When an Instigator takes time to over explain…The Empathizer perceives trust.
- When an Instigator is unhurried, not rushed, and breaks off focus…The Empathizer perceives being cared for.

These are some of the trade secrets to consciously trigger your opposite type to work closely and respectfully with you. By controlling moods and giving helpful feedback the true value of win-win solutions is brought to life.

Confident Empathizers

If you're an Empathizer, how can you act confidently when fearful moods linked to inaccurate critical feedback are getting you down?

- Know your solutions need to be heard.
- Skip the self-criticism.
- Be kind to yourself.
- Speak up more.
- Be focused on a single goal and stay on track.
- BE DECISIVE.
- Walk and talk with a self-confident air.

- Move from task to task with ease.
- Tell a joke or listen to something funny.
- Let go of needing approval for what you know is right to do.
- Don't sweat the big or small stuff.
- Leave work at work as best you can.

Calm Instigators

If you're an Instigator, how can you find your calm center when you're spinning from impatient moods linked to accurate critical feedback?

- Know toxic words alter team moods.
- Skip critiquing or blaming anything or anyone.
- Speak kindly to others.
- Listen more and speak less.
- Act nice and play nice.
- Change the mood channel when irritated.
- BE APPROACHABLE.
- Name that mood to change that mood.
- Ask for help when you feel vulnerable or "less than."
- Take time to do the "extras" or "feel-goods."
- Be patient with your progress.
- Open your mind to new beliefs and more effective ways of doing things.
- Tolerate different approaches to solving problems.
- Be receptive.

Be a Confident, Calm and Competent PRO Communicator

Gaining experience planting fertile fields of feedback will make you a mixture of both types. That's because in your super-conscious brain, you have easy access to both Empathizer and Instigator toolkits and mindsets.

By being a blended "Empagator" or "Instithizer" you will create a calm and confident attitude to:

- Shake off bad moods and stimulate good moods in others.
- Fight against bad moods instead of fighting with others or faulting yourself.
- If you're an Empathizer, practice walking and talking like an Instigator.
- If you're an Instigator, practice walking and talking like an Empathizer.
- If you're an Instigator, listen intently to others with whom you disagree and don't argue to win.
- If you're an Empathizer, speak up for your rights and interrupt others with your insights.
- Periodically ask your spouse or boss for a mixture of critical feedback with a little credit sprinkled in.

Being a flexible communicator is a top trait of PROs. You might go to extremes at first when you engage the tools, but your behavior will even out as you gain experience.

Effective communication ignites change. In our last chapter together, we are going to show you how to embrace change instead of being afraid of it.

💬 Key Takeaways: Critical Feedback Isn't Critical of the Person

- Apply Law 6: Critical feedback is critical to your growth.
- The loudest voice often makes the least important point.
- The master communicator has become proficient at giving accurate and helpful feedback.

- Sad Empathizer moods block giving and receiving accurate and helpful feedback.
- Mad Instigator moods block giving and receiving accurate and helpful feedback.
- A balanced diet of positive and negative feedback cultivates change.
- In any feedback session, stick to one key point or criticism at a time.
- Package and flexibly customize your feedback by Instigator vs. Empathizer receiver.
- Change occurs when feedback is heard.
- I-Types require more *constructive criticism*.
- E-Types require more *constructive recognition*.
- Instigators blurt out words that hurt Empathizers, words they later wish they could take back.
- Empathizers withhold criticism only to explode later like a volcano.
- Interrupting disrupts the reception of helpful feedback.
- Instigators need to pause and pre-package their feedback before speaking.
- Empathizers need to put facts over feelings and speak up more assertively to Instigators.
- Interrupting is seen as a cheap power play and will be met with listener resistance.
- Interrupting defeats the reception of helpful feedback.
- Don't give feedback when you're frustrated.
- In a dispute, pause to write out your message so you think before you speak.
- In a conflict, show you understand before you demand to be understood.
- If you're afraid to say something, that might be the very thing you need to say.
- Confident Empathizers need to be more decisive about feedback.
- Calm Instigators need to be more approachable about feedback.
- Delivering quality feedback is common sense but not commonly done.

Critical feedback doesn't cause resentment or retribution. It's not what you think you said but how your message was received that matters. You have a better chance of having your feedback heard when you blend the feedback styles of both Empathizers and Instigators.

💬 Law 6: Sharpen Your *TALK2ME©* Skills

Activity 1- Call for a Feedback Session: Ask your partner, "Can we have a feedback session?" Do not say, "Can we talk about something?" which causes fear and defensiveness. Obey the mood rule, "No giving feedback in a frustrated mood." And follow the focus rule, "Take on only one issue at a time!" Stick to one issue per feedback session when you're in a reasonably calm mood. Disallow piling on multiple complaints or criticisms. Make a safe space where focused criticism is about behavior not character. Listen instead of lecture. Disclose your inner feelings.

Activity 2- Feedback Conflicts I've Wrestled With: Improper feedback causes unneeded conflict. Think a moment about conflict situations that you've wrestled with. Some are inside you, many are with people you care for, some with institutions and even technology.

Accurate partner feedback is invaluable: 70% of partner pairs are I-E, 15% are I-I, and 15% are E-E. Think of you and your partner. Are you and your partner an I-E, I-I, or an E-E pair?

Now, share with your partner your feedback habits and preferences. Select from the list below or create your own questionnaire.

1. Share a situation where positive feedback has inspired you.
2. Share a situation where constructive criticism has helped you.
3. Share how you handle compliments, and whether or not they are hard to hear.
4. Share how listening to critical feedback is challenging for you.
5. Share the conflict styles of your parents and how they influenced you today.

6. Share how you will package your feedback based on your Instigator or Empathizer partner's preferences.
7. Share how you would like constructive criticism and constructive recognition to be handled in your relationship going forward.

Self-disclosing can make people nervous. Just chat. Have some fun, and go off on tangents. You're not interrogating each other. It's OK to use humor during these exercises to handle feeling uncomfortable.

Now on the serious side, hurtful feedback often triggers fears of abandonment. This causes standoffs and broken rules. Overall, determine with your partner how you want them to address conflicts.

Decide in advance what mood attitude you will use in response to a disagreement. If you're talking to an Empathizer, can you use a slower calmer approach? If you're talking to an Instigator, can you use a faster directive approach?

Activity 3- Interrupt Your Interrupting: Interrupting causes unnecessary relationship tensions that disrupt intimacy. Instigators who interrupt put Empathizers in bad moods and trigger prejudices. Empathizers who don't speak up are perceived as ineffective. This week, flip the switch:

• If you're an Instigator, go without interrupting anyone. When you slip up and do interrupt, simply say: "Sorry about that. I interrupted you. Please continue with what you were saying."
• If you're an Empathizer, repeat your point when interrupted. Simply say: "I need to interrupt you here and say something before you move on to your next point."

Not listening, interpreting, and misinterpreting a sender's message are correctable communication mistakes. Listening instead of interrupting promotes emotional agility, is a key problem-solving ability.

Activity 4- Statements to Say During a Feedback Conflict: Offensive feedback causes a standoff. Try some of these transactions when conflict rears its ugly head and ears are getting clogged up:

1- "That's a valid point." This respectfully acknowledges an Instigator's point of view without condoning it.

2- "Did I do or say something that offended you?" This clarifies and confirms what point that's being overlooked but needing to be heard.

3- "Thank you for speaking up." This builds trust with shy Empathizers who feel their point of view has been bulldozed.

4- "What's on your mind?" This is a good feedback starter question that gets to the heart of the issue if you are sensing something is wrong. This allows the other person to again share with you what they are thinking instead of assuming you know or accusing them.

5- "You're probably right." This reduces frictions that are heating up with Instigators who are getting mad.

6- "Any input?" This taps into solutions an Empathizer is keeping safeguarded or stashed away due to fear or lack of trust.

7- "Would you say that in a different way?" This transaction slows down the speeding freight train of the Instigator mind.

8- "Let's meet in the middle." This helps your Empathizer trust in knowing that it's not going to be your way or no way.

Depending on your Communicator Type, select from the list above or create short go-to statements or questions that reliably defuse conflicts.

Activity 5- Feedback Trade Secrets of Empathizers vs. Instigators: Critical feedback is not critical of the person. Each communicator type has trade secrets of how to handle difficult feedback. Empathizers follow the rules of being nice while Instigators follow the rules of being blunt during feedback sessions.

Instructions: Take turns. The Empathizer will read the "Nice People" section to an Instigator partner who listens carefully. Then the Instigator partner will read the "Blunt People" section to the Empathizer partner. Afterwards, ask and answer the following questions:

- How are you impacted by hearing your opposite types' trade secrets?
- Were you aware of the hidden feelings lurking behind the social scene?

- Do these sayings generally fit the inner experiences of both partners?
- What light bulbs turned on, if any, from honestly discussing these insights?

💬 Nice People

If you're an Empathizer, you are perceived as being a nice person who is a pushover. That's true…and prejudicial, because:

Just because I'm quiet…doesn't mean I'm weak.

Just because I'm silent…doesn't mean I'm in agreement with you.

Just because I'm reserved…doesn't mean I have nothing to say.

Just because I stumble over my words…doesn't mean I'm not right.

Just because I don't look confident…doesn't mean I'm not competent.

Just because I look away…doesn't mean I'm intimidated by you.

Just because I'm sad…doesn't mean I'm not content.

Just because I'm cautious…doesn't mean I avoid taking risks.

Just because I'm smiling…doesn't mean I'm happy.

Just because I'm talking…doesn't mean I'm saying what I want.

Just because I'm nice…doesn't mean I don't feel resentful.

Just because I'm a pushover…doesn't mean I won't or can't push back.

If you're an Empathizer, or know someone who is, challenge them to speak up quickly when things aren't going right.

💬 Blunt People

If you're an Instigator communicator, you are perceived as being a blunt person who won't be pushed around. That's true, but also prejudicial because:

Just because I'm direct...doesn't mean I'm strong.

Just because I'm loud...doesn't mean I'm sure of what I'm saying.

Just because I'm outgoing...doesn't mean I have something important to say.

Just because I use a few words...doesn't mean I'm right.

Just because I sound confident...doesn't mean I'm competent.

Just because I look intensely...doesn't mean I'm not intimidated by you.

Just because I'm mad...doesn't mean I don't appreciate you.

Just because I'm reckless...doesn't mean I avoid taking precautions.

Just because I'm frowning...doesn't mean I'm not happy.

Just because I'm talking over you...doesn't mean I'm saying what I feel.

Just because I'm blunt...doesn't mean I don't feel vulnerable.

Just because I'm pushy...doesn't mean I don't feel sad when I don't get my way.

Blend the strengths of both Empathizer and Instigator communicators today, and you'll notice positive changes almost immediately.

Activity 6- Parachuting in Constructive Recognition and Compliments: Pick a random day to surprise your partner with affection and compliments. Think of creative ways to just "drop in" or parachute in needed supplies of recognition to a partner who is starving for your recognition and attention.

- What text can you send that will surprise and delight?
- What handwritten note can you leave on the table?
- What loving and fun voice message can you share with your partner that brightens their day?
- What picture and short message can you send that will make your partner feel happy? For example, a pet photo.
- What task or chore can you take off their plate?
- What big hug and smile can you lay on your partner when you greet each other after a long day?
- What song can you share with your partner that sends a message of love?
- What humorous card can you take time to pick up at the store that will amuse and delight?

Being a blended Instigator-Empathizer mood-balanced communicator works best to reduce your stress. The light bulb will come on when you creatively use *TALK2ME©* tools.

SEVEN

EVERYBODY WANTS TO BE A BETTER COMMUNICATOR, BUT NOBODY WANTS TO CHANGE

> *"Be the change that you wish to see in the world."*
>
> —Mahatma Gandhi

💬 Becoming Your Own Change Agent

Now that you understand in your head how to be a better communicator, here comes the hard part. You actually have to change how you listen, speak, and interact with other people in your life every single day. Change is good. Change is hard. Change requires you to make these new concepts completely tangible—minute-by-minute and day-by-day, until this new way of communicating becomes your new norm. Are you ready?

Growing up, my (Riley) after-school routine was to walk down our street from the bus to our home in a cul-de-sac. I enjoyed listening to music on my portable CD player, thinking about the school day and looking at the towering trees that would change with each season. As I walked, I could be totally alone with my thoughts, able to explore self-reflection.

As I walked, some of my thoughts were extraordinarily deep, such as contemplating my place in the world. Others were charmingly shallow and echoed my age, including the note I once dropped into the locker of a crush. The note had three little boxes that said, "Do you like me?" "Yes" … "No" … or "Maybe." Written notes were our form of texting back then. That's how I got my first boyfriend, who checked the "maybe" box.

Self-reflection promotes your growth, too. Life *is* change. The dictionary definition of change is "to be different." You will go through seasons of change in your life, too.

> **PRO Rule:** The only constant in life is change.

Along our long and curving driveway, was a dinner plate-sized paving stone with a Gandhi quote carved into its surface. "Be the change that you wish to see in the world." I loved to read that quote each day. As a ritual, I would mentally recite a pact with myself as I walked past the stone that I would make a difference in the world, whatever it took.

Creating change starts within. So, taking stock of what's changing around you just might as well start with a good look at yourself in the mirror. If you want better communication, don't wish it upon others, embody it in yourself. Become your own catalyst. I know, I know. It sounds corny, but life won't let you deny this truth for very long. Conflicts and crises signal a change is needed.

Be a student of change. Study change. Life is always changing. You might as well be, too.

Law 7: Everybody Wants to be a Better Communicator, But Nobody Wants to Change

It's a simple truth. Change is tough. Everyone wants to be better, but most people are hesitant to change. Humans are more eager to change other people. On some deeper subconscious level, you might believe your personality is set in stone. It seems impossible to do things differently. This prejudice is warped social scripting not reality. You're free to change, ready or not.

But don't get discouraged when you hit a rough patch. Rewiring your brain can feel like it's one step up and two steps back. Expect it. You're going to be using new parts of your brain.

If you're an Instigator, you will become more sensitive to how you make others feel. You will discover the hidden strengths of your "Inner Empathizer." This also means you will likely hit unexpected roadblocks and notice a stirring of unfamiliar feelings. Pent-up sadness could give way, like a dam that bursts open, releasing an uncontrollable flood on a valley below.

If you're an Empathizer, you will become more desensitized to sad moods that don't serve you. You will discover the hidden strengths of your "Inner Instigator." This also means you might go to the extreme of your opposite. Anger might come spewing out like a dormant volcano that was suddenly awakened, startling those who witness this unexpected eruption.

You will start experiencing new things if you open yourself up to change. You might be unsure if you're "doing it right" or perhaps you will start questioning if it's all really worth it. This requires digging deep into your inner resources. Never forget that a hidden opportunity awaits within any crisis.

Fear of change is normal. Change is a process. By using *TALK2ME©* tools, you sign up to create deep change in your life instead of feeling angry or resigned that others aren't changing around you. The major drain on your forward movement comes from wasting your efforts doing what doesn't work. This amounts to beating your head against a brick wall and expecting the wall to change.

In the Ohio springtime, a robin builds a nest in the dwarf pine tree by my (Dennis) window. When it sees its reflection in my window, it pecks and pecks at his own reflection, perceiving it to be an enemy aggressor. His flurried pecking leaves white beak marks on the window, and sometimes it seems as if he might knock his brains out. My solution? I taped a piece of colorful paper to the window pane. It changed the robin's view of what to fear; a new perspective changed his automatic response.

But humans have bigger brains. Humans tend to do more of what isn't working to make it work the way they think it should go. Trying to screw a round peg into a square hole will bloody one's fingers. Law 5 is a friendly reminder to pause, take a step back and a deep breath, when what you're doing isn't working. Then clearer heads prevail in a conflict instead of reacting with a prejudiced perception that's going to knock your brains out.

In therapy sessions, conflicts between family members are commonplace. Each aggrieved party complains that the other party isn't accepting or showing respect for their view. What resolves the objectionable behaviors of the "difficult" spouse, sibling, father, mother, etc. is to change how you think of them and thereby change how you react to them. For example, changing how an adult son speaks confrontationally to his elderly mother reduces the number of times the mother gets angry and criticizes her adult son for acting like a selfish spoiled brat. Conflict patterns indicate that you are reacting like the robin who pecks repeatedly at the same window, to no avail. A change is in order.

What to do when what you're doing isn't delivering the expected results? When others aren't changing, and you're feeling repeatedly frustrated? Change your expectations of *who* should change. The only person you have the power to change is you. Change *you* by letting go of trying to make the other person change. And then change your expectations of what the results should be. As you've previously learned, you must accept the reality that the solution isn't in your current, emotionally compromised view.

At heart, inner peace is ultimately what most people strive for. Changing old ways of thinking isn't easy, but change is necessary to transform your frustrations into peace of mind.

💬 You Can't Teach Old Dogs New Tricks?

Subconsciously, people don't think they can change after a certain age. In truth, not changing makes you feel old and tired. Changing, however, makes you feel young and free.

But as the antiquated excuse goes, "You can't teach an old dog new tricks." But that's BS and you know it. It's never too late to change.

Communicate Like a PRO

The truth is you *can* teach old dogs new tricks when the master is patient. Even if you don't want to change, or have failed to change before, you can change today. By allowing the *7 TALK2ME© Laws of Effective Communication* to permeate your life, you purposefully take charge of change.

As a metaphor, if you're standing in the sand at the edge of the ocean, and you're being beaten down by high surf waves, you can make small steps to move your life in a new direction. You can step back onto the safety of the beach, or you can move out beyond the breaking waves on your surfboard. You can smooth out the stress waves in your life.

Your attitude about change is more important than your age or history. Let's say it a different way: Your age has little to do with your change capabilities. In fact, research on neuroplasticity suggests that we can change our minds, literally—biochemically and structurally—all life long. We can grow new pathways in our brain and learn at any age. Change isn't frozen; it is a fluid event. And all change first begins with changing your mind. You can even change something people closest to you have been bugging you for eons to change.

Brutal self-criticism and critiquing others are the major ways you resist change. Ego-driven fights about who's right and who's wrong in the form of "Opinion Wars" are the second major way you resist making personal changes. Change isn't a rigid fixed view that demands the other guy or gal to change—but not you. In those situations, the only thing that remains static or still are repetitive fights that go nowhere.

You've also learned the insightful truth that the solution resides not in your view but in their view. Change is fluid. It's not hard, like ice. Much of your change efforts are fixed in place by your beliefs, such as, *"I can't change...*or *"I won't do it right so I might as well not try."* In this chapter, you will be changing your ideas about change.

Blaming yourself for not changing is self-sabotaging. Blaming others for not changing is relationship-sabotaging. This suggests that you stick to crappy communication habits because you don't like to change, not because it's not possible to change. Truth is you have the freedom to choose change or resist change. Effective communication creates change in your life. Why gripe about it? Being free to change is at the root of every victory.

Only you and those close to you can make the important decision. Choose wisely. Choose change.

🗨 Taking Advice to Change Your Life

Rejecting advice doesn't benefit anyone. Taking good advice will change your life. It sounds corny, but it's true.

Hardly anyone likes being told they're doing something wrong. Heck, many people have difficulty swallowing genuine compliments about their character strengths. But humbly accepting accurate helpful advice changes you. Accepting instead of resisting helpful feedback is a strength.

Empathizers need more constructive recognition, while Instigators need more constructive criticism. And as you've learned, critical feedback is critical for your growth. But in your new blended reality, a balance of both positive and negative feedback encourages you to keep on changing when the going gets tough.

> **PRO Rule:** Change happens whether you worry about it, or not.

Here's a professional feedback example that underscores your freedom to choose or refuse change. In my leader manager role, I (Riley) needed to give corrective feedback about the inappropriate behavior of a senior supervisee. This isn't so easy when the supervisee—in a subordinated position—is four decades older than you and reminds you that she has more experience. So I carefully planned out how to give constructive criticism to the older Instigator female. I'll call her Ruth. The problem was that Ruth could come across abrasively in her emails to our trainee group, a trait that turned people off. In fact, the harsh emails were at risk of causing volunteers to drop out.

> **PRO Rule:** Honesty solves problems.

I packaged the feedback as you've been taught to do in Instigator language so it had the best chance of being heard. And I delivered the feedback calmly and concisely. But Ruth rapidly fired back, dismissing my constructive criticism that our volunteers weren't responding well to her scolding emails. Ruth firmly deflected the feedback, by saying, "I'm German. I just have a German temper. *I am who I am.* If you don't like the way I send emails and communicate, then you might as well find a replacement for my position." As a classic Instigator, Ruth feared appearing weak or making mistakes that would take away her feelings of self-worth.

Ruth kept resisting the critical feedback that was critical to her growth. When you quit listening, you quit learning. To change, you need to accept your part in the problem with dignity. What is your attitude about hearing critical feedback that will change your customary way of doing things? My job was to give the feedback honestly. I can't "make" or force someone to change, and I wouldn't if I could. The power to change resides within us.

Ruth tried to turn the tables on me, and complained, "I did nothing wrong. There was nothing wrong with my email. If you have a problem with it, then I shouldn't be contacting people. Why don't you just do it if you don't like how I do it?" Confidence comes from making small positive changes in your life in spite of the fear of change. The first step is to hear accurate feedback that you might not want to hear. Be a change expert who doesn't fear failure or fear appearing foolish.

Instead of changing, Ruth stubbornly threatened to quit her volunteer role instead of changing her ways, even though there might be better ways to travel. When you quit listening, you quit learning and you quit changing. Demanding an apology is not changing yourself. Looking at the speck in their eye while ignoring the plank in your own eye blinds you to change possibilities. Criticizing another is not changing yourself. We encourage you to be a competent communicator who takes 50% co-responsibility for solving your side of the relationship equation.

PRO Rule: Blaming and complaining aren't changing.

"I am who I am. You've just got to take me as I am!" is showing your fear of change. Ruth represents every human being who gets defensive. Hers is the mother of all change-avoidant excuses. It stubbornly says that you can't change who you are, how you communicate, and basically that you can't be better. This might be fine if you're getting along happily and perfectly with everyone you know. But for all remaining Earthly humans, continuous improvement of communication skills is important.

You are wise to keep changing even when everything's going well. Always strive to change more than you blame or complain. Remember: Complaining isn't changing. Complaining fools your mind into believing that complaining alone will change your circumstances. But the truth is that complaining rewards you for not changing and it reinforces a feeling of powerlessness.

Be a changer not a complainer. Although the feedback I gave to Ruth was a hard pill to swallow, several weeks after the conversation, she showed significant improvement. Sometimes you don't know what impact you might have on another person until they've had time to lick their wounds and decide to apply the change in their life.

Working with our clients over the years (Dennis and Riley), we've discovered that the flame of growth can never be completely extinguished. Good moods give birth to good changes. Until the day we die, humans are blessed with repeated opportunities to change and choose the life we wish to live.

You are capable of change until the day you take your last breath, but why should you wait that long?

💬 Advice About Advice

So much priceless free advice is given but not taken. But by using the *TALK2ME©* Laws and PRO Rules, something quite astonishing is going to happen to you. Creative ideas will come out of nowhere. Our clients experience the "lightbulb came on" effect. You will see things in a new light that will change your life.

As a change expert, you infrequently give advice but frequently take advice freely given. So get ready. How can you keep your mind open to the "lightbulb came on" effect? Here are handy rules about giving advice:

- Just because people complain doesn't mean they want to change.
- Never give advice or feedback when you're in an angry mood. Never!
- Before offering advice, say: "Do you want my advice?"
- Empathizers change when they take their own advice.
- Instigators change when they hear the advice of others.
- Empathizers need to learn to stop listening to bad advice.
- Instigators need to learn to give advice infrequently.
- When offering advice, ask yourself: "Am I giving this advice with no strings attached?"
- Listen courageously to fair constructive criticism that comes up when you least expect to.
- When you get a "Yes, butttt…." reaction to your advice, simply ask: "Do you just need to vent?"
- Take your own good advice. Your intuitive advice is customized for your current situation.
- Don't throw your pearls of wisdom in the mud to be trampled by pigs.

Accept that you don't have to change. Decide for yourself when to make a change. Don't be too prideful. Take pride in accepting others' and your own good advice.

💬 A Battle of Opinions: What's the Right Way to Load a Dishwasher?

The hardest thing to change is your mind. It's also one of the few things you have total control over.

Much life-changing advice and helpful feedback dies on the vine. When you *have* to be "right" and *can't* be "wrong," you lose the freedom to change your mind. Remember that "right" or "wrong" are simply opinions or preferences informed by habit or family scripting. More important than your being "right or wrong" is whether your behavior is "effective or ineffective" in the situation.

Would you rather be right or would you rather be an effective communicator? Getting into a "battle of opinions" distracts you from the courage to look into the mirror of change. People often focus on stupid little stuff to upset themselves, such as grumping about doing the dishes or taking out the garbage. But judging what another person is doing wrong doesn't help you do more things right. Where's the give and take in that? Where's the equal effort to meet in the middle?

Affixing blame doesn't fix anything. As a marriage counselor, I (Dennis) have witnessed and interceded in many senseless couple feuds. One pretty common partner complaint is not putting the dishes in the dishwasher, or not loading the dishwasher correctly according to the rules. It would be funny if it didn't make partners so spitting mad and put a wedge between them in bed.

Couples now come in all different gender combinations. Not to worry. We think in terms of types, not sexual orientation. Our principles work equally well with any couple from any corner of the globe. Let's take a look at patterned moves of one Instigator couple who could be gay or straight and still act and sound the same way:

Instigator-1: "I don't want to fight with you about this. But you could put the dishes in the dishwasher for a change without my asking."

Instigator-2: "I was getting around to it. But you don't like my way of doing it. I don't see why it has to be your way. The dishes come out clean either way."

Instigator-1: "That's my point. Why can't you just put the dishes in the dishwasher right away so they won't get all gross? Why does it always have to be such a big deal with you?"

Instigator-2: "I can't stand you always nagging me. I come home after working a 12-hour shift at the hospital, and you act like dishes are a life-and-death matter. If you don't like how I do it then you can just do it yourself."

Instigator-1: "That's always your go-to place. Just walk away and throw up your hands and make threats. Is that too much to ask, or is it too difficult for you to do? If you don't want me to get on you, then why don't you just put the dishes away in the first place?"

Instigator-2: "Yes, but... when I do put the dishes away right away it's still not good enough for you. You always come right behind me and rearrange the dishes your way. It makes me feel like a child."

Instigator-1: "There's a right way and a wrong way to put the dishes in the dishwasher. I don't see why someone as intelligent as you are can't get that through your thick head."

Instigator-2: "See! That's what you always do. You put me down when you don't have it your way. That's your solution to everything. Why does it matter if the large plates are placed together and the small plates put in the dishwasher in a separate spot? Is it really that big a deal to you?"

Instigator-1: "You're the one who's making this into a big deal, not me. I've told you the right way to arrange the dishes and that the utensils go down in the rack except for the knives which are to be standing up. This isn't rocket science. If you did it right in the first place, I wouldn't have to go behind you and straighten up your mess."

Instigator-2: "Fine. Then do it yourself from now on if the dishes are so important to you." (Walking away from the dishwasher and leaving the kitchen.)

Instigator-1: (Projecting his louder voice aimed at the back of his partner who is leaving the kitchen.) "Fine. That works for me. You're useless!"

A metaphor for the clashing of wills is two mountain rams head butting. During ram mating season, males will charge one another fiercely, striking and pummeling their large, horned heads together. The sound can be heard for miles across a canyon. Each ram shakes its head before rearing back and charging again to head-butt even harder the next time. This pattern goes on over and over again. It's "I'm right because you're wrong!" in primitive form. Two wrongs don't make anything right.

It's the dumb things that destroy couples. We've all had a variation on this theme of being wed to our opinions instead of being married to our spouses. One wise Instigator said, "We Instigators need to go light something on fire so we have something to put out. I need something to work on...to stay engaged...I love adventure. I guess being a fixer who gets bored easily has its downside."

It's the dumb things that destroy couples. Truth be told, as a clinical psychologist, I've heard many different couple argument stories like this one. They all have in common a "battle of opinions" about "the right way" and "the wrong way," whether to load a dishwasher, do the laundry, make a bed neat and tidy, mow the lawn, and even whether the toilet seat is to be left up or down.

Oh, and don't forget how the toilet paper folds over or under on the dispenser roll. Little things are a big deal. Positive change happens when one kindness deserves another kindness.

💬 If *You* Would Change Things Would Work

"It's not me, it's them!" is a mood-wrecking ball that will tear down the home of your happiness.

All "opinions wars" demonstrate this fatalistic thinking error, "If you would change, things would work." The truth is, "Changing *you* will make *you* happy." Tactful criticism motivates people to change their behavior. Useless debating is deadly.

Do you paste your internal prejudices on the face of your difficult antagonist, the person who has disappointed your expectations? Everyone does. Much conflict is caused by people not behaving as you think they should. Namely, you get mad that people aren't doing what you want them to do when you want them to do it.

Empathizers think, "Why aren't they acting like me? Something must be wrong with *me*." In reverse, Instigators think, "Why aren't they acting like me? Something's wrong with *them*."

How you view someone dictates how you act toward them and how they react toward you. Are you the main cause of difficulty in your life? Of course you are. Seek to view things from a new point of view. "It's not me, it's them!" is a blame game fueled by subconscious prejudices. Blaming the other party avoids putting the responsibility squarely where it belongs: internal prejudices. The enemy is within and you will go without peaceful co-existence until you realize this fact.

Opinions are like belly buttons. Everyone has one. One type isn't better than the other, just different. What false idea do you feed yourself that prevents your changing? Is it "I can't change." And, "Why should I have to change when my partner isn't doing their part?" Or, "They've got to see it my way instead of doing it the wrong way."

When what you're doing isn't working, do something different. In our case example, the dishwasher problem masked the real hang-up. The real problem was the "unspoken rules" learned in childhood about the right vs. wrong way to load a dishwasher. Actually, dishwashers come with manuals, but who reads them? His mother taught him the "right" rules, and her father taught her the "right" rules. The two sets of rules didn't match.

A third higher option is to come up with new rules to suit the present day. Just because we have been taught certain rules as children doesn't mean they're right for all situations. It's more important to know what's effective than who's right.

What goes around comes around. Are your dishes more important than your happiness and peace of mind? If you expect respect and acceptance, then be the first to give it during a difficult change passage or life transition.

The Chinese Finger Trap

What can you do to get out of a rut? As one Instigator client put it, "I've tried hard to fix my partner for 15 years and that hasn't worked. I'm here to change *my* behavior to make *us* work better. Changing me changes the pattern."

A frustrated mood shuts down change. You do more of what doesn't work, instead of doing something, anything, new and different. When you feel irritated or stuck, you push harder in the same direction instead of doing the opposite, like letting go. To change, you must do something different, and that includes changing your view of what will fix the conflict.

Case in point: Riley and I will pass out a gag toy known as a Chinese finger trap to participants in our workshops. The colorful woven bamboo tube traps the victim's fingers. Did you ever put your index fingers in a Chinese finger trap as a child? Trying to pull your fingers out only tightens the trap. The harder you try to pull your fingers apart, the more stuck they become. You get frustrated. You squirm. You feel stupid. Then you want to break out of the trap pronto.

Do you remember the solution to the finger trap? It isn't using brute force and pulling harder. Pulling harder and harder doesn't work because it makes the bamboo trap tighten around your fingers—and escape all but impossible. To remove your fingers from the trap, you need to go in the opposite direction that your logical mind is telling you to go. This is an emotional puzzle. You need to relax your fingers and move them toward each other to the middle of the bamboo cylinder to free them. Isn't that a great metaphor? You need to pause and think calmly when what you're doing isn't effective. Overall, you need to move toward—not against—your opposite communicator type in order to gain freedom from the emotional traps of prejudicial ignorance.

Workshop participants doing this exercise often start laughing, sweating and gritting teeth. They say if they only had child-size fingers they could easily exit the trap. Some start looking for scissors. Some question why they signed up for our seminar in the first place. Some remember that the way to escape the trap is to push their fingers from the ends toward the middle. Everybody gets a good chuckle. But it's a takeaway tool that our trainees remember to use when solving relationship puzzles.

The downward spiral of poor communication is caused by continuing to do what isn't working. Continuing to do more of what isn't working is the definition of insanity. Doing the same thing over and over again while expecting different results doesn't work. It's the same as putting your car in reverse gear and expecting it to go forward. Then when you crash, it isn't fair to blame the car. When your mood is off, you're vulnerable to doing the reverse of what works.

Relationship problem-solving is the same. If what you're doing isn't working, think outside the box, and get outside feedback about what you can do differently. Then apply the tools without debate and measure the results. Asking for help is the rational thing to do when stuck in an emotional trap that is draining your life energy.

Your awareness is growing. The tools work when you use them. Hope is here. The path ahead is clear.

💬 Transformational Communication

Change creates transformation. Look at the chart. It shows how you become a relationship problem solver by bringing out new traits and hidden strengths.

In these final pages, if you're an Empathizer, we are going to help you anticipate and work with your "Dormant Inner Instigator." If you're an Instigator, you will engage and bring out your "Dormant Inner Empathizer." The chart visually shows that both types are accessible within you to activate and blend. The dashed line on the chart indicates that you can activate and blend the strengths of both types because the boundaries are permeable. By using *TALK2ME©* tools, your hidden strengths are no longer walled off from you.

TALK2ME© Transformational Communication

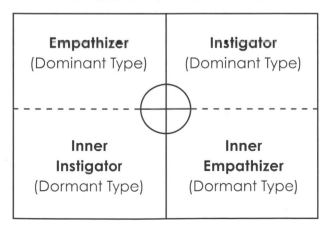

Empathizer (Dominant Type)	**Instigator** (Dominant Type)
Inner Instigator (Dormant Type)	**Inner Empathizer** (Dormant Type)

Transformation requires work and courage. Think of a difficult person in your family or work life. Acknowledge that people who are frustrating you actually call out your Dormant Type from hiding to be better integrated into your daily life. The effective blending of the "yin and yang" of both types is a key giveaway of Transformed Empathizers and Transformed Instigators. Their communication goes to a higher level during conflicts and is adaptive to who they are speaking with and what their purpose is during the interaction.

Both mindsets are inside of you. Your less dominant type naturally emerges when you use I-E thinking laws, mood rules, and language tools.

🗨 TRANSFORMING INTO YOUR OPPOSITE TYPE

As a teen Empathizer, I (Riley) changed from being a "pleaser" to acting the role of a "rebel." My Dormant Inner Instigator came bursting out of the closet.

I developed the opposite extreme response. Instead of having a "flight response" I would have a "fight response." I would display my disgust of their negativity or fake confidence through quick, sassy, or rebellious behaviors and comments. I seemed to think someone needed to teach these people a lesson, and that someone was going to be me. I often would overcorrect and become more of an Extreme Instigator.

So, you're not going nuts if you experience this type of thing, too. You may go to extremes when you first bring out your opposite Dormant Inner Instigator or Dormant Inner Empathizer. Think of it as analogous to the awkward teenage years. It's normal, healthy, and shows you're changing.

In my junior year of high school, I despised my math teacher, a negative and "difficult" Instigator. One day she handed back our tests. Almost all the students got a question wrong because of an error in the way the question was worded. I spoke up. I told her this was unethical and that she needed to take ownership for her mistake. "We don't deserve to be penalized," I said. Some students clapped in approval, while others looked at me with wide eyes and gaping mouths.

You can disagree without being disagreeable. Although there exists a natural tension between Instigators and Empathizers, you can voice your opinions without getting into a battle of wills. Contrasts between Empathizers and Instigators don't have to turn into conflicts. Actually, difficult people can serve you well by bringing out your opposite dormant communicator type from hiding.

I was lucky to not be sent to the principal that day. Two weeks later, I got re-seated in the back of the classroom. This was probably the best for both of us.

At the time, I felt very proud of my speaking up. I felt I was doing what was "right." Plus, this was a big difference from the timid and quiet child I used to be. Looking back on it today, especially having been a high school teacher myself, I could have spoken to the teacher after class. If this didn't resolve things, I could have voiced ethical concerns with my principal.

In truth, I find negative people of both types to be difficult, but I-Types who are negative have always been especially challenging for me. What I learned from this is that it's important to speak up, but to do it in a way that I'm aware of the other person's insecurities so that I don't tap into them. I don't need to teach people a lesson by humiliating or outsmarting them. Clearly, proving you're right at the expense of a relationship is all wrong.

Evaluate how people treat their relationship with you. During a conflict with someone you care for, words matter even more and are more heavily weighted and impactful. If you find you have gone too far or to an extreme, pause before you react with prejudice. Then, reel yourself back in to match the other person's communication style.

It should be noted that when you get a shocked reaction from others to what you're saying, chances are you have gone too far in your efforts to transform your Dormant Inner Instigator or Dormant Inner Empathizer style.

This is a lifelong transformational process. Don't get discouraged. You won't suddenly become a 100% perfect communicator. It takes daily work. Don't trust the quick fix. Personally, I feel much more confident in the accuracy of my feedback.

In the next few sections, we are going to explore case examples of the metamorphosis or transformation that occurs in both "Recovering Empathizers" and "Recovering Instigators." We use the term recovering because there can be pain or resistance. It's not an easy process.

Our next case follows the emotional awakening of a Recovering Instigator who is transforming his marriage to his Empathizer partner by blending his communication style. You will notice that when Instigators let go of their anger habit they become aware of their underlying tender-heartedness, sadness, or grief that requires processing.

The Need to be Right: Case of a Recovering Instigator

Instigators who begin to tap into their Dormant Inner Empathizer experience emotional vulnerability. There is an upsurge of emotional sensitivity and defensive hypersensitivity to perceived criticism. Emotions of anxiety, sadness, fear, sorrow, jealousy, joy, and many others come pouring out. They learn the world of emotions is run by different rules than the rules that work in the world of logic.

Danny came to me (Dennis) for personal growth therapy right after becoming a first-time new father. He felt feelings he had never felt before. Danny was hypersensitive that he wouldn't be a good dad because he didn't have a good relationship with his father. Worrying about the future was dragging him down into the pits. Getting frustrated was a defense he erected in order to feel in control and not overrun by rampant emotions. Danny was afraid of these new emotions of vulnerability and tenderness.

Here's how Danny described his "awkward" hypersensitivity. "When my wife states any opinion about taking care of the baby, I take it personally and stop listening. I take it as some kind of criticism that I failed to be as effective as I should. Then I interpret she's disappointed and disapproving of me as a father. I will interpret her tone as shaming even when it has no bearing on the matter. I realize now this is a false way I distance myself from feeling deeper feelings that are new to me." You will recall that extreme self-criticism and magnifying negatives are hallmarks of Empathizer views.

Intense emotions caused Danny to lose his confidence. Insecurities emerged that he had to cope with. He doubted himself and had difficulty making quick decisions. This scared Danny because he felt he was becoming someone he didn't recognize. Anger was his old coping mechanism and comfort zone. Danny had to leave his anger comfort zone and learn how to communicate with his wife openly and honestly about what he was feeling in the present moment.

Transformed Instigators access the power of sadness to heal conflicts and resolve resentments. Instead of being defensive, Danny learned to use "I feel ____" statements with his wife. He stopped automatically resorting to his compulsive anger habit. Self-disclosing emotions became a new tool that built trust and respect with his wife. For example, when Danny felt sad and uncertain about being a new dad, he would share with his wife, "I feel vulnerable right now." The word "vulnerable" is a keyword or command that opens locked doors for Instigators. The "I feel vulnerable____" prompt opens a buried treasure chest that Instigators can then put to good use.

Danny learned to apply Law 5: "In a conflict, pause before you react with a Communicator Prejudice." In his case, the prejudice was reacting with false anger and saying things he didn't mean that hurt his partner's feelings. "I get aggressive when I don't feel good," Danny said. Then they wouldn't talk for days and the pattern would repeat itself. So, Danny pre-planned his response. Instead of getting mad, Danny made a point to look his wife in the eye, step back mentally and take a deep breath, and reveal vulnerable emotions instead of concealing them from his partner. Danny tapped into his Dormant Inner Empathizer. By revealing his real feelings, Danny was able to build bridges of connection when times got tense.

Frankly, Danny was shocked at how well these simple timely emotional disclosures worked with his wife. In this case, she smiled and gave him a quick hug of reassurance, then said, "You're a great dad.

You're a different and better dad than your dad was to you. Let's give us both some time to get used to this parenting thing. I don't know what I'm doing half of the time, either. Babies don't come with an operator's manual." Then they would both laugh a little and feel stronger and more bonded with a little more energy.

When Instigators feel vulnerable, they deflect soft-hearted feelings with anger. By bringing out their Inner Empathizer, Instigators become aware that defaulting to anger is an unhealthy habit, and they seek to change it. Instead of deflecting their vulnerability with eruptive anger, Enlightened Instigators peel the onion and express what they're honestly feeling, helping them feel calm and in control. The irony is this technique is the opposite of what they would typically do to regain "emotional control."

> **PRO Rule:** Engaging your Dormant Inner Instigator or Dormant Inner Empathizer transforms your life.

Danny engaged in a new PRO attitude. He would ask himself, "My mission is peaceful coexistence with my wife. Is what I'm about to say or do going to bring me more or less inner peace? Is it going to be effective or ineffective with my wife to address my concerns in this way?" He would repeatedly ask, "Is what I'm about to say necessary or helpful?"

The ability to engage the sweet sorrow of being a new dad strengthened Danny. "I'm a better listener and can learn from advice I wouldn't think of on my own. Now I get my wife's suggestions and requests aren't a critique of me. If she has a preference or a preferred way of doing something, I now realize she's not criticizing me. She's telling me her preferences, her way, what she needs and wants to feel OK. We have very different views but they aren't disputes that put a wall between us in bed."

Peace is not the absence of conflict. Growth comes through healthy conflict.

🗨 How to Deal with Sad Feelings as an Instigator

To review what Instigator Danny did differently to integrate his Dormant Inner Empathizer into his life as a new dad:

- I need to say "I feel _____" more often to reveal what's going on inside of me.
- I need to let go of wanting to be all things to all people.
- I need to accept what I'm capable of and not capable of.
- I need to talk directly about the emotional issue and not skirt the problem.
- I need to steer clear of overthinking what or who is the cause of the problem.
- I need to accept that "I'm not trustworthy" when I don't reveal my feelings.
- I need to accept my Empathizer partner's identification of the problem and her view of the solution.
- I need to remember my reputation is not being slurred and I'm not being condemned.
- I need to view my partner as asking for a simple change in behavior.
- I need to let go of feeling pressured to surgically remove the offending gene.
- I need to accept I don't have to be right.

Another Instigator client took a long hard look in the mirror of change, and concluded, "I have a tremendous messiah-martyr complex. I play both roles well. But it's false remorse. I need to really change that."

If you're an Instigator, when you start to unlock the treasure chest of your Inner Empathizer you might experience a flood of feelings or a sudden onset of guilt. This does not mean that it's time for you to panic. It doesn't even necessarily mean there is anything to feel bad or ashamed about. Don't be afraid of this newness. Feelings are just feedback, they are not to be feared. Feelings are just feelings, they aren't behaviors or actions. Feelings aren't facts. Feelings are energy.

You have to learn to walk before you can run. This "strengths adoption" process is a bit jarring at first. And as an Empathizer or Instigator, expect to swing to an extreme initially when you are busy blending and intermixing your communicator strengths. You'll swing back to the middle in no time at all. Just get back up and keep going forward. Or talk to your coach to get your bearings.

Like a toddler learning to walk, you will find your own blended way to bring out your opposite Inner Empathizer or Inner Instigator as you gain experience at creating more harmony than chaos.

🗩 Blended Instigator Sadness

As you recall, Instigators divert to a mood state of anger to feel safe when things feel outside of their control.

If you're an Instigator, you will feel a surge of sad feelings underneath your usual grievances and frustrations. There is no longer defaulting to anger but a deeper experience of vulnerability and sorrow. You will feel the grief of working so hard on your "to-do" list to "earn" feelings of worth that your life unfolds without you enjoying it.

Here are some practical guidelines to give yourself a chance to feel the power inside of your vulnerability:

- Good feelings don't make you good.
- Bad feelings don't make you weak or inferior.
- People who make you feel bad aren't necessarily bad.
- When you're sad, there isn't anything wrong with you.
- You don't have to conceal vulnerable feelings for fear of being shamed.
- When you say "I feel vulnerable because…" people will connect with you.
- True empathy is the willingness to feel the sorrow of tears without fear.

- When you feel sensitive, you will pick up the mood of any room you walk into.
- You don't have to fix anything when you hear what others are feeling. Listening is the fix.
- You are strong and good enough when your heart is filled with grief.
- The courage to change your mind shows the strength of character.
- Real men cry and tears are healing for one's physical health.
- You can't stay stuck in swamps of grief when you use mentors or guides.

As an Instigator, dishonest habitual anger can take years off your life and limit the joy you do find. Softer feelings don't make you a sissy or cause rejection from the people who love and respect you. Tears are healing. Don't feel ashamed. Take pride in being strong enough to cry.

Instead of "It's my way or no way!" being more sensitive creates "It's my way...your way...and our way. Okay?!" This allows you to feel less judging and more loving. Less grumpy and more grateful. Less pressured and more pleased with your partner and children. You feel more content and feel more at home in your own skin while walking in those blue suede Empathizer shoes. You leave people feeling better off as a result of knowing you.

This next equivalent case study looks at a "Recovering Empathizer" who came into psychotherapy to reduce her anxieties, self-criticism, and fears of being more assertive in her relationships and career life.

🗩 Anger Outburst: Case of a Recovering Empathizer

The classical Freudian definition of depression is "anger directed toward the self." Self-anger causes Empathizers to feel down, blue, and uncertain of their talents and strengths.

As a custom, Empthizers are extremely self-critical. This self-flogging restricts their ability to give constructive criticism. Unleashing their Dormant Inner Instigator traits frees Empathizers from their low self-opinions. The "Transformed Empathizer" learns to magnify positives and minimize negatives, just as Instigators characteristically do.

If you're an Empathizer or Instigator, you will bring out sides to your personality that have been unused and hidden from view when you begin accessing new rooms in the mansion of your mind. That's both the good and the bad news.

The good news is that you have a whole new way of being and succeeding in the world. The bad news is that you might overdo it at first. That's OK. You will get used to experiencing firsthand what it's like to walk in the shoes of your opposite type in real time. Anger comes out in Empathizers, and they have to get honest with it. Using healthy anger is a life skill. In a confrontation, you might be surprised when you react from the extreme of your hidden opposite type. Anticipate and plan for it but don't indulge fears of change.

Tiffany, a millennial client, found this out when she came out of her Empathizer shell and roared like a lion during a confrontation with her older brother. Although super close growing up under the watchful eye of a single dad, they weren't seeing eye-to-eye as much as young adults with new partners and careers. In Empathizer Tiffany's view, her Instigator brother had become an opinionated jerk who was a terrible listener.

If you're an Empathizer, swinging to the Instigator side of the spectrum can be both unsettling and terribly freeing. Tiffany was highly capable and had worked hard to drop her inferiority and shyness act. She just lacked confidence in speaking up for herself, telling her truth, and pushing back when the situation called for it. Tiffany had always been close to her Instigator brother and her Instigator father. She didn't want to lose that. Tiffany was shocked when her easy-going attitude toward her brother burst into fiery anger.

This is how Empathizer Tiffany described her concern when her Dormant Inner Instigator came charging out like a bull in a china closet.

"I blew up at him. I said spiteful things. I know I'm in the wrong. I didn't know how I felt so I just got mad and said what I was thinking. There was no filter.

"I feel angry because nothing is ever going to be the same. The arguing is like me and my mom. Every time we're together we end up arguing. My brother, Stu, believes everything around him is at fault and he's not. It's so stupid. He thinks he knows all the answers. I used to stay quiet because I didn't know what to believe or how to behave around him.

"I was screaming inside during a fight when he said, 'Now that I see your true colors, I don't know if we can ever be friends.' Stu said what I was thinking! But I got mad instead of hurt. Maybe being angry is my true color. I feel like I'm losing so much now. I thought things were going really well and I was growing and changing. This makes me feel insecure and not worthy as a person.

"I don't like the person I am right now. When I get angry I yell. It's not right but I can't help it. When I get angry, I yell, and I can't stop myself. It feels good to be yelling. When I used to get mad I would shut down. It feels good to be yelling and letting out all the emotion in the moment. Anger makes me feel strong and powerful instead of sad. But then I feel like a terrible person. It's not being very mature. At some point, I stopped being anxious and I got relief by getting really angry.

"Blow ups aren't rational. I wish we could come together and support each other as we used to and not be at each other's throats. We're going in circles, stuck together in fight loops.

"Looking back, I don't think I was mad. I'm angry in general. But peeling the onion, I really feel scared. That's the true feeling, not dishonest fake anger outbursts. I felt scared that I don't have control over my life. I don't feel I'm truly angry at Stu. As an Empathizer, I have so many feelings going through me in a day it can be confusing. Being angry gives me a temporary sense of control, but it comes at too high a cost."

In therapy, Empathizer Tiffany took stock of her emerging Dormant Inner Instigator and was able to modify the extremes and learn to channel her anger assertively. And her understanding of the transformational power of Instigator anger grew and deepened. Some anger management lessons both Empathizers and Instigators need to address:

- Anger masks the fear of loss.
- When feeling things are out of control, Instigators default to anger as a habit.
- Underneath anger, is hidden a more vulnerable emotion, such as grief or sadness.
- "Anger orgasms" or blow-ups feel good at the time but make you feel guilty later.
- Arguing when using alcohol or other drugs is like throwing gasoline on anger fires.
- Anger feels strong, but the real strength is in saying, "I feel sad and scared right now."
- A single "anger attack" can completely drain the relationship savings account of trust and respect.
- Healthy anger means using compassionate energy to change a hurtful scene into a healing one.
- Resentment is a form of anger you can live without to live longer.

Empathizers who tap into the hidden transformational power of their Dormant Inner Instigator will feel less sensitive to criticism and more confident. They will use healthy aggression to push their own agenda by getting things done fast. Put simply, they will be more of a pusher instead of being a pushover.

The Transformed Empathizer gains an awareness of, and appreciation for, the inner workings and power of the Instigator mind.

Empathizer Worries: How to Activate Your Inner Instigator

As an Empathizer, your Dormant Inner Instigator is a treasure chest of strengths ready for you to unlock and activate whenever you choose. The goal for both Empathizers and Instigators is to use the standard traits of your opposite type to blend your response and excel in relationship problem solving.

One Empathizer said, "It consumes me when my I-Type is upset, bothered, sad, or unhappy. It bothers me if I can't fix it because it's out of my control. I want to give and help but have trouble setting boundaries. I give too much and expect too little which overextends me. You're right. I can be nice to a fault and give too much when others need to pull their weight."

You alone are responsible for your mood. Every time you feel yourself getting pulled into the energy black hole of another person's bad mood, repeat these words: *Not my circus, not my monkeys.* What assertive thoughts can Empathizers use to activate the dormant strengths of their Inner Instigator?

- "If I were an Instigator, I wouldn't care as much."
- "If I were an Instigator, I wouldn't carry their problems and pain as much."
- "If I were an Instigator, it wouldn't bother me as much."
- "If I were an Instigator, I would put a time limit on how long to worry about it."
- "If I were an Instigator, if there's nothing I could do about it, I would let it go and move on."
- "If I were an Instigator, I would define the problem as the other person's responsibility to solve."

Moods spread like the flu. Be responsible for self-care and set firm boundaries.

Co-dependency occurs when you work harder to solve a problem than the other person works to solve it. "Not my circus, not my monkeys!" signals both types to stay away from attempting an emotional rescue that's none of their business. Quipped one Empathizer client, "This is going to take a lot of practice!" Exactly.

In practice, Transformed Empathizers don't absorb others' bad moods. They also don't take responsibility for other people's poor actions.

🗩 Blended Empathizer Anger

As you recall, Empathizers characteristically divert to a mood state of sadness when hit by unexpected stressful changes.

If you're an Empathizer, you will notice that anger lurks underneath your sadness and hurt feelings. Healthy anger is an emotion that signals you that something needs to change in a more positive way that supports your goals. Stuffing anger isn't the fix.

Let's talk about healthy anger. Your healthy anger strives to:

Anger Power
Force a change in the status quo.
Get someone to do something differently.
Let go of the old.
Make something new happen in your business or personal life.
Receive a response instead of being ignored.
Be treated as an equal instead of a subordinate.
Make your family function better as a team.
Live a life of meaning instead of a life of quiet desperation.
Make your voice count to leave the world a better place.
Redress grievances through healthy discourse.

Whew! It's refreshing to see the positive side of anger for a change. How you think about anger dictates what you do about it.

Let's next cover some healthy ways to view your anger and anger directed at you:

Anger Attitudes
You aren't bad when you feel mad.
The purpose of healthy anger is to promote needed change.
Complaining is socially acceptable anger that is corrosive.
Self-criticism is anger directed at the self.
Blaming others is stubborn anger that stymies change.
The need to be right by making others wrong fuels hurtful anger attacks.

Feeling angry doesn't justify saying hurtful things.
When you feel really angry you can still speak calmly and rationally.
No one can make you stay angry without your co-dependent consent.
"Anger orgasms" or blow-ups feel good but later cause guilt.
There is a time to give yourself the gift of forgiveness.
Feeling sorry for yourself is passive anger that retards your growth.
Empathizers and Instigators are equally powerful in using their anger wisely.

You are 50% co-responsible for the mood of any relationship you're in. Empathizers get mad when their feelings aren't heard. Instigators get mad when they can't fix things. You can remain civil when you're raging inside. You can be temperate with your temper and set a loving mood temperature in your home.

You are in charge of all of your moods. Anger is normal. However, being angry for long periods of time is not healthy and indicates a long-overdue change needs to be made.

What Does a Transformed Communicator Look Like?

A frequent question we get in our workshops is, "But can't I be both communicator types?"

Initially, we teasingly answer "No" because you are born as one type or the other then shaped by family forces and upbringing. And certainly that's true. But after using the 7 *Laws of Effective Communication* in your everyday life, we can answer "Yes" because you have experienced what it's like to truly walk in the shoes of your opposite type in our *TALK2ME©* world. You now see conflicts clearly through Instigator eyes and hear what's being said through Empathizer ears. You are an "Empagator" or an "Instithizer" who changes colors like a chameleon to fit the background you find yourself in while always remaining true to your real colors.

A main goal of your *TALK2ME©* training has been to help you understand and appreciate your own dominant style as an Instigator or Empathizer communicator and how you impact others without being aware of it. Predictive empathy is knowing in advance how your words and feedback will impact others.

Another outcome of your enlightened listening and mood management skills has been to activate your dormant style. Having both toolboxes to work from provides you more flexibility and options during tough times and tense talks. You now know what works and why.

Here's how it might look when you reverse roles and effectively bring out your dormant Inner Empathizer or Inner Instigator to blend with your dominant style:

Decision-Making

- Blended Empathizers: You make decisions faster and more independently.
- Blended Instigators: You make decisions slower and more interdependently.

Anger

- Blended Empathizers: You focus your frustrations on solving problems and taking action.
- Blended Instigators: You feel patient and laid back because you control your temper.

Corrections vs. Recognitions

- Blended Empathizers: You courageously give more constructive criticisms.
- Blended Instigators: You regularly give more unconditional compliments.

Time Zone

- Blended Empathizers: You move into the future and let go of the past.
- Blended Instigators: You look to past patterns to find problem-solving clues.

Script

- Blended Empathizers: You are able to be an outspoken strong leader.
- Blended Instigators: You are able to be an easygoing peaceful listener.

Listening

- Blended Empathizers: You speak up and hold your ground when the situation calls for it.
- Blended Instigators: You make time to listen, paraphrase, and ask good questions.

Mood Managing

- Blended Empathizers: You believe that rational thinking can change moods.
- Blended Instigators: You believe deep emotional dialogues foster intimacy.

Goals Focus

- Blended Empathizers: You give direct concise answers and don't beat around the bush.
- Blended Instigators: You give empathetic thoughtful answers and fuller explanations.

Love Languages

- Blended Empathizers: You take care of your needs and put yourself first when you're feeling depleted.
- Blended Instigators: You elect to bring a good mood home to make family members feel important and cared for.

Social Approval

- Blended Empathizers: You are committed to giving honest feedback with less fear of hurting the feelings of others.
- Blended Instigators: You are cautious giving sharp feedback and instead focus on carefully pre-packaged corrective feedback.

Problem-Solving

- Blended Empathizers: You seek more control of difficult situations by having more of your ideas implemented.
- Blended Instigators: You seek to show compassion in difficult situations by being open to trying out others' ideas.

Fault Finding

- Blended Empathizers: You blame others or the situation now when issues aren't fixed.
- Blended Instigators: You are self-critical and analyze your part in a problem.

Co-Parenting

- Blended Empathizers: You are a stricter parent.
- Blended Instigators: You are a more permissive parent.

To come full circle, the above items roughly correspond to the PRO Inventory you took upfront in this book to begin our journey together. What a long way you've come! When you have a minute, glance back at the NICI-A items and compare them with this list of blended traits. Give credit where credit is due *you*. You're a more balanced Instigator or Empathizer communicator than you've ever been.

Happiness means never putting the aliveness of your life on freeze-frame. A smart-aleck coffee-cup motto said, "Reality is a major source of stress." When you keep changing, you will progress. When you stop changing, you will regress.

Change means life. In reverse, fighting change means predictable failure and stagnation. You will feel stuck in a trap of your own making.

Blending your dominant and dormant Instigator and Empathizer strengths and talents gives you maximum flexibility. Use the following checklists to judge for yourself how effectively you're tapping into and blending your Dormant Empathizer or Dormant Instigator strengths.

Instigators Who Tap into Their Inner Empathizer Strengths

As a Transformed Instigator who is approachable, you will tap into and blend these latent hidden strengths of Empathizers, wherein:

- Adopt a relationship mood of approval. Need to feel adequate.
- Smile approvingly. Use friendly eye contact and softer voice tones.
- Allow yourself to feel sad. Feel the loss of trust when you preach. No debating. No battles about right and wrong.
- Seek first to understand. Paraphrase what you've heard. Ask good follow-up questions.
- Use more compliments. Don't critique or offer suggestions unless you're asked to.
- Let go of needing to be the lone ranger fixer. Ask how you can be of help. Ask for help.

- No debating. No battles about right and wrong.
- Use brief corrections, not redundant criticisms.
- Ask often for others' input. Make everyone you come into contact with feel important.
- Slow down. Relax. Know you'll get all the improvements done in due time.
- Do not raise your voice ever...ever...EVER.
- Remain approachable: Appreciate and feel grateful for what others do for you.

Empathizers Who Tap into Their Inner Instigator Strengths

As a Transformed Empathizer who is directive, you will tap into and blend these latent hidden strengths of Instigators, wherein:

- Adopt a relationship mood of respect. Need to feel worthwhile.
- Joke and tease more to socially feel at ease.
- Allow yourself to feel mad. Feel the frustration when you aren't heard. No shutting down. Be strong, hold your ground. Raise your voice a bit louder. Interrupt.
- Humbly strut your stuff and feel confident. Repeat points that are brushed off.
- Get straight to the point. Control the conversation using your goals.
- Compliment sparingly, criticize specifically.
- Share your big ideas with confidence. Give one-suggestion feedback.
- Care less about what others think of you, and say what you're afraid to.
- Don't take the shiny bait of false feedback that will make a "bass" of you.
- Remain firm. Stay true to your point of view and speak up.
- Be direct. Don't beat around the bush. Get to the point and get on with it.

The communication spectrum is like a piano keyboard. You will come back to the middle from the high or low notes to reach a balance that is satisfactory.

Just Say Yes to Change

How do you keep on changing when you hit barriers? You keep moving forward one small step at a time. Listening creates change. As Law 3 states: "Pretending to listen isn't really listening."

As Heraclitus, a pre-Socratic Ionian Greek philosopher put it, "The only constant in life is change." Change means life. Your transformation is a constant in life. If you're an Empathizer, it gives you the gift of confidence. If you're an Instigator, it gives you the gift of calmness. Blending types creates calm confidence in your life even during times of conflict and crisis.

You can't rest on your laurels. When you get too comfortable, keep on changing. Having potential and not engaging your potential means you're not changing. Don't brag about what you can do in the future. The only thing that matters is what you do today. As one of our family business CEO clients told new employees, "Your potential will get you fired." This implies you have to walk the talk or you will be shown the exit door.

Resisting change is like slogging up a fast-moving river with cement boots on your feet. Using *TALK2ME©* Tools brings out the strengths that lie dormant within you. You will now be able to change what you dislike in your life. Saying yes to change means saying yes to a better life.

You're bound to have trying times and setbacks. When you are stuck and feel like giving up, actively apply Law 1: "Who am I talking to? An Instigator or an Empathizer?" Communicating like a PRO isn't about perfection or not making mistakes. It's about a constant pursuit of improvement. A daily dedication to transform yourself into a better and better communicator.

Stay the course. Enjoy being on the road less traveled. You now have the guidelines for getting through tough life transitions. Be a continual life-long learner.

⌕ Signs You're on a Transformational Track

Generally speaking, as a self-actualizing Instigator *and* Empathizer PRO of any age, these are the positive attitudes you will use when you're on the right track:

- High enthusiasm and optimism.
- Inner Cynic or Inner Critic have been fired or retired.
- Steady positive mood attitudes.
- Free of need to exert control over others to control your own mood.
- Rich enjoyment of life, nature, and appreciation for the beauty of all kinds.
- Independence of decision-making. You make up your own mind.
- Not needing to be liked or obtain the approval of others to feel OK.
- Welcome change. Are a student of change. Don't fear failure.
- Free of relationship enslavement or co-dependencies.
- Self-love: Rich inner world. Seek expert help as needed.
- Life career enjoyment and expanding responsibilities and opportunities.
- The continuing curiosity of Instigator-Empathizer language styles.

Perception is reality. Different feedback strokes for different folks. You now "see" the previously hidden I-E communication rules that compulsively rule the world of different folks.

In the past, resentment accrued when people didn't follow your I-E Rulebook. As you've learned, the rule book of Empathizers differs from the rule book of Instigators. Although each has a different set of fair play rules and expectations, it doesn't mean you don't have to fight about who's right and who's wrong. You remember Law 2, "The solution isn't in your view, it's in their view." You can switch your beliefs when what you're doing isn't working.

Becoming a better communicator opens the door to known and unknown possibilities. A metaphor that Albert Einstein used was, "Life is like riding a bicycle. To keep your balance you must keep moving."

The same applies to you. Just like riding a bike, you have to keep moving forward to stay balanced. Growing. Changing.

💬 Transformed Instigators

As a Transformed Instigator, your Inner Empathizer potentials are realized. Daily you take these small steps to reach the summit of peak communication:

- Listens first.
- Talks later.
- Won't interrupt.
- Practices patience in the face of frustration.
- Shares good moods.
- Attitude of problem preventer vs. problem solver.
- Private feelings divulged.
- Open to not knowing.
- Changes self, prior to criticizing others.
- Learning as a team is more important than winning.
- Self-confidence isn't faked.
- Won't use a clique of chest thumpers.
- Freely gives positive feedback.
- Smiles warmly and approvingly.
- Allows self to be helped and influenced.
- Secure in selfless performance.
- Talks on a two-way street of dialogue, no lecturing.
- During relationship strife asks: "How can I be of help to YOU?"

💬 Transformed Empathizers

As a Transformed Empathizer, your Inner Instigator potentials are realized. Daily you take these small steps to reach the summit of peak communication:

- Exudes confidence when doubtful.
- Interrupts arrogant monologues.
- Speaks out loud and proud.
- Keep others' moods out of you.
- Talks first...Listens later...Interrupts...Talks over...Repeats key points.
- Be impatient with broken promises.
- Let go of people you love but who aren't good for you.
- Feed your mind positives to begin, during and end your day.
- Insist people around you change, too.
- Promote your intuitive ideas and solutions.
- Confronts life dissatisfactions and problems head-on.
- Willingness to hurt others when nothing else works to resolve a key issue.
- Gives less around energy drainers.
- Change what you hear yourself repetitively complain about.
- Strive to please yourself first when irritated or frustrated.
- Respectfully disagree persistently.
- Better yourself by not downing yourself.
- Gives corrective negative feedback as a habit.
- Mindfully shares obvious solutions to the team.
- Divulges hidden insights and feedback.
- During a relationship, strife asks: "How can I treat ME better?"

Strengths and weaknesses are two sides of the same life coin. Choose positive changes by utilizing the strengths of both types to achieve your worthy goals. Transformation is a process.

The Truth About Becoming a PRO Communicator

As a junior psychotherapist, I (Dennis) was made to believe I could change people. In fact, it was an unsaid expectation in graduate school that everything we were learning could change our clients for the better. Ironically, in the 90s when I was writing my first book, *Taking the Fear out of Changing*, I came to the gradual realization that I couldn't change others. They had to make a choice to change themselves. I noticed my clients resisted changes when I took accountability for their change efforts. It was like taking away their dignity. The change expert knows it's not possible to change others. It's important to honor and not take away the choice of change from another person.

By now you realize, perhaps ruefully, that you can't change anyone but yourself. You perceive the difficult people in your life, typically your opposite type, in a new light. At the beginning of this book, you thought the other person was crazy and needed to change. But now you realize you're living by unrealistic expectations when you expect others to be like you or to change for you. Consequently, you experience greater inner peace and a calm confidence during conflicts.

Why can't we all just get along? We *can* all get along better when we choose to use Instigator-Empathizer tools that build bridges of trust and respect. Instead of blindly stumbling into unnecessary conflicts, you now know in advance how your words will impact others. As a team, together you come up with creative new solutions to old problems. The lightbulb has come on. You now know why what you're doing works.

This book hasn't been about making sparkling presentations, working a room to your financial and social advantage, or pretending to get along with people to get your way. It's been about everyday communication. How to talk with people in novel ways, how to view stressful situations through a new lens, and how to rally during a conflict when you feel knocked down.

You now have the discipline to disagree without being disagreeable, and to be kind to others and yourself when you feel mad or defensive.

Two minds joined together have three times the power. By learning and practicing these powerful breakthrough tools, you are now a more competent *and* confident communicator, someone who will no longer unintentionally lose friends and tick people off. You believe everyone deserves to feel trusted and respected, seen and heard, and you are able to fully embrace the freedom to grow and change.

Continuing to be a *TALK2ME©* PRO communicator requires constant, conscientious, and consistent practice. Without this, your shiny new communication skills will grow dull over time through lack of use. Always look for ways to spontaneously be better and work at developing new communication strengths until they become a habit. Be a lifetime student of changing communication patterns.

Change occurs when critical feedback fosters critical growth. Change occurs when you pause before reacting with a communication prejudice. Change occurs when you pick a mood that fosters a better reputation. Change occurs when you truly listen instead of pretending to listen. Change occurs when you view the solution through their view instead of your own. And finally, change occurs when you determine who you're talking to, an Empathizer or Instigator. Let's be honest, these Communication Laws don't create change if everybody wants to be a better communicator but nobody wants to change. But you know that being a PRO Communicator starts and ends with changing yourself.

We have thoroughly enjoyed the unique privilege, as an adult daughter and senior father, to discover and teach *TALK2ME©* Laws and PRO Rules. The process of writing this book has deepened our own personal insights, strengthened our relationship, and further honed our *TALK2ME©* Effective Communication Skills. We hope joining us in this work has cultivated the same positive changes for you, too.

We feel deeply grateful for you, our dear reader. Hopefully, someday soon we'll have a chance to greet you on the Two-Way Communication Highway. Be well and travel peacefully on your exciting journey to new destinations.

In this era of transformational communication, leave everyone feeling better off as a result of knowing you.

Behold a new world of communication awaits for you and yours!

💬 Key Takeaways: Be the Change

- Apply Law 7: Everybody wants to be a better communicator, but nobody wants to change.
- The only constant in life is change.
- A crisis holds an opportunity within it. Flow with change don't fight it.
- Change is normal. You don't have to fear it.
- You *can* teach old dogs new tricks by using *TALK2ME©* Tools.
- Blaming yourself for not changing is self-sabotaging. Blaming others for not changing is relationship-sabotaging.
- Your attitude about change is more important than your age or history.
- Change happens whether you worry about it, or not.
- Honesty solves problems.
- Blaming and complaining aren't changing.
- Accept you can't change others. Focus on yourself.
- Good moods give birth to good changes.
- Don't give any critiques when you're mad.
- Affixing blame doesn't fix anything.
- Opinions are like butt holes. Everyone's got one.
- Give advice only when asked. Remember, advice and feedback are two different things.
- When what you're doing isn't working, do something different. Go back to Law 1.
- Moods of fear and frustration cause you to do the reverse of what works.
- When stuck, ask: "Do I want to be right, or do I want to be effective?"
- Blending your dominant vs. dormant Instigator-Empathizer styles activates change.
- Predictive empathy is knowing in advance how your words will impact others.
- Little steps you take today create momentum that adds up to big changes tomorrow.

- By using your Instigator and Empathizer communication tools, you are guaranteed to become a PRO communicator.

💬 Law 7: Sharpen Your *TALK2ME©* Skills

Activity 1- Change your Prejudicial "I'm Right and You're Wrong" Language: For a week, whenever you hear yourself say the fault-finding words "right/wrong" or "good/bad" stop in your tracks. Then mentally substitute the words "effective" or "ineffective" and rephrase the thought into a question. For example, "It was the right thing to do!" transforms into, "But was it the effective thing to do?" Or, "They have a bad attitude!" transforms into, "But was their attitude effective in this situation?" How does that change your mood, outlook, and energy? The problem is not the person, the problem is the pattern.

Activity 2- Stop Giving Your Opinion or Advice Unless You're Asked: Go one whole week without giving any advice or suggestions unless you're specifically asked to. How does that deepen your listening skills? Does that make you aware of when you reject your own good advice? Can you let go of needing to be the fixer? Count the number of times you hear, "Yes, but…" in response to your ideas shared or suggestions. Then observe whether you can stop yourself from giving more unwanted advice that causes a conflict in the relationship.

Activity 3- Change Your Expectations That "They" Should Change But Not You: Whenever you're getting all worked up about why someone isn't doing what you think they should, change your expectations. They don't have to be like you, do they? Pause and reflect. Ask yourself, "What is my main mission here?" Remind yourself that your purpose is to have inner peace. Then say to yourself, "Not my circus, not my monkeys." Or, "Not my pigs, not my farm." Disallow yourself to stay mad when someone is living in your head rent-free. Living up to your own expectations is tough enough.

Activity 4- Practice Acceptance: When you feel that you're beating your head against a wall, recall the metaphor of the robin. You're seeing the difficult person as the enemy who is aggressing against you and invading your mental territory. Ask yourself, "What are they seeing when they look at me and my behavior?" Then inquire within, "Instead of expecting them to change, what small change can I make that might make a big difference to resolve this conflict?" Try it out and then measure the results.

Activity 5- Don't Meet Negative With Negative: The sick rule "I do back to you what you do to me" must be disrupted. That's how energy-draining cycles escalate chaos and cause everyone loss. Little things are a big deal. Use the healthy rule, "One kindness deserves another kindness." And be the first to be kind. Change the one thing you have total control over... you. Be kind when you feel frustrated, and let kindness boomerang back to you. This simple adjustment creates a positive energy loop.

Activity 6- Give Credit Where Credit is Due: As you allow yourself to travel into unknown regions of your emerging dormant Inner Empathizer or dormant Inner Instigator, give yourself credit for the courage to change. Process this with a coach, psychotherapist, or mentor how you are walking in new shoes that still feel a bit tight and awkward and need to be gradually broken in. Dress for success. Give yourself permission to alternately wear your burnt orange Instigator hat or your ocean blue Empathizer hat as the occasion calls for. Analyze which approach works best for different people and situations. Enjoy your new mastery. Admit it: You are now part of a new world of communication.

Activity 7- Create Your Million Dollar Talk Tool: At the end of *TAL-K2ME©* Communication Workshops, we have participants reflect on their Leadership 360 and assess areas where they will most likely get dinged in the future. Then, participants create a *"Million Dollar Talk Tool"* as an action item to address this area of concern. For example, if they struggle with giving accurate feedback, they will focus on delivering timely constructive criticism and compliments. How will you take action to prevent problems and get better results? Action to change the self ironically creates the change you wish to see in others.

May Blessings of Better Communication Abound for You and Yours!

TALK2ME© PRO RULES

32 *TALK2ME©* TOOLS FOR TAKING ON TOUGH TALKS

💬 Law 1: Know Who You're Talking To: An Instigator or Empathizer.

- **PRO Rule:** Treat others the way *they* want to be treated: As an Instigator or Empathizer.
- **PRO Rule:** It's not how you meant the message that matters, but how it was received.

💬 Law 2: The Solution Isn't in Your View. It's in the Other Person's View.

- **PRO Rule:** Know how your opposite communicator type views you from their world.
- **PRO Rule:** We're all difficult in the eyes of our opposite type but not in our own view.
- **PRO Rule:** Change your view to change your outcomes.
- **PRO Rule:** Resentment respects no one.
- **PRO Rule:** Don't view the person as the problem. It's the pattern, stupid.

🗨 Law 3: Pretending to Listen Isn't Really Listening.

- **PRO Rule:** Listening is the fix.
- **PRO Rule:** Intentional listening is the greatest gift you can give another human being.
- **PRO Rule:** Problems can't get solved until hot emotions cool off.
- **PRO Rule:** Listening doesn't mean agreeing.
- **PRO Rule:** Talking to yourself isn't listening.

🗨 Law 4: Your Mood Dictates Your Reputation.

- **PRO Rule:** You will prosper by putting yourself and others in an upbeat mood.
- **PRO Rule:** Instigators are Mood Pitchers, while Empathizers are Mood Catchers.
- **PRO Rule:** Empathizers who don't absorb others' moods feel more confident.
- **PRO Rule:** Instigators who set a positive mood tone at home feel calmer.
- **PRO Rule:** What you say and do in a high-pressure situation forms your reputation.

🗨 Law 5: In a Conflict, Pause Before You React With a Communicator Prejudice.

- **PRO Rule:** You can't fight the predators of invisible prejudices when you can't see how they're stalking you.
- **PRO Rule:** Emotional safety during a conflict is of utmost importance to Empathizers.
- **PRO Rule:** Combatting relationship issues first starts with disarming yourself.

- **PRO Rule:** Tense moods trigger prejudices that fuel conflicts.
- **PRO Rule:** See *yourself* the way your I-E opponent *fears you*.

⤷ Law 6: Critical Feedback Is Critical to Your Growth.

- **PRO Rule:** The master communicator has become proficient at giving accurate and helpful feedback.
- **PRO Rule:** I-Types require more *constructive criticism* while E-Types require more *constructive recognition*.
- **PRO Rule:** Interrupting defeats the reception of helpful feedback.
- **PRO Rule:** Don't give feedback when you're frustrated.
- **PRO Rule:** If you're afraid to say something, that might be the very thing you need to say.

⤷ Law 7: Everybody Wants to be a Better Communicator, But Nobody Wants to Change.

- **PRO Rule:** The only constant in life is change.
- **PRO Rule:** Change happens whether you worry about it, or not.
- **PRO Rule:** Honesty solves problems.
- **PRO Rule:** Blaming and complaining aren't changing.
- **PRO Rule:** Engaging your Dormant Inner Instigator or Dormant Inner Empathizer transforms your life.

REQUEST A WORKSHOP

You can transform your workplace with the *TALK2ME©* System. *TALK2ME©* workshops are highly interactive and engaging events that help participants navigate relationship challenges with calm confidence and respond effectively to tense conversations.

Built on more than 15 years of extensive clinical and real-life leadership research, *TALK2ME©* is an original communication system that has been proven to work for couples, companies, and family-owned businesses.

Participants use these seven words most frequently to describe their *TALK2ME©* workshop experiences: *Eye-Opening, Thought-Provoking, Enlightening, Informative, Engaging, Interactive, and Positive.*

New Insights Communication provides organizations with a broad range of *TALK2ME©* Communication services, including:

- *TALK2ME©* Communication Workshops
- *TALK2ME©* Leadership Development Programs
- *TALK2ME©* Team Communication Assessments
- *TALK2ME©* Mood Management Programs
- *TALK2ME©* Critical Feedback Programs
- *TALK2ME©* Creative Conflict Management Programs
- *TALK2ME©* Change Management Programs
- *TALK2ME©* Executive and Leadership Coaching

For more information, e-mail info@drogrady.com or call 937.428.0724.

You can also visit New Insights Communication websites at drogrady.com, effectivecommunicationworkshopsdayton.com, or marriagecounselingdayton.com.

UNLEASHING THE POWER
OF *COMMUNICATE LIKE A PRO*
RECOMMENDED READING:

- *Codependent No More* (Melody Beattie)
- *Crucial Conversations* (Kerry Patterson, Granny, McMillan, Switzler)
- *Games People Play* (Eric Berne)
- *Getting The Love You Want* (Haville Hendrix)
- *How to Win Friends & Influence People* (Dale Carnegie)
- *Taking the Fear Out of Changing* (Dennis O'Grady)
- *Talk To Me* (Dennis O'Grady)
- *The 7 Habits of Highly Effective People* (Stephen R. Covey)
- *The Art Of Communicating* (Thich Nhat Hanh)
- *The Art Of Loving* (Eric Fromm)
- *The Coaching Habit* (Michael Bungay Stanier)
- *The Dichotomy of Leadership* (Jocko Willink, Leif Babin)
- *The Five Love Languages* (Gary Chapman)
- *The Highly Sensitive Person* (Elaine Aron)
- *The One Minute Manager* (Ken Blanchard, Spencer Johnson)
- *The Servant* (James C. Hunter)
- *The Seven Principles for Making Marriage Work* (John Gottman)
- *Verbal Judo: The Gentle Art of Persuasion* (George Thompson)
- *When Everything Changes, Change Everything* (Neale Donald Walsch)
- *Wooden on Leadership* (Coach John Wooden)

ABOUT THE AUTHORS

✎ Dr. Dennis O'Grady

Psychologist Dr. Dennis O'Grady is Riley's proud dad and the father of the *TALK2ME©* System. Dennis is a veteran 40-year leadership trainer, marriage counselor, family business consultant, and president of the Dayton Area Psychological Association. Dr. O'Grady received his doctorate in psychology degree in 1982 from the School of Professional Psychology at Wright State University.

Since 2008 in 143 highly interactive classes, Dr. O'Grady has personally trained over 496 diverse IQ Leaders of Dayton Freight Lines to tap into the Instigator-Empathizer playbook. The *TALK2ME©* leadership training programs in effective communication build and maintain a positive, companywide culture of trust and respect. By investing in their resource of people, Dayton Freight has grown from 37 Service Centers to 56 Service Centers with 4,500+ employees. Taking the fear out of feedback has improved Dayton Freight's productivity and netted skyrocketing profits, including happiness at home.

In 2018, Dr. O'Grady was commissioned by Dayton Freight to develop and implement a new course and write a 257-page workbook called *The Communication Highway: Drive the Fear out of Feedback.*

Book 1: Our Communication Culture. These highly rated, three-day workshops are customized to deliver increased performance when the pressure is on. Dr. O'Grady also designed and taught *Managing Mood In The Workplace* day-long seminars for Premier Health to improve patient satisfaction scores while reducing the stress of caregivers. He is grateful to have worked with many outstanding organizations and associations over the years.

In 2005, Dennis authored the groundbreaking textbook *Talk to Me: Communication Moves to Get Along with Anyone.* In it, he explored the brave new world of Empathizer and Instigator communicators based on his client clinical research. Additionally, in 1997 he developed and recorded an anger management audio program called *No Hard Feelings: Managing Anger and Conflict in Your Work, Family, and Love Life.* In 1992, his first book, *Taking the Fear Out of Changing: Guidelines for Getting Through Tough Life Transitions,* provided guidance on moving successfully through emotional tides of unexpected change to feel renewed hope and connection to life.

Dennis is the happy single dad of three adult daughters: Erin in Boston, Riley in Cincinnati, and Kasey in Phoenix. At 69, Dennis continues to work with couples, individuals, and families at his company, New Insights Communication in Centerville, Ohio. For relaxation and pleasure, Dennis enjoys riding his three-wheeler motorcycle, night walking on the golf course paths where he lives, hiking in the Glen Helen Nature Preserve in Yellow Springs, bicycling on the Miami Valley's top flight paths, and reading or listening to audio books on spirituality... and, of course, writing books on solving relationship problems to become better communicators.

 Riley O'Grady

Riley O'Grady is an interpersonal communication professional, educator, and instructional systems designer who grew up with the *TALK2ME©* system. An entrepreneur and educator at heart, Riley is recognized for impassioned approaches, colorful ideas, and a mission to transform the workforce of tomorrow. She designs and delivers career education, life skills, and workforce solutions in one-on-one, small group, and corporate training settings. She has experience as a North Carolina middle and high school teacher, psychology research coordinator at Miami University (Ohio), career coach, and business owner. Riley is currently the founder and executive director of a Cincinnati youth nonprofit called LEAD Training and owns her own career coaching business called Valiant.

Her youth programs help young people develop self-efficacy—a belief in their own capacity to succeed—by providing opportunities to learn and practice these skills in safe, real-life settings. Riley has developed and delivered career and life-skills educational programs for YMCA, Cincinnati State Technical and Community College, United Way, and various other schools and nonprofit organizations in Ohio and Northern Kentucky.

Riley is also a *TALK2ME©* Trainer and instructional designer for New Insights Communication and enjoys being involved with workshops and corporate training activities. She is deeply passionate about the *TALK2ME©* system and spreading word of its impact on school systems, youth confidence, personal relationships, and corporations.

Riley fiercely loves teaching scuba diving, her dogs Teddy and Kai, her partner Tyler, her two sisters Erin and Kasey…and, of course, her dad (her words). Riley is a PADI Master Scuba Diver Trainer and teaches scuba certification classes mostly to university students and teens. Since 2009, she has been an active leader in Civil Air Patrol, where she gained first-hand exposure to the power of youth programs on soft-skill development and confidence-building in young people. Riley enjoys crazy adventures such as diving with sharks at the Newport Aquarium, flying with Tyler, and traveling. As her sisters say, she is free-spirited—which explains her love of not wearing shoes, driving to be her own boss, and believing that with a bit of courage, it's possible for people to create almost anything they want in life.